Resort Development and Management

Resort Development and Management

Mahendra Singh Chabbra

RANDOM PUBLICATIONS
NEW DELHI (INDIA)

Resort Development and Management

ISBN 978-93-5111-549-6

Published in 2015 in India by

RANDOM PUBLICATIONS

Reprint, 2017

4376-A/4B, Gali Murari Lal, Ansari Road
New Delhi-110 002
Phone : +9111-43580356, 011-23289044, 011-43142548
e-mail: sales@randompublications.com,
info@randompublications.com, randomexports@gmail.com

Type Setting by : Friends Media, Delhi-110089
Digitally Printed at : Replika Press Pvt. Ltd.

Preface

A resort is a place used for relaxation or recreation, attracting visitors for vacations and/or tourism. Resorts are places, towns or sometimes commercial establishment operated by a single company. The term "resort" is now also used for a self-contained commercial establishment which attempts to provide for most of a vacationer's wants while remaining on the premises, such as food, drink, lodging, sports, entertainment, and shopping. The term may be used to identify a hotel property that provides an array of amenities and typically includes entertainment and recreational activities. A hotel is frequently a central feature of a resort, such as the Grand Hotel at Mackinac Island, Michigan. A resort is not always a commercial establishment operated by a single company, although in the late twentieth century this sort of facility became more common. Towns which are resorts - or where tourism or vacationing is a major part of the local activity - are sometimes called resort towns. If they are by the sea they are called seaside resorts. Inland resorts include ski resorts, mountain resorts and spa towns. Towns such as Sochi in Russia, Sharm el Sheikh in Egypt, Barizo in Spain, Cortina d'Ampezzo in Italy, Druskininkai in Lithuania, Cancún in Mexico, Newport, Rhode Island, in the USA, Ischgl in Austria, St. Moritz in Switzerland, Blackpool in England and Malam Jabba in Pakistan are well-known resorts.

I would like to thank my team for standing beside me throughout my career and writing this book. My special thanks go to "Random Publications" who have published the book.

– Mahendra Singh Chabbra

Contents

1

Development of Resort

IN SMALL METROPOLITAN REGIONS

Everywhere in North America, suburbanization has caused a relative and, in many cases, absolute decline of downtown areas. The effect on the downtowns of small metropolitan regions (small-metro downtowns) has been particularly severe, for they possess fewer assets than those of larger metropolitan regions to resist the effects of suburban development. This identifies the few healthy small-metro downtowns in order to draw lessons that can aid the other downtowns within this urban size category, all of which are struggling. Our study concentrated on downtowns of North American metropolitan regions with populations between 100,000 and 500,000.

There are 177 metropolitan statistical areas in the U.S. and 25 census metropolitan areas and census agglomerations in Canada in this size range (excluding U.S. primary statistical areas that are part of consolidated metropolitan statistical areas, all with populations exceeding our threshold). In the U.S., these metropolitan areas have a total population of 40.8 million, roughly one of every seven Americans. Small Canadian metropolitan regions register an overall population of 5.08 million, which represents about one sixth of this country's population.

Our objectives in this study were fourfold: (I) identify successful small-metro downtowns across the U.S. and Canada; (2) explore reasons for their success; (3) from their experience, draw lessons for less successful downtowns; and (4) generate information on a category of downtowns that has been neglected in the literature.

To meet these objectives, we surveyed planners and other urban professionals from the United States and Canada who have an interest in downtown revitalization. Respondents were first invited to define what are, in their opinion, the features that contribute to the well-being of successful small-metro downtowns. Then, they were asked to identify successful ones and justify their selections. As expected, we found that few such downtowns were perceived as successful. And these districts nearly always cumulate advantages that are exceptional among small-metro downtowns—close proximity of a university, a state capital (in the U.S.), or provincial legislature (in Canada); a strong historical character; and a powerful tourist appeal. The article closes with a discussion of the implications of these findings for the vast majority of these downtowns, which are in a poor state of health. This latter part of the article is based on interviews with informants from the cities whose downtowns were selected in the survey.

Downtown Decline and Revitalization Efforts

In downtowns across North America, whether in large or small metropolitan regions, attempts at revitalization can be grouped into three phases. The first phase concentrated on adaptation to automobile accessibility, the second on head-on competition with suburbs, and the third on the accentuation of a distinct core area identity. Early strategies of the 1950s and 1960s aimed at maintaining the pre-eminence of the downtown within a changing transportation environment.

Planners sought to preserve or restore the dominant position of the downtown by replacing or complementing transit accessibility focused on the core area with similarly advantageous automobile-oriented access patterns. Radial expressways and widened arterial roads were meant to channel flows of cars towards downtowns, increasingly well provided with parking space.

It soon became clear, however, that accessibility alone would not safeguard the primacy of central business districts.

Policymakers became convinced that to stem the retail hemorrhage towards the suburbs, downtowns had to gloss their image and embrace suburban shopping formulas. This phase, which ran from the late 1950s into the early 1980s, consisted largely of attempts at ridding CBDs of eyesores and tailoring downtown shopping to the tastes of the day.

Sectors seen as blighted or merely obsolete were razed with the hope of replacing them with up-to-date developments apt to fuel downtown growth. This was also the time when indoor retail malls, an already well established suburban shopping formula, were introduced in CBDs. This strategy was grounded in the assumption that by replicating conditions found in suburban shopping centres, downtown areas could compete successfully with suburbs.

The 1970s marked a radical departure from earlier approaches to downtown revitalization. The shift was induced by a growing recognition of the ineffectiveness of previous efforts at reversing CBD decline. In fact, earlier revitalization attempts were often held responsible for downtowns' downward spiral.

For example, in small-metro downtowns, most enclosed retail malls were economic failures, and even prosperous malls tended to generate little retail activity beyond their walls. Also fueling the 1970s transformations were public expenditure cutbacks, the opening of planning to public participation, and a rediscovery of the merits of pre-World War II built environments, most notably the traditional pedestrian-oriented retail street.

Increasingly, planning interventions emphasized preservation or enhancement of the uniqueness of the physical features of downtowns within rapidly suburbanizing metropolitan regions and the targeting of markets where CBDs enjoyed competitive advantages. This reorientation signaled a mounting sentiment that downtowns could no longer compete with the suburb on its own terms and that their salvation rested instead on their distinction from the suburban realm in terms of the nature of their activities, a more compact built environment, and the predominance of pedestrian movement for intradowntown journeys.

The post-1970s attempts at revitalization did not, however, mark a clear break with previous efforts. Large redevelopment projects continued to be a mainstay of revitalization strategies. While redevelopment projects did not lose their allure, the process leading to this outcome underwent transformations. With the demise of large, federally funded urban renewal programmes, reliance on partnership-based approaches gained in popularity.

Projects included, for example, convention centres, professional sport venues, and aquariums. Meanwhile, in downtowns, or portions thereof, that were not subjected to redevelopment, increased importance was given to the preservation of the traditional built environment and its occupation by activities targeting markets congruent with the attributes of core areas—festival places and hospitality and recreational establishments.

In small metropolitan areas, there was a lag in the succession of these phases due to the tendency for revitalization strategies to be first devised and tested in larger metropolitan regions (urban renewal in Pittsburgh, Philadelphia, and New Haven in the late 1940s and in the 1950s, for example). Moreover, the impact of these phases was attenuated in small-metro downtowns by a lesser availability of public- and private-sector resources.

The foremost consequence of limited resources was a weaker involvement in urban renewal and a resulting preservation of much of these CBDs' traditional built environment. Another effect was a tendency in all phases to rely on small- rather than large-scale interventions.

Small-metro downtowns deserve distinct treatment because the circumstances they face are different from those encountered by CBDs of smaller urban areas or of larger metropolitan regions. They are more complex than downtowns of small urban areas (with less than 100,000 residents) and thus require more diversified revitalization strategies. In small urban area downtowns, the problem is often one of main street revival and can lend itself to targeted remedies such as the introduction of a farmers' market, an unusual attraction (such as the carousel in Mansfield, OH), or the adoption of a theme for the street.

At the same time, small-metro downtowns are more often in a state of decline than those of large metropolitan regions. While large-metro downtowns that perform poorly on all fronts (employment, retail, services, housing) are the exception, the opposite holds true for small-metro CBDs. One reason for this discrepancy is the absence in small-metro downtowns of assets widely distributed among their large-urban-area cousins, such as important employment and retail concentrations, world-class attractions, and elaborate public transit networks.

Another factor of decline among these CBDs is the higher decentralization propensity of small-metro downtowns due to their limited critical mass, their near total dependence on the automobile, and the relative ease with which different destinations, including peripheral ones, can be reached from anywhere within these metropolitan regions.

Method

With the expectation of poor health generally among small-metro CBDs, we engaged in a study purporting to identify the exceptional ones that are vital, with the intention of drawing lessons that can be of use to less successful CBDs. The study relied on a two-pronged methodology. The first phase consisted of an Internet survey.

E-mails with a link to the Internet survey form were sent to the 1,076 persons in our sample: 371 (34.5 per cent) to university planning, urban studies, and urban geography faculty members; 503 (46.8 per cent) to planners employed by the central cities of small metropolitan regions; and 202 (18.8 per cent) to professionals with a possible interest in downtown revitalization who are associated with government agencies (such as regional HUD offices) and economic development and research institutes with an urban focus.

This sample was not constructed with a probabilistic objective, but rather in a fashion that would maximize the information on small-metro downtowns across the continent. Of the sent e-mails, a total of 859 reached their destination (217 were undeliverable). The number of answered questionnaires after two reminders was 295—a 34.4 per cent response rate.

As do all surveys, this one reflects the values of its respondents. Far from being a challenge to the validity of its findings, we see the expression of these values as an important contribution of our survey. The values it picks up are indeed those of people who are among the best informed on the state of downtowns. Its respondents are also active in the framing and deployment of downtown revitalization strategies and in the advancement of knowledge on downtowns. Directly or indirectly, their values thus become embedded in downtown revitalization policies.

Moreover, in most cases these values have been influenced by firsthand experience of downtowns and past revitalization efforts. Respondents answered the three-question survey on a Web site. Question 1 listed 19 factors potentially influential in the success of small-metro CBDs. Respondents were invited to rate each factor on a scale of 1 to 4, from 1 = very important to 4 = not important at all. Comments were solicited at the end of this question.

The Web site used information about a respondent's state or province to generate, in question 2, a list of all small metropolitan areas in their region, defined as their home state or province and contiguous states or provinces. Respondents were asked to rate each downtown within their region. The adoption of this approach was based on the view that, contrary to the knowledge of downtowns of large metropolitan regions, which is continental or global in scope, awareness of those of small-metro downtowns is mostly regional. Space was provided for comments on each CBD.

Respondents were also offered the opportunity to rate small-metro downtowns within their own region that were not listed in question 2. Because our roster included only the names of metropolitan regions with a 100,000-500,000 population, respondents readily used the space reserved for unlisted downtowns and for comments on enumerated metros to single out the successful downtown within multicentreed metropolitan regions.

In question 3, respondents were asked to mention and comment on any successful small-metro downtown, irrespective of its regional location in North America. There was no limit on the number of downtowns that could be identified as very successful or successful in question 2's list, in the space made available in question 2 for additional downtowns within the region of a respondent, or across the continent in question 3.

The second phase of the study consisted of interviews with urban professionals (mostly planners) from the urban areas identified in the survey. These interviews were intended to cast additional light on the conditions accounting for the healthy state of the selected downtowns, including the revitalization strategies deployed there. We carried out 10 face-to-face and 24 telephone interviews. Two more respondents answered our questions in writing.

Factors in the Success of Downtowns

There was a great deal of agreement among survey respondents about the important attributes of successful downtowns. Together, factors believed to account for the success of small-metro CBDs rated as "very important" by at least half the respondents evoke features of traditional pre-World War II downtown areas: an active, street-oriented retail scene; cultural activities; concentrations of jobs; and a pedestrian-friendly environment with busy sidewalks.

The "important" category adds a further characteristic associated with traditional downtowns: Well preserved neighbourhoods indeed constitute a significant component of traditional downtowns. The other factors ranking high in the "important" category can be perceived as amenities and activities likely to attract and retain people in downtown areas—historical character, distinctive architecture, green space, civic events, and tourist activities.

For 18 of the 19 factors listed in the questionnaire, the sum of the "very important" and "important" ratings exceeds 50 per cent. The exception is the presence of an indoor retail mall, which was rated in these two categories by less than one quarter of respondents. This negative attitude towards indoor malls is consistent with the attachment to the traditional perception of downtowns and with the resistance to attempts at bringing downtowns closer to suburban development norms expressed in the choice of many factors categorized as "very important."

Anti-mall sentiments can thus be construed as a commitment to the preservation of the distinctiveness of downtowns within the contemporary urban environment. Another explanation may be the abovementioned failure of most of these malls. When asked for other factors (*i.e.*, factors not listed by us in question 1), many respondents emphasized the importance of a resident population and of a wide variety of land uses to assure 24-hour activity.

Another common response was the need to find a market niche for downtowns. Some mentioned the importance of distinctive, often locally owned shops apt to create a retail environment that departs from the one produced by chains found in the suburbs. Others stressed the role that food, entertainment, and the arts can play in this regard.

But the most frequently voiced comment concerned the need to properly blend and integrate the identified success factors. Numerous respondents observed that more important than the presence of individual activities is how they interact.

In this same vein, many comments concerned the role of small-scale developments, short blocks, and judicious urban design in maximizing pedestrian-based synergy between downtown activities.

Certain attributes are disproportionately present among these downtowns. Seven of them have a large university that is either in or adjacent to the CBD. In five more cases, while not immediately downtown, a university is located within 2 miles of this district; and in two additional cities, Savannah, GA, and

Asheville, NC, there is a smaller college in or close to the CBD. Moreover, five of the selected downtowns host a state capital or provincial legislature.

Another common feature among selected downtowns is their historical character. It is noteworthy that virtually none of the chosen CBDs have undergone a profound alteration of their traditional built environment resulting from redevelopment initiatives. This is due to avoidance of or limited reliance on urban renewal in most selected downtowns and a celebration of this historical flavour. (One exception is downtown Boise, ID, where several blocks were torn down to make way for a regional mall, which never materialized.)

Older, architecturally significant buildings have been restored and parts of these CBDs have received historical district designations. In fact, historical flavour has turned many of these downtowns into major tourist destinations. The importance of tourism can be gauged by the presence of unusual concentrations of resort/motel rooms.

Most of the 19 downtowns register a high ratio of resort/motel rooms to central-city population. Asheville and Santa Fe have 70 rooms per 1,000 residents, and all but three of the remainder have at least 20 rooms per 1,000 residents. For comparison, central cities within metropolitan regions with a modest visitor orientation register scores in the 5-10 per 1,000 range. For example, the ratio is 6 in Kitchener, ON; 8 in Flint, MI; and 9 in Columbus, GA, and Regina, SK.

Nearly all selected downtowns are further advantaged by the easy accessibility of natural amenities, generally bodies of water, untarnished by defacing developments such as waterside freeways. These amenities have usually been the object of restoration projects intended to enhance their appeal and accessibility, ranging from the creation of large waterfront parks, as in Chattanooga, TN, to the naturalization of the banks of the San Luis Obispo, CA, creek.

As indicated, all chosen downtowns share the presence of continuous street-oriented retail facades. This characteristic is hardly specific to successful downtowns, however. By virtue of its age, this built form is found in most downtowns, whether they are successful or not. But the successful CBDs are distinguished from other such areas by the occupation of street-facing premises by well patronized retail and hospitality establishments and by high levels of pedestrian movement. Chosen downtowns were able to substitute activities targeting niche markets for mainstream retail activity, which historically had dominated these districts but in most cases plummeted in the face of suburban competition.

Department and chain stores have generally been replaced with boutiques, restaurants, bars, cultural activities, and entertainment. The adaptation of these activities to downtown markets—the university community, government employees, and tourists, for example—is a factor of synergy within downtown areas, as is the pedestrian friendliness of their street-level environment. The quality of walking space receives considerable attention in downtowns chosen in the survey. Six of the selected downtowns possess a pedestrian mall, a rare occurrence in contemporary North America, and number ban parking lots.

In summary, in addition to a pedestrian-hospitable environment, all highly rated CBDs possess at least one of the following assets: a university that is in or close to downtown; presence in a metropolitan region with a strong visitor orientation; a well preserved historical district; and a state capital or provincial legislature. In justifying their selection of successful downtowns, respondents also alluded to the presence of cultural activities—art galleries and live entertainment—and natural amenities.

Yet for all their shared features, downtowns selected in the survey present many differences. If all these downtowns are perceived as historically rich relative to the remainder of their metropolitan regions, some of them, Chattanooga, TN, and Savannah, GA, in particular, possess an exceptional historical character.

The markets they cater to represent another difference among downtowns chosen in the survey. While most draw several markets, in some places activities are narrowly focused on university students. This is the case in Athens, GA, and State College, PA. Downtown State College, for example, contains 42 bars and 50 fraternity houses. These downtowns are further differentiated by the extent to which they have suffered the retail assault of the suburbs.

In a few instances, thanks to the underdevelopment of suburban retail establishments or the long distance from the downtown of large suburban shopping concentrations, downtowns were able to retain some mainstream shopping. This happened, for example, in Kingston, ON, Santa Barbara, CA, and Rochester, MN. Finally, a few downtowns—Victoria, BC, and Madison, WI, for example—break from the ranks by posting relatively high public transit patronage.

Answers to question 3, where respondents were asked to name successful small-metro downtowns irrespective of their location in North America, added five CBDs to our list. These are downtowns that were mentioned by a minimum of three respondents, had not been selected in the previous question and approximated our size criteria.

All enjoy the presence of a nearby university campus. Portland, ME, and Knoxville, TN, feature well restored historical centres that are popular with tourists. Boulder, CO, has created a downtown pedestrian mall, and downtown Lincoln, NE, is the site of the state capital. Question 3 findings thus confirm those of question 2.

At first glance, observations from this study do not seem to be of much use to the majority of small-metro CBDs, which did not make the list of successful downtowns.

It indeed appears that only those downtowns blessed with extraordinary assets that do not lend themselves easily to duplication (such as core area university campuses, seats of government, or exceptional historical character) can aspire to be successful. But closer examination reveals that extensive efforts were made to revitalize these successful downtowns, which served to create or enhance some of their advantages or to extend the benefits of existing assets.

After all, these are not the only downtowns with a built environment that is distinctive within its metropolitan region or with historical merit. Moreover, it is not unusual to find deteriorated downtowns with universities or government employment close by. Somehow, these less successful downtowns have not been able to take advantage of such features to the same extent as those picked by our survey respondents.

Comments from the survey and subsequent interviews reveal six categories of measures used in successful downtowns. Note that none of the downtowns relied on the full roster of revitalization measures and, indeed, that a number of CBDs made very little use of any of them.

In the first category we find initiatives intended to stimulate development, such as public-sector financial support to private investments in the form of tax increment financing, loan guarantees, and different forms of incentive funding. Within this category also fail public-sector involvement in land assembly and brownfield rehabilitation. The second category groups different types of streetscape, urban furniture, facade improvement programmes, and the introduction of public art.

The third category includes the erection of public buildings such as convention centres, courthouses, and municipal offices. The next group deals with transportation and parking issues. We find under this rubric traffic calming measures, the creation of pedestrian malls, the provision of municipally run parking, as well as control—occasionally banning—of parking lots.

The fifth category concerns the restoration of natural amenities, essentially waterfronts, and the opening of pedestrian-friendly corridors to these sites. And the final category groups efforts at increasing the visibility of the downtown through marketing and event programming.

While most of the selected downtowns enjoy the active involvement of a vast array of organizations, including the planning department, the chamber of commerce, downtown business associations, citizen organizations, private foundations, and arts groups, in other downtowns organizational support is virtually absent.

This is the case in downtown Victoria where, since the dissolution of the Business Improvement Area for lack of interest on the part of property owners, the planning department is pretty much alone in fending for the downtown area.

We now briefly explore how listed measures and the involvement of different organizations congealed into revitalization strategies. To this end, we rely on the content of interviews to picture the strategies adopted by three of our downtowns—Asheville, NC, Chattanooga, TN, and Kingston, ON—chosen for their representation of different types of approaches. Asheville, NC. Following the 1972 opening of a regional shopping mall in the suburbs, downtown Asheville entered a cycle of decline that lasted into the 1980s. Many buildings were boarded up and remaining businesses were often left struggling. This situation prompted a broad collaborative approach involving the City Development Office, whose primary function is to assure downtown revitalization; the Downtown Commission appointed by the city; the Downtown Association, which is responsible for programming and retail marketing; the Arts Council; and strong merchant and resident organizations.

From the mid 1980s, downtown issues assumed a prominent position on the municipal political scene and mobilized multiple interest groups. Since then, local government support for downtown revitalization initiatives has been unwavering, with the exception of a hiatus in the early 1990s when municipal leadership was taken by suburban interests for one term.

Asheville has relied on a variety of financial inducements to stimulate private investment in its downtown, and thereby bolster the commercial and residential function of the district and the rehabilitation of historic buildings. For example, loan guarantees from the municipal administration allowed the restoration of 11 adjacent historic buildings and the erection of a parking structure. Overall, the revitalization of downtown Asheville was not so much the outcome of a few major projects as that of numerous local entrepreneurial initiatives and small-scale improvements to the built environment.

Chattanooga, TN. In Chattanooga, as in Asheville, interest in the downtown was triggered by the severe damage caused by suburban retail development. Downtown Chattanooga lost its department and chain stores to the regional mall, but was able to preserve its office employment base.

The revitalization process was initiated in the early 1980s by three distinct initiatives: one focusing on urban design, the second on the waterfront, and the third on the promotion of specific projects in the CBD. The Chattanooga approach to downtown revitalization parallels characteristics of the "urban regime" model documented within large metropolitan regions. This model involves the presence of stable alliances, driven by private economic interests with the means to carry out their own revitalization efforts.

The Lyndhurst Foundation, set up by a pioneer of the Coca-Cola bottling business, has played a leading role in launching and funding downtown renewal initiatives. What is more, banks have been active in the renovation of historic buildings. Like Asheville, Chattanooga has made extensive use of public funding support to leverage private investment in the downtown and has taken a multipronged approach to revitalization. But more than most other downtowns selected in the survey, Chattanooga has relied on large projects.

This is the case of Warehouse Row, consisting of the restoration of eight historic warehouses; Charleston Place, which includes a resort, conference centre, 30 stores, and an athletic club; the Tennessee Aquarium; and the $120 million waterfront plan presently being implemented. This plan involves the creation of public parks, streets, and the expansion of a museum and the aquarium. The revival of Downtown Kingston began in the late 1960s when railroad lines and derelict industrial structures along Lake Ontario made way for a park, marina, resorts, and luxurious apartment buildings.

Along with the failure of a downtown shopping mall proposal and citizen mobilization against threats to historic structures, this concentration of new developments on the waterfront contributed to the preservation of downtown Kingston's traditional built environment. In comparison to Asheville, Chattanooga, and many other downtowns selected in the survey, the last decades have witnessed little public sector intervention in downtown Kingston.

After involvement in waterfront redevelopment, public sector efforts were pretty much confined to streetscape beautification and an upgrading of the downtown's urban furniture. Still, the district remained healthy and even held on to some of its mainstream retail activity, thanks to the distance of the regional mall from the downtown and a large close-by population. In addition, the Business Improvement Area is effective in marketing the downtown and recruiting new stores to fill empty premises.

And with different community organizations using the downtown as a venue for their events, there are activities programmed over all summer weekends. Asheville and Chattanooga mirror the high level of interventionism shared by most successful downtowns identified in the study. Kingston, on the other hand, figures among selected downtowns where public sector involvement has been lowest.

The contrast between these downtowns can be interpreted as a consequence of differences in the severity of threats confronting them. Again, in a fashion that is common to most downtowns rated as successful in the survey, Asheville's and Chattanooga's revitalization efforts were reactions to manifest signs of downtown decline in the wake of advancing retail suburbanization.

Kingston, on the other hand, is more representative of the minority of successful downtowns where damage inflicted by suburbanization was limited.

Many interviewees and a number of comments made in the survey stress the fragility of vital downtowns.

They underscore the need for constant vigilance to safeguard the health of these districts, and thus the importance of durable political support and stable downtown alliances. Sustained mobilization around downtown issues is needed to secure municipal government interest in downtown matters and willingness to tailor interventions to CBD realities. Downtowns indeed require a different approach to planning and development from the remainder of their metropolitan regions, most particularly suburban areas.

Financial incentives are frequently necessary to lure investments to the core, and in contrast to most other parts of metropolitan areas, the vitality of downtowns demands an environment that is stimulating for pedestrians. But the risk always looms that the special needs of downtowns will be overlooked by city councils, especially if they are dominated by pro-suburban interests. The outcome could then be extreme difficulty in attracting investments and, over time, a less distinctive built environment.

In addition, despite the stabilizing effect of universities and government, the replacement of mainstream by specialized retailing and heavy reliance on hospitality and tourism make the downtowns selected in the survey acutely sensitive to economic cycles. Less capable than mainstream suburban retail to withstand recessions, the economies of successful downtowns risk being devastated by a severe downturn.

These downtowns would then require economic rebuilding strategies to take advantage of the subsequent recovery. Successful downtowns must also constantly stay on top of the frequent fashion shifts characteristic of their niche retail markets and of the hospitality and entertainment sectors.

When considering the duplication potential of lessons drawn from our selected downtowns, we must keep in mind that these are the bright stars in the constellation of small-metro downtowns, and that it is unrealistic to expect a generalization of their level of performance across CBDs of similar size urban areas. There are obviously wide variations in the extent to which such downtowns can benefit from the experience of their successful counterparts.

For example, many lessons from the downtowns chosen in the survey are pertinent to other downtowns where the traditional built environment is still in place. In contrast, such lessons are of little relevance to those downtowns where the pre-World War II layout has been severely compromised.

Still, the situation for small-metro downtowns is not as somber as it was in the earlier phases of suburbanization, when the lure of the periphery was fuelled by generalized aspiration for a car-oriented lifestyle. For the many individuals for whom this lifestyle has since lost its luster, the traditional layout of downtowns can be attractive, provided these districts contain activities adapted to their needs and preferences.

Demographic trends are also in part favourable to downtown areas. The prevalence of small, predominantly childless households in downtowns and surrounding neighbourhoods has long been documented. The bulge of aging baby boomers, some of whom are ready to trade their suburban homes for smaller dwellings in a pedestrian-friendly area, provides ample potential residents for core areas. This is also the case for the growing proportion of childless households in all age categories.

What is more, interest in downtowns may be bolstered by present-day environmental and economic development thinking. The compact and pedestrian-oriented characteristics of downtown areas are consistent with smart growth principles presently in vogue. Downtown revitalization figures prominently among measures that the smart growth movement advances to contain urban sprawl and reduce automobile dependence. From an economic development perspective, lively, entertainment- and culture-rich downtowns are depicted as appealing to the "creative class," broadly defined to include people engaged in professional, product development, entrepreneurial, artistic, and management occupations. According to the perspective expounded by Richard Florida, the creative class assumes a leading role in economic growth.

This view therefore implies an enhanced ability on the part of metropolitan regions possessing a healthy downtown to attract members of the creative class and thereby enjoy resulting economic rewards. Revealingly, metropolitan regions whose downtowns were selected in our study figure prominently among urban areas in their size category posting a high presence of the creative class.

The foremost generalizable lesson that can be distilled from our selected downtowns is disarmingly simple: Their success can be attributed to an ability to attract people and assure that they remain in their midst to pursue many of their activities. Chosen CBDs possess magnets (a university, government presence, historical character, and specialized retail establishments) and provide reasons for people to spend time downtown.

Selected downtowns indeed offer a synergy-rich environment consisting of activities that are well adapted to core-area markets and are set within a pedestrian-hospitable environment. In reality, however, it is difficult to distinguish between magnet and retention features, because the presence of many people and of the activities they support itself adds to the allure of downtown areas.

If typical small-metro downtowns cannot improvise the university campus, seat of government, or exceptional historical character commonly found in the downtowns selected in our survey, they can nonetheless make efforts to draw employment and, perhaps with most promise, new housing. Lessons from successful downtowns underscore the need for strategies that are both multipronged and well coordinated. In typical small-metro downtowns, revitalization strategies would at once need to attract employment and housing and create an environment that is hospitable to downtown workers and nearby residents.

Ideally, such an environment will possess historical flavour and lively street life, two characteristics that will differentiate it from the suburbs. It will also harbour retail and services that are suited to the needs and tastes of people who are attracted downtown. For example, to cater to the needs of nearby residents and encourage further housing development, a downtown must provide a variety of food outlets.

Given the nature of the markets they are susceptible to lure, success for typical small-metro downtowns is a function of their ability to provide activities and settings that are unique within their metropolitan regions. These downtowns should attempt to launch a virtuous cycle whereby the attainment of a critical mass of users and activities within a distinct environment will make them attractive to a growing number of visitors. This type of cycle is a major factor in the success of the downtowns selected in the survey.

Our research findings are generally in accord with the transition over the last decades in the perception of the role of downtowns and of appropriate revival interventions. They resonate with the recent literature's emphasis on the preservation and enhancement of the traditional layout and historical character of downtowns. Our results also mirror the importance recent writings give to people places, pedestrian connectivity, variety of land uses, and, generally, quality of life within downtown areas.

Likewise, many of our selected downtowns have adopted revitalization strategies that are consistent with those documented in recent writings. These strategies are inclusive, drawing on diverse constituencies such as property owners, merchants, residents, governments, and historic preservationists and rely extensively on private/public sector partnerships.

Yet, findings from our research are occasionally at variance with the literature. This is mostly a consequence of the scant coverage it gives to downtowns belonging to metropolitan regions with populations of 100,000-500,000. Whereas the revitalization strategies of large-city downtowns can benefit from extensive public transit systems, national- and world-scale attractions, the enduring presence of mainstream retail, large office space concentrations, and the key role of big corporations, most CBDs of small metropolitan regions cannot count on such advantages.

This explains in large part the differences between our findings and previous literature depictions of large-metro downtown revitalization strategies. More than those of their larger counterparts, successful downtowns of small metropolitan regions tend to target niche markets, make use of small- rather than large-scale revitalization interventions, and rely on the public sector.

The results of this research were not surprising insofar as they confirm the observation that the vast majority of small-metro downtowns have not recovered from the severe damage inflicted by suburbanization. Findings also mirror the conceptual turn that has run through the planning profession over the last decades. The emphasis of revitalization strategies on features of traditional downtowns, such as street-oriented and pedestrian-friendly environments, is in agreement with current thinking within the planning profession.

The assets respondents associate with a successful downtown paint the picture of the traditional downtown, harking back to the pre-1950 period. This depiction is consistent with the present popularity of built environment preservation and new urbanism within the planning community. The usefulness of these findings lies in lessons derived from the downtowns identified as successful, which can be of aid to ailing CBDs. The proposals generated by this research stress the need to emphasize the distinction of downtowns from the suburban realm.

First, this type of revitalization strategy should involve an accentuation of historical character and street-level activity, two features that distinguish these districts from suburban-type developments.

Second, with the irrevocable loss of mainstream retail activity to the suburbs, downtown revival strategies are compelled to capitalize on the few markets where this sector holds a comparative advantage over suburban locales.

Acknowledgements We acknowledge financial support from the Waterloo Community-University Research Alliance and thank the planners who answered our questionnaire and who agreed to be interviewed. We are also grateful to the anonymous referees for their helpful comments.

Because of the limited literature on small-metro downtown revitalization and considerable overlapping in the nature and sequence of revitalization phases in both large and small metropolitan region downtowns, the following four paragraphs draw on writing pertaining to both categories of downtowns.

The sample was constructed from several sources: rosters of both the American Institute of Certified Planners and the Canadian Institute of Planners; the Web sites of North American university planning, urban studies, and geography departments and programmes; and the Web sites of organizations involved in downtown revitalization and urban research in the U.S. and Canada. All identified academics were included in our sample.

As regards planners employed by small-metro central cities, two names were incorporated in the sample from those administrations with less than seven accredited planners, and where there were more than seven planners, every fourth name was added to our list. All professionals with a possible interest in downtowns who are associated with government agencies or economic development or research institutes with an urban focus were surveyed.

The presence of a retail mall was rated as "not important at all" by 33.9 per cent of respondents, by far the highest score within this category. The second highest factor rated as "not important at all"—abundant parking—was selected by a meagre 5.4 per cent of respondents.

Irrespective of the 20 per cent rule, cores that were placed in either of the two categories by less than four respondents were not included. The few cases where the 20 per cent threshold was attained with less than four citations are due to a strong reliance on the "don't know" option. The important proportion of tourist- and university-oriented downtowns within those given highest rankings could be interpreted as an artifact of the method used in this research. The presence of academics in the sample would favour the reporting of downtowns with a university, because of the evident familiarity of this group of respondents with such CBDs.

And tourist destinations are obviously better known by everyone, including our respondents. Two features of the methodology reduce the likelihood of such biases, however. First, academics amounted to only a little above a third of our sample. Second, and most importantly, to assure that as many downtowns as possible would qualify as successful, we set low thresholds—citation by 20 per cent or more for the cores on the regional lists and three mentions or more for the continent-wide selection.

The only selected downtown that does not fully share the historical features and intense street orientation of the highly rated core areas is that of Rochester, MN, where the main focus has been on a modernization of the downtown through the building of an indoor mall and of a skyway and underground passageway system. The resort/motel room to central-city population ratio was calculated from American Automobile Association and Canadian Automobile Association tour book resort/motel directories.

This method somewhat underestimates the presence of resort/motel rooms, because the directories exclude lower-end facilities. In the case of Burlington, VT, the central city was combined with a suburb. This is because while close to City of Burlington boundaries, this metropolitan area's main concentration of resort and motel rooms is in South Burlington.

There are two explanations for the exceptional presence of pedestrian malls in these downtowns. First, by virtue of their success, we can assume that some of the downtowns selected in the survey are among those that have been most engaged in revitalization efforts, one form of which was the creation of a pedestrian mall.

Second, and perhaps most importantly, these downtowns are among the few that can generate sufficient numbers of pedestrians and activities to bring malls to life, thanks in large part to the presence of tourists and university students. Elsewhere, the use of pedestrian malls as instruments of revitalization has generally failed lamentably.

In Rochester, MN, the Mayo Clinic and the Methodist Hospital attract many visitors—patients and their families—which explains the high resort/motel room to resident ratio. Rochester ranks fifth in this regard among core areas. Moreover, the Mayo Clinic, with its intense medical research activity, maintains with downtown Rochester a relationship that recalls the one prevailing between centrally located universities and their downtown areas. Respondents listed a total of 170 downtowns in question.

f these, only 17 were part of metropolitan regions that come close to our size criteria and were mentioned by at least three respondents. Twelve of these downtowns were also ranked highly in question 2, thus lending additional credence to this question's regional selections. Of the five additional downtowns mentioned in answers to question 3, two had been listed as options in the previous question, but had not been selected by a sufficient proportion of respondents from their home region to be included among successful CBDs. Of the remaining three downtowns, one was excluded from question 2's options because the population of its metropolitan region is slightly above the 500,000 limit. The other two are part of larger consolidated census metropolitan areas, Detroit and Denver.

A survey carried out in Kitchener-Waterloo, ON, a highly suburbanized urban area belonging to a 414,284-resident metropolitan region, has revealed that close to half the population would consider living in a neighbourhood close to a downtown.

This interest in central area living was, however, conditional upon the downtown being revitalized into a safe, pedestrian-friendly environment where respondents could find activities compatible with their tastes, and on the availability in central neighbourhoods of their preferred types of housing.

Many of these individuals were attracted to central neighbourhoods by their mature character and the possibility of reducing dependence on the automobile. The results of the Kitchener-Waterloo study are consistent with those of recent studies documenting a housing renaissance in numerous central areas.

2

Industrial Relations and Resort Professionals

INDUSTRIAL RELATIONS

'Human resource management' and the 'new industrial relations', like most terms in the field of management and organization, originated in the United States. Those using the terms were not doing so with a concern for precision; nor were they proposing any tight distinction between them. Rather, they were seeking to convey to a predominantly management audience a sense of innovation and change. There appear to be no compelling reasons why we should therefore seek to impose artificial boundaries of our own.

However, 'human resource management' generally conjures up an image of a high technology non-union environment while the use of the term 'industrial relations' inevitably implies that trade unions or some other form of workforce representation are involved. In considering human resource management and the new industrial relations, it is on this absence or presence of a trade union and its consequences for policy, practice, and performance that we will concentrate.

The 1981 *Newsweek* article which perhaps more than anything else proclaimed '*The New Industrial Relations*' in the USA suggested that it had arrived almost unnoticed, and until then unannounced, accelerating the demise of the traditional adversarial industrial relations and its replacement by a new collaborative system. In keeping with the spirit of the times, the article went on to claim that the influences on the new approach came not from Japan or from any European system of codetermination but from a uniquely American tradition with its roots in the work of Mayo, Maslow, and McGregor.

In the kind of system outlined in the *Newsweek* article, the role of trade unions was rather blurred. The work of Kochan, Katz, and McKersie presented a positive view of the trade union contribution by focusing on cases where successful union-management collaboration had resulted in significant change.

They celebrated the 'new' by entitling their book *The Transformation of American Industrial Relations*. What they showed was the possibility of bringing about marked improvements through management-union cooperation. What they could not do was indicate if this yielded better performanace than non-union arrangements.

Alongside the debate on the new industrial relations, human resource management was emerging in the 1980s in the United States as a possible solution to the challenge of an increasingly competitive national and international industrial environment.

Although the concept had been around for some time, often as an alternative to the rather jaded image of personnel management, it was given a major boost by the rediscovery of the human side of enterprise in Peters and Waterman *In Search of Excellence*. In this book, trade unions scarcely merited a mention; unlike the debate on the new industrial relations, it relegated unions to a minor historical role. Certainly we are left with the impression that they played no significant part in any 'excellent' companies.

As human resource management gained prominence in the United States, it was possible to discern three main strands of work. The first, captured in the work of writers like Tichy, Fombrun, and Devanna, Miles and Snow and Schuler, was primarily concerned with the relationship between business strategy and human resource management strategy. This implies that the key issue in human resource management is the question of strategic choice and recognition of the importance of considering human resource management issues in terms of their integration with wider business strategy. Driven by business and market considerations, this perspective treats trade unions as irrelevant and they are rarely if ever mentioned.

The second strand of work is captured in what might be termed the Harvard view of human resource management. This is essentially a generic approach which attempts to make the subject area comprehensible and interesting to Harvard MBA students and to general managers who have often been more attracted by the quantitative, financial, and strategic aspects of business. It is therefore an approach which tries to capture and re-present the field of what by tradition had been personnel management.

Apart from providing a much more contemporary 'feel',) the resulting analytic and descriptive material does not differ significantly from a number of personnel texts. Furthermore it explicitly acknowledges the role of trade unions in its conceptual framework by introducing the concept of 'stakeholder interests' as one of the key contingent variables helping to shape policy choices. However, once the more detailed material and the case studies are presented, trade unions are relegated to a very minor role. It was left to Kochan and his colleagues at MIT to present a more comprehensive framework which made explicit both the influences in the wider economic system and the potential role of trade unions.

The third strand, which perhaps links in more directly to Peters and Waterman as well as to the non-union case studies of Foulkes (1980) and some of the work of academics such as Lawler presents human resource management as an approach which is concerned with the full integration and full utilization of the workforce. This overlaps with the initial new industrial relations interest in the work of people like Maslow and McGregor. Indeed it is captured perhaps best in the writing of Walton and his contrast between the old control philosophy and the preferred new philosophy of high commitment.

Both Lawler and Walton acknowledge that in high commitment organizations trade unions could have a role to play, but they tend to pass on quickly to consider non-union environments. Foulkes is explicitly writing about policies in large non-union companies. This perspective maps out the potentially distinctive features of human resource management which have been developed and presented elsewhere. With its focus on an integrative, unitarist perspective, in which emphasis is placed on commitment to the organization, the role of trade unions is called into question. Indeed, one of the key research questions which emerges is whether it is possible to display commitment to both company and trade union.

This discussion of the emergence of human resource management and the new industrial relations in the United States is relevant partly because, at a key period in the 1980s, the United States was held up as the model to emulate in the UK. This was reflected in the warm relationship between Reagan and Thatcher at a political level and in the interest in monetarist free market economies at a policy level. Another source of interest was the legislative framework for industrial relations which in the United States reflected the dominance given to the operation of the market economy and made it more difficult for the unions to act as a significant economic constraint. Of course, as Beardwell has emphasized, there are dangers in taking the comparison too far.

The context in the UK in the early 1980s was different in some important respects from the United States; in particular, the trade unions were more powerful and membership was much higher. However, there was a vacuum created by the apparent failure of the pluralist industrial relations strategy to deliver either good industrial relations or an efficient and productive industry. This resulted in a major policy debate about the need for new legislation and about the appropriate role for trade unions. As Beardwell acknowledges, much of the rhetoric of the debate was drawn from America.

What this meant was that the UK became susceptible to American ideas about human resource management and the new industrial relations. Beardwell has drawn a distinction between two approaches to the new industrial relations.

He sees one as concerned with the reform of industrial relations, manifested in interest in job control, single union agreements, pendulum arbitration, and the like. The second approach is concerned with the new ideology of human resource management, with its focus on individualism and therefore it's potential to replace the traditional pluralist system.

The typical illustration of the reformist approach is the new Japanese manufacturing site, perhaps Toshiba or Nissan where management appears willing to accept a single union on their own terms. The American high technology firms such as IBM, Hewlett-Packard, Texas Instruments, and DEC represent the stereotype of the second approach.

However, as Garrahan and Stewart have argued in the case of Nissan and McLoughlin has shown in the case of high technology companies, the two approaches overlap, implying that the idea of the two perspectives existing Janus-like is too sharply drawn. Recognition of overlap has also been apparent in some of the debates about industrial relations and human resource management. What this implies is that managements' broad policy choices are not about a reformist industrial relations or human resource management but about options along two dimensions.

The first dimension is concerned with industrial relations. Following the Beardwell analysis, the type of industrial relations sought by management may range from the unreconstructed pluralism still found in some corners of the public sector, through a reformist type of new industrial relations complete with single union deal and pendulum arbitration to an absence of trade unions.

The second dimension is concerned with human resource management. Managers must decide how far they wish to embrace it. If they consider the issue strategically, they may opt to pursue a full-utilization model through policies designed to generate employee commitment, flexibility, and quality; and they may choose to do this for all or part of their staff. Alternatively, they may deliberately set out to pursue a strategy of cost-minimization, seeking high flexibility through short-term contracts and a policy of hire and fire. In such contexts, there is no pretence of seeking workforce commitment to the organization.

Considering the policy choices using these two dimensions takes us away from the conventional debates about the new versus the old or industrial relations and trade unions versus human resource management. Instead it opens up a variety of possible arrangements including trade unions operating alongside a set of human resource management initiatives. Alternatively, management may try to abandon any semblance of either traditional or new industrial relations and at the same time avoid any of the mutual commitments implied by human resource management.

Any consideration of this wider set of choices forces us to look at the key contextual influences in the economy and the market place. It also requires a reconsideration of the ideological framework. The contrast between pluralism and unitarism may need to be replaced by notions of coexistence or complementarity. The possibility that some managers may choose to avoid both trade unions and human resource management opens up the question of the black hole of non-unionism, for too long neglected by researchers.

At present we know too little about the policy choices that managers actually make, about what influences them and about their consequences. In our view the debate about human resource management and the new industrial relations has probably gone on long enough and the best way to take the debate forward is to generate empirical data which can inform it. The kind of research required must be both sufficiently wide-ranging to detect key trends and developments and sufficiently detailed to explore beneath the surface. Both surveys and case studies are required.

We need to know more than whether unions survive; we need to know whether they play an active role or have become an empty shell. We need to know more than whether an organization has introduced single status or quality circles. To explore any comprehensive theory of human resource management we need to understand how these techniques combine to provide some sort of integrated approach.

Researchers have already embarked upon this task. The breadth is provided in the WIRS. WIRS3, carried out in 1990, can find little evidence of major advances in human resource management. Such advances as there have been are more likely to have occurred in unionized workplaces. Non-union workplaces apparently avoid human resource management practices, preferring, it seems, to treat the workforce harshly with consequent costs for both employer and employees.

Such evidence further reinforces scepticism about the value of debates about trade unions or human resource management. Looking at the impact of human resource management, Fernie*et al.*, in their analysis of WIRS3, have shown that those workplaces that adopt single status and employee involvement are more likely to report better performance. However we can only take the debate about human resource management and the new industrial relations forward a little with WIRS3 because the survey omitted large areas of human resource management policy and practice.

McLoughlin and Beardwell, in their research on non-union establishments, have met the research criteria spelt out above by combining survey and case study material to highlight the diversity of practice in the non-union sector. They explore the question of whether a human resource management strategy reduces the propensity of workers to join a union. The conclusion appears to be that although this may contribute, a range of other factors, centring around the low perceived instrumental value of union membership and lack of encouragement from trade unions, are more important.

Whatever the reasons, only 5 per cent of the establishments in their sample of high technology companies in South-East England recognize a trade union. Useful as it is, their research concentrates on issues of union joining and related management strategy rather than the detailed application and impact of human resource management.

In many respects their work is reinforced and complemented by the findings of the CLIRS2. For example, this survey reports diversity of practice about trade union recognition at new sites. Recognition is more likely where there is centralized pay bargaining and less likely in companies which, strategically, can be classified as financial controllers. Perhaps predictably, the decision about whether or not to recognize a trade union at a new establishment is usually taken centrally. This survey also finds that only a few companies practice what can be described as 'sophisticated' human resource management, reflected in eight indicators, but those that do are more likely to recognize a trade union.

These major surveys, together with a certain amount of detailed case study work, help to shed some light on the relationship between aspects of the new industrial relations and human resource management. However, they are unable to explore in sufficient detail the issue of the impact of trade unions on human resource management policy, practice, and performance. If we take the range of practices associated with human resource management, are there any which are more likely to be found in union or non-union workplaces?

Are unions inhibitors or facilitators of human resource management initiatives and, keeping an eye on the new industrial relations, does it matter whether the presence of a union is based on traditional UK multi-unionism or a single union deal? The aim of the remainder of this is to report research which helps to answer these questions.

In seeking to answer the question of whether human resource management is compatible with trade-unionism, we will operationalize the two dimensions described above. Along the dimension concerned with industrial relations policy and the union role we group establishments into four categories according to whether they recognize no union, recognize a single union in the context of a single union deal, recognize a single union but without any special deal, and whether they recognize multiple unions. On the human resource management dimension, we identify four categories acccording to whether they have an explicit human resource management strategy and the extent to which they make use of a range of human resource management practices. This provides us with a classification which we have initially applied to non-union establishments but which can equally well be applied to any workplace.

Those with an explicit human resource strategy and a high use of human resource practices we label the Good. They adopt an approach close to the kind of 'high involvement' management espoused by Lawler. At the other extreme, those with no human resource strategy and a low adoption of human resource practices we label the Bad. This could be construed as cautious pragmatism, but it is more likely to be poor, ill-thought through management. Those with an explicit strategy but one which results in a low take-up of human resource practices we label the Ugly.

By implication, since they claim to have a strategy, they have thought through how they wish to manage their human resources and decided not to adopt a 'full utilization' approach. They fit the pattern outlined by Millward of bleak environments and limited rights. The Good and the Ugly have some parallels with the 'soft' and 'hard' versions of human resource management identified among others by Keenoy and Storey. Finally, those with no human resource strategy but a high use of human resource practices we label the Lucky. They are lucky in that they have stumbled on a set of practices, perhaps through outside guidance, perhaps through emulation or perhaps by following fads.

The potential value of a classification of this sort is that it explicitly takes into account the issue of strategic integration, emphasized by many writers on human resource management. Good human resource management should be based on a strategy and on extensive rather than narrowly focused application of human resource management practices. The research can explore the association between the two dimensions.

The second central research question is whether the trade unions act as a drag or a spur to performance. To explore this we will again use the same classification but add data on outcomes. Three types of outcome will be explored since they are the most central to the debates on the new industrial relations, the role of the unions, and the efficacy of human resource management.

These outcomes are those predicted as first level outcomes by human resource management theory such as levels of commitment, staff quality, and flexibility. The second are employee relations outcomes such as industrial conflict, labour turnover, and absence. The third are performance outcomes including resilience in the face of recession and benchmark estimates of establishment quality and productivity.

The Method of Analysis

The data reported here are part of a larger study of human resource management in greenfield sites—new, often purpose-built factories and offices. The main study has three central aims; it examines what happens when greenfield sites turn brown; that is, as they age. The second part is concerned with the impact of ownership and in particular foreign ownership on the nature of human resource management.

The third question is concerned with the impact of human resource management. An overriding question is the extent to which human resource management has become established as a preferred management option, on the assumption that this will be most dearly manifested in new establishments where managers have greater freedom to express their preferred choice. There are three parts to the study; the first is a reanalysis of part of WIRS3; the second is a survey of greenfield sites in the UK; and the third is a number of case studies in some of the surveyed establishments.

For our present purposes we will use data collected from the survey of greenfield sites. The survey was conducted in mid-1993, when a postal questionnaire was sent to just over 1,000 establishments in the UK employing more than fifty staff, including about 800 set up since 1980. We received responses from 393 establishments, subsequently reduced to 344 since some had less than fifty employees. Of the 344, 96 are purpose-built greenfield sites, new plants or offices being used for the first time; 152 are 'refurbished' sites, where there had been a major change of ownership and usually of activity, often following a shut-down period for the refurbishment; and 96 were set up before 1980.

For this analysis, we have restricted the sample to the greenfield and refurbished sites set up after 1980. This cut-off date was chosen as it marks the point at which Thatcherism began to have an impact at work, launching the debate about the new industrial relations. Establishments started since then provide what is arguably the best setting in which to explore the choices managers make about how to operate in the new industrial relations environments.

At new establishments, unconstrained by history and tradition in the workplace, managers are most free to introduce the policies and practices of their choice. Equally, they provide the most exacting test of how far trade unions are able to respond to the challenges they face in the new industrial relations. If they can flourish in such settings, then we can be more confident about their ability to retain a viable long-term role. In operating with new establishments we recognize that there is a different argument that could be made about looking at processes of change in older establishments. However, we believe that the cutting edge of innovations and emerging patterns in human resource management and the new industrial relations is likely to be found in new establishments.

The sample therefore contains 248 post- 1980 establishments of which 166 (66.9 per cent) are non-union and 82 (33.1 per cent) are unionized. These figures are in line with what we might expect from the analysis of WIRS3. Analysis by ownership reveals 104 UK owned establishments, 45 American-owned, 52 Japanese-owned, 19 German owned, and the remaining 24 owned by companies from the rest of the world which in practice means predominantly European Union and EFTA countries.

Comparison with WIRS3 shows that the sample is broadly representative in size, based on number of employees and allowing for exclusion of those employing less than fifty staff. It is weighted towards manufacturing industry; indeed 84 per cent are manufacturing establishments, 10 per cent are in financial services, and 6 per cent are other services. The questionnaire contained four sections. The first asked for background information on issues such as size, ownership, sector, age, and location.

The second contained items about the presence of mission statements, human resource management strategy, and the degree of 'parental' influence. The third contained twenty-six items describing a range of contemporary human resource management practices and asked whether they are currently in existence at the establishment and whether they were used one year after start-up. The final asked about a range of outcomes.

These fall into three groups concerned with human resource management, employee relations, and establishment performance. The vast majority of questionnaires were completed either by the head of personnel at the establishment or by the most senior line manager with special responsibility for personnel issues, which in practice often meant the Managing Director, General Manager, or Plant Manager.

Management and Unions

In this subsection we examine the impact of trade unions on human resource management strategy and human resource management practices. We do this by comparing the establishments falling into the four trade union categories. These are those with no union (n = 166), those with a single union deal (n = 31), those with a single union but no single union deal (n = 18), and those with multiple-unionism (n = 33). In the questionnaire we were unable to explore the content of the single union deals, so there are risks in assuming that they are similar in nature. However, the question was quite explicit in asking whether there was a single union agreement.

How helpful is a union presence? One indirect way of exploring the impact of the unions was to gauge whether managers considered their presence to be helpful to the achievement of company goals. Sixty-six per cent of managers in establishments where unions were recognized considered the unions to be helpful. This ranged from 70 per cent in the case of single union deals to 55.6 per cent where there are single unions but no special deal.

Multi-union establishments fell between the others with 62.5 per cent considering them helpful. The differences are not significant so we must be cautious, despite the apparent trend, in concluding that unions in the context of single union deals are seen as more helpful. This is a somewhat surprising result if we accept the popular assumption that single union deals are explicitly designed to foster cooperation. It suggests that single union deals, assuming they have been correctly identified, do not have the clear-cut advantages sometimes claimed for them by their enthusiastic advocates.

On the other hand, with two-thirds of managers taking the view that the unions are helpful, it is possible that new establishments provide an opportunity for managers to develop the kind of cooperation they want irrespective of whether or not they have a single union deal.

Unions and human resource strategy The questionnaire contained a section of items on aspects of policy and strategy. The responses in this section are important in setting a key part of the context for human resource management. It is hypothesized that those who take strategy more seriously will have better outcomes.

However, as noted elsewhere the content of the strategy will be as important as having a strategy. The comparison of the 166 non-union establishments with those where various union arrangements were recognized. In this table we present the descriptive statistics, together with a Chi2 test of differences between the categories.

This controls for background variables and is a more rigorous test of differences between the categories. All types of unionized establishment are more likely to have a mission statement than non-union establishments. However, when we control for factors such as size and ownership, the difference is only significant for establishments with single union deals. Where there is a mission statement, it is more likely to include explicit reference to human resource issues in non-union establishments.

Although the Chi2 result falls just short of significance, the multivariate test is significant and reveals that once again the differences can be accounted for mainly by the establishments with a single union deal. The third key issue is the presence of a human resource strategy, formally endorsed and actively supported by the top management team at the establishment. Once again the unionized establishments are more likely to report the existence of such a strategy, although in both tables the results fall just short of significance.

The differences can be accounted for mainly by the establishments with single union deals. One indication of an effective strategy is that it is reasonably consistent over time. Although the differences are not significant, the results indicate that where a mission statement or a human resource management strategy exists, the non-union establishments tend to be more likely to have altered both. The results from this first set of data are reasonably clear-cut. Those new establishments where a union is recognized are more likely than non-union establishments to have a mission statement and to include in it specific reference to human resource issues, and more likely to have an explicit human resource strategy.

These differences remain when we control for a range of background factors so they cannot be accounted for by variations in size, sector, or ownership. However, the presence of all these reflections of a strategy varies within the unionized establishments and is much the most likely to be found where there is a single union deal.

We cannot establish cause and effect. It is possible that those who think strategically opt for a single union deal. Alternatively, agreement to consider a single union deal forces establishments to confront related strategic human resource issues.

It is probably most plausible to suggest that since we are dealing with new establishments, the development of human resource strategy and the planning of a single union deal go hand in hand. In this context, the role of the parent, as Marginson et al, have indicated, appears to be important in shaping attitudes towards trade union recognition and the form it takes. Whatever the reasons, the key finding is that it is the unionized rather than the non-union establishments that take the lead in developing human resource strategy.

Unions and Human Resource Practices

The data indicate that a union presence is associated with a greater likelihood of a human resource strategy and a mission statement. However, it is wise to be somewhat sceptical about both unless they are clearly reinforced by a set of relevant practices.

This subsection therefore takes us a step further by examining the presence at the new sites of the sort of practices commonly associated with human resource management.

The list is not exhaustive and it concentrates on human resource practices rather than some of those that might be associated with the more narrowly defined industrial relations aspects of the new industrial relations. This reflected the key focus of the study and also our knowledge that most of the establishments in the sample would be non-union and therefore issues like pendulum arbitration would be irrelevant.

Perhaps the most interesting result is the lack of consistent differences between union and non-union establishments. In both sets of new establishments, the use of a majority of the innovative human resource management practices is now the norm. Nevertheless significant differences emerge on seven of the items. Two of these concern status and harmonization. Here the differences are not so much between union and non-union as between non-union and single union deals on the one hand and other forms of union recognition on the other. However, in both cases it is the non-union establishments that are most likely to report these practices; and, the differences between the non-union and single union deal establishments are significant.

Therefore, although establishments with single union deals are more like the non-union establishments, they still fall some way short on single status. The pattern is somewhat similar for two other items, merit pay and appraisal. Non-union establishments are well ahead of all forms of unionized establishment in the use of merit pay. The differences are much less marked on appraisal where it seems that the multi-union establishments are less likely to operate it. The three remaining items are those where establishments with a single union deal stand out as most likely to have adopted a practice. One is the use of trainability as a major selection criterion; the others are concerned with integration of strategy.

Establishments with single union deals are much more likely to claim that human resource policies are integrated with business strategy and that the various human resource policies are integrated with each other. This would fit with the earlier claims to be more likely to have a human resource strategy.

Taking the set of practices as a whole, it appears that they are most likely to be reported in establishments with a single union deal, closely followed by non-union establishments. However, the other unionized establishments are often little different, indicating that a union presence is no bar to most human resource practices.

Despite this, the exceptions may be important. Unionized establishments are less likely to have progressed towards single status and less likely to be using appraisal-linked merit pay. These touch on traditional trade union territory and it would seem that in this territory they are still able to exert some influence on workplace practices.

Unions and Types Strategy

There is some evidence from the preceding analysis that unionized workplaces, and more particularly those with a single union deal, are more likely to have developed a coherent human resource strategy. However, not all establishments have a strategy and not all have introduced human resource management practices. To explore whether a union presence is compatible with the kind of high utilization human resource strategy sometimes associated with best human resource practice but also often seen as inimical to a trade union presence, we can reclassify establishments. The basis for this classification was introduced earlier. Those establishments labelled Good have a human resource strategy, defined in the questionnaire as being formally endorsed and actively supported by the top management at the site; and also a high use of human resource practices, defined arbitrarily as more than half of those listed.

The Bad are the opposite in that they have no strategy and use less than half the practices listed. The Ugly have a strategy but use less than half the practices while the Lucky have no strategy but use more than half the practices.

If strategic integration is at all important, we would expect the Good to report better outcomes than the Bad. If strategic integration around a distinctive set of human resource practices confers an advantage then we would also expect to see the Good report better outcomes than the Ugly and Lucky. By comparing across the groups we can also identify whether adoption of practices without a strategy—the approach of the Lucky—also has an impact on outcomes. In our total sample of 245 establishments, 107 (43.7 per cent) were classified as Good, 70 (28.6 per cent) as Bad, 28 (11.4 per cent) as Ugly, and 40 (16.3 per cent) as Lucky.

The key question for the debate about human resource management and the new industrial relations is whether the Good are compatible with unionism.

The results confirm that a union presence is compatible with a high utilization model of human resource management. Indeed, if we examine the distribution, a higher proportion of union than non-union establishments fall in the good category. This is due to the greater likelihood that they will have a human resource strategy. In contrast, more of the non-union establishments fall into the lucky category.

They have adopted the practices but have not developed a strategy. The multivariate analysis confirms this pattern but reveals where the differences lie. It is the establishments with a single union deal that are significantly more likely to fall within the Good category while the non-union are significantly more likely to be Lucky. No group stands out as more likely to be Bad or Ugly, although, contrary to expectation, there is a slight tendency for them to be unionized rather than not.

Summarizing the results to date, we have shown that at new establishments, those set up in the 1980s or more recently, industrial relations, manifested in a trade union presence and human resource management are able to exist side by side. However, we can go further than this. It appears that, more particularly in the case of single union deals, it is less a matter of the systems coexisting as of being integrated through a coherent strategy.

Indeed, unionized workplaces are more likely than their non-union counterparts to have a human resource strategy. There do appear to be some differences between the types of union presence. Without a single union deal, there is a slightly lower use of human resource practices and slightly less evidence of the sort of strategic pursuit of a high utilization policy categorized as the Good.

We have shown that with perhaps two exceptions, represented by single status and appraisal-related merit pay, the unions do not inhibit human resource management practice. The next key question is whether they have any impact on performance.

The Impact of Unions

If we wish to conduct a rigorous test of the impact of unions on performance and other outcomes, it is firstly necessary to see if there are links between human resource policy and practice and outcomes. If there are, then it will be necessary to hold this factor constant in order to ascertain the effect which unions have on performance *per se,* irrespective of the policies which are being used. The wider and controversial literature concerning the impact of unions on performance suggests that on balance they act as a drag. However, it is plausible to hypothesize that where a union presence is part of a planned human resource strategy in a new workplace, this is less likely to be the case.

The first step is to examine the impact of human resource policy and practice on outcomes. This is an important and interesting topic in its own light. For this purpose, we retain the integrative distinction between the Good, the Bad, the Ugly, and the Lucky. These results show that there are consistent differences between the policy types and it will therefore be necessary to hold policy effects constant when testing for union effects.

It shows the strength of the links between the use of strategically integrated human resource policies and performance. Specifically, the good establishments, those with a human resource strategy and a high uptake of human resource practices, consistently report better outcomes. At the other extreme, those with the poorer outcomes, revealed most clearly are the Bad, those without a strategy or much use of human resource practices.

The Ugly and the Lucky both report consistently poorer performance than the Good on all three types of outcome. This result will be of great encouragement to those who are attempting to implement a high utilization human resource strategy. This is the first UK. study to date which demonstrates the benefits of such a strategy so clearly.

We can now hold the human resource policy variable constant while examining the impact of unions on outcomes. The resulting multivariate analysis is shown. First, however, we can examine the descriptive results.

The results reveal few significant differences between the various categories. There are some exceptions. Establishments with a single union deal claim to have weathered the recession more successfully than multi-union establishments. Industrial disputes are predictably less likely in non-union establishments. Finally there is a trend towards higher quality of staff in single union deal establishments compared with the multi-union.

Only when the controls are imposed do the differences become clearer. The unionized establishments, taken as a whole, report poorer outcomes on almost all variables.

On a number they are significant. However, as expected, there are variations according to the type of union arrangement. The rest indicates that the poorer outcomes are most likely to be found at the multi-union establishments. In particular, they appear to have poorer human resource outcomes. In contrast, the only significant factor among the single union establishments is the greater likelihood of industrial conflict compared with the non-union establishments. Indeed, on issues associated with flexibility they appear to be at an advantage.

What these results indicate is that the presence of a union still acts as a modest but sometimes significant drag on performance. The effects are greater for multi-unionism and least for single union deals.

Despite the earlier evidence of a willingness on the part of union establishments to embrace human resource practices, it seems that the unions still exert some influence on workplace outcomes. Finally, it is worth noting that the human resource strategy types appear to exert more influence than the unions. Performance is poorer in the Bad establishments than in the multi-union establishments.

The first key question we set out to explore through the study of greenfield sites is whether human resource management and trade-unionism can coexist. The answer from this study is an unequivocal yes. Most human resource management practices are just as likely to exist at unionized establishments as at those without unions. There are some variations on this general pattern.

The first important variation is the finding that the presence of a trade union is associated with a greater use of a human resource management strategy and a mission statement, which, in addition, is more likely to refer explicitly to human resource issues. This needs to be qualified by the analysis of types of trade union presence. A strategy and mission statement is particularly likely to exist where there is a single union deal. We cannot tell from this cross-sectional data whether the union presence encourages managers to think strategically or whether those who think strategically opt for a single union deal.

Although we suspect that the causal direction varies from context to context, since the choice of whether to recognize a union is an increasingly open one, we suspect that management thinks strategically about both human resource management and the new industrial relations and decides to opt for a single union deal.

Multiple unionism, by contrast, may come into operation in those establishments where a parent company already has a central collective agreement with a number of unions. It follows that the majority of such cases are likely to be British-owned. Examination of the national ownership patterns confirms that this is indeed the case. The UK- and USA-owned establishments where any union is recognized are the least likely to report a single union deal.

The pattern across the range of human resource management practices also reveals some specific differences and helps to sharpen the distinction between the new industrial relations, reflected in single union deals, and the traditional industrial relations reflected in multi-unionism. Any type of trade union presence is associated with less use of single status and use of performance appraisal and merit pay for all staff.

Single union deals on the other hand are associated with a set of practices broadly similar to non-union establishments but with the added advantage of having a more coherent human resource strategy. These results are strongly supported by Millward's analysis of the new industrial relations based on WIRS3. He finds that establishments with single union deals are consistently more likely to have a range of innovative practices, implying once again that they think strategically about single union deals and human resource management issues together.

The second major question we have explored is whether a union presence facilitates or constrains aspects of performance. The general conclusion is that unions inhibit performance and multi-unionism inhibits it more. However, this conclusion requires some qualification since single union deals have far less impact on performance, compared with non-union establishments.

The similarity between non-union establishments and those with a single union deal brings us back to the question of whether this type of unionism is an empty shell. It does not appear to constrain management. Indeed, it is associated with what managers believe to be greater commitment to the organization among lower level staff and with greater flexibility than even non-union establishments. In contrast, multi-unionism is associated with poorer outcomes on all variables except labour turnover and absenteeism; and on five of the outcomes, the differences with non-union establishments are significant. Thus multi-unionism is associated with poorer performance. This confirms the economic research on the impact of unions.

Before reaching the general conclusion that multi-unionism is bad for performance, we should recall the data on human resource management types.

The Bad establishments are more clearly associated with poor outcomes than the multi-union establishments, implying that decisions about human resource strategy are more important for outcomes than decisions about multi-unionism—assuming that managers take decisions about these issues and that in practice the two can be disentangled. In one sense, this marginalizes the union issue. On the other hand, unions may always have been marginal to performance in the great majority of organizations although industrial relations specialists, with their distinctive focus on unions, have been understandably reluctant to acknowledge this.

To summarize, the new trade-unionism, reflected most strongly in single union deals, is compatible with human resource management. There is more of a question mark against multi-unionism. This raises the question of why any company will recognize a trade union at a new establishment. A single union deal has very little impact compared with non-union establishments suggesting that they turn unions into empty shells.

Multi-unionism has a somewhat negative impact. In our sample of post-1980 establishments, approximately a third recognized one or more trade unions. However, this fell to 20 per cent in the 'pure' greenfield sites compared with 42 per cent in the refurbished sites. The great majority of managers have already decided that there is no value in recognizing a trade union. So why do others do so?

The evidence from our case studies supports the more extensive data from the CLIRS2. This indicates that unions will be recognized in those companies which have a centralized system of collective bargaining which they wish to retain. Secondly, as our comparison of greenfield and refurbished sites suggests, unions may be recognized at those workplaces which are taken over, even if shut down for a while and refurbished, and where a union was already recognized.]

It is possible that in some cases there may be scope for the operation of individual values. Some managers, including perhaps personnel managers in particular, may value the presence of a trade union as a counterweight to arbitrary management treatment. Since we have found little evidence of any trade union official presence in our case studies, it appears that the personnel manager may act as promoter and recruiter for the union. However, this is likely to become less common. The evidence from this study suggests that as we learn more about the impact of the new industrial relations, in the absence of any change towards a government that more actively encourages them, the outlook for trade unions is bleak.

The practices and process of 'new industrial relations' and human resource management have become the primary agenda of industrial relations research and teaching whether prescriptive or critical; notwithstanding this primacy new industrial relations and human resource management are of no use in themselves; they are propagated as mechanisms to rejuvenate the British economy, its manufacturing sector in particular, and connect with current dynamics in capitalist production. Without an evaluation of the problematic nature of the wider dynamics of capitalist production new industrial relations and human resource management are both abstract and decontextual.

In the period since 1945 the dynamics of capitalist production have been generalized under two broad headings. The post-war period is generalized as 'Fordism', centred on the mass production of standardized commodities, institutionalized collective bargaining, and Welfare State capitalism. The contemporary period is generalized as 'Post-Fordism' premissed on the demise of mass consumer markets, the rise of niche markets, and the erosion of social democracy in the institutional base of the State. In particular, it has rejected collective bargaining and trade union recognition as 'good' industrial relations.

If we accept that Fordism and Post-Fordism generalize periods in capitalist production it is equally necessary to question the degree to which national pathways in capitalist production measure up to the generalization. We contend that national pathways predominate over generalized descriptions in the development of capitalist production. In consequence we must evaluate the relationship between capital, labour, and the State within national pathways in order to illustrate how historical formation within particular nation states weakens the viability of generalized description.

We suggest that the British State has been subject to a formative influence of libertarian *laissez faire* which emphasizes freedom and liberty from centralized and institutionalized measures enacted by the State. In the post-war period plural industrial relations and voluntary regulation epitomize this influence. Equally during the post-war period the British State was subject to the contextual influence of social democracy and plural public policy manifest in 'good' industrial relations as collective bargaining and trade union recognition.

The contemporary erosion of social democracy and 'good' industrial relations has separated the State from an active interest in capitalist accumulation; in fact the disengagement of pluralism in industrial relations has wound up the contextual influence of social democracy and returned the formative influence of libertarian *laissez faire* as contemporary contextual influence in the State, its accumulation strategy, and public policy on industrial relations.

However, the disengagement of pluralism, an accumulation strategy based on flexibility, and redefined 'good' industrial relations are all caught in the permanent yet unfolding contradiction of libertarian *laissez faire*; that is, a continuity in historical formation within a particular nation state and the predominance of this over generalized pathways in capitalist production. We contend that new industrial relations is in the British case isolated and disengaged from contemporary material dynamics other than promoting what can be termed 'extra flexibility'.

This isolation illustrates the weakness of prescriptive generalization in capitalist production because Post-Fordism and Fordism are based on a presumed role for the State, which we suggest never developed in the British State. This seeks to illustrate the isolation of new industrial relations as informed by human resource management from market and production strategies which are portrayed as the (future) basis of capitalist production in the UK.

This develops a wide-ranging polemic and is eclectic in its discussion with references to the State and its current strategy of disengagement from active involvement in capitalist accumulation. Since 1945 'good' industrial relations have been a central feature of public policy. For much of the post-war period 'good' industrial relations was constituted in terms of plural State institutions presiding over an economy where collective bargaining and trade union recognition were functional elements within an accumulation strategy centred on Fordism. By 1979 'good' industrial relations had become 'bad' industrial relations; almost overnight the Thatcher Government rejected the pluralism in the post-war settlement between capital and labour. More significantly the Thatcher Government came to power when the period of capitalist development generalized as Fordism was exhausted.

The contemporary State has initiated a libertarian, that is individual accumulation, strategy, disengaged pluralism in industrial relations, and sought to roll back much of its previous social democratic orthodoxy in areas such as employment policy, the Welfare State, nationalized industry, and industrial relations. Good industrial relations have been reconstituted and now emphasize the managerial prerogative and less industrial action as the basis of good.

This contends that the contemporary State's method of operation, disengagement from social democracy, actively frustrates its efforts to generate a positive flexible Post-Fordism in the UK. This asserts that flexibility is a means to an end in the movement between stages of capitalist development whereas in the UK it has become an end in itself.

In consequence, in the UK, flexibility is not a bridge between Fordism and Post-Fordism but a method of making the entrails of Fordism more flexible, thereby contributing to the development of a neo-Fordist low wage, low productivity, yet flexible, economy. Hence our contention that sovereign national pathways to capitalist development predominate over generalized periodizations. In order to develop this overall argument the discussion which follows is divided into four sections.

In Section 2 formative and contextual influences on the British State are briefly introduced in order to specify the limited nature of the British State. Section 3 evaluates the process of contemporary State disengagement from the post-war social democratic orthodoxy; the strategy of Conservative governments and their attempts to reconstitute good industrial relations is located in the process of disengagement.

Section 4 evaluates new industrial relations, new market and production strategies, and suggests that institutional disengagement by the State isolates new (improved) industrial relations from new market and production strategies. In consequence typology-normative description of market and production strategies are removed from their actual constitution in the UK's national pathway.

Section 5 builds on the arguments of the previous sections to illustrate the limited nature of new industrial relations in the generation of flexibility and sustainable improvement in productivity.

Formative and Contextual Influences

As a precursor to a more detailed evaluation of new industrial relations we briefly discuss formative and contextual influences on the British State. The aim of this section is to illustrate how a renaissance of formative influences on the State in terms of its public policy actually frustrates overall economic performance. The formative influence on the development of the British State is libertarian *laissez faire*.

As an economic and political doctrine it eschews a centralized state and highlights voluntary regulation in all spheres through contract and status. Notwithstanding its formative influence, *laissez faire* was discredited as the industrial revolution progressed during the nineteenth century.

From the 1870s a contextual influence emerged on the State; social democracy and collectivism developed in response to industrialization and collective experience in the employment relationship. For example, between 1871 and 1906 trade unions were legalized so that their activities were given immunity from prosecution in specific instances. Additionally between 1832 and 1928 the franchise was extended to all adults over the age of 21. Lastly, between 1908 and 1911 the Liberal Government introduced the beginning of what later becomes a fully fledged Welfare State. In addition to these examples of collectivism and social democracy both concepts reached their height in the formulation of plural industrial relations as public policy in the post-war period.

For much of the period since 1945 industrial relations were worked out plurally between employers and employees free from substantive legislative interference by the State. In substance pluralism in industrial relations was extra-contractual and socio-political in its constitution.

By extra contractual we mean it operated beyond the influence of individual contract, in consequence its method centres on the negotiation of collective agreements on the individual enforcement of contract. Pluralism was socio-political in its constitution because in public policy it was geared towards collective bargaining, trade union recognition, and State absenteeism with minimal negative use of the law; Kahn-Freund referred to this as 'collective laissez faire'.

The formative influence of libertarian *laissez faire* on the British State facilitated the development of voluntary industrial relations, projecting freedom from the State in the institutional base of industrial relations. Voluntary method in industrial relations illustrates the political foundation of *laissez faire* which prescribes a preference for voluntary regulation over State regulation. In the post-war period this equated to autonomous collective bargaining between employers and employees.

The central point in the making is the contradictory effect the formative influence of libertarian *laissez faire* has had. In many respects voluntary industrial relations replicated the formative influence of libertarian *laissez faire* by limiting active and positive State regulation of industrial relations, in particular the negative use of the law. By this we mean that voluntarism, that is collective *laissez faire,* encouraged a form of decentralized production politics where capital, labour (and the State) sought to keep the State out of their internal affairs and relations. Perkin argues that a pattern of preindustrial class-formation, emphasizing maximum material freedom from the State was reproduced in industrial society.

Barrington-Moore refers to this as a peaceful bourgeois revolution expressing a continuity of interests in and between capital and free labour *vis-a-vis* the centralized State apparatus in the form of Monarchy or Parliament. I. Clark (forthcoming) illustrates this argument in relation to the development of State policy on productivity in the post-war period.

Notwithstanding the above, institutional freedom only extends to the method of industrial relations. Within a capitalist economy the State is always present in the institution of industrial relations; the State apparatus defends and maintains private property, capitalist reproduction, and the contractually determined employment relationship, that is the naturalized framework of capitalist production.

A contradiction in industrial relations is its complete separation from the dynamics of capitalist production. Rule-making in capitalist production is beyond economics but central to industrial relations, this defines the fictitious nature of voluntary industrial relations; their method may be voluntary but their institution results from the framework of capitalist production.

Since 1979 the State has not been rolled back *per se,* it is the contextual influence of social democracy and collectivism which has been curtailed. As a result the formative influence of libertarian *laissez faire* has been repopularized in order to halt socio-political advances made by labour during the post-war period.

In essence the Thatcher-Major Governments have sought to restructure capital by eroding social democracy and reconstituting public policy as individual and liberal. A major element in this policy has been the removal of 'market rigidities' such as trade unions, elements of the public sector, and within employment inflexible collective agreements constituted beyond contract.

A by-product of reconstituting public policy has been an effort to generate new industrial relations informed, initially by macho management and latterly by new management techniques amalgamated in 'human resource management'. In both cases individual contractual reward and regulation are highlighted. We now proceed to a more detailed discussion of new industrial relations.

3

Reflections on the Significance

INTEGRATING PERSPECTIVES

A resort is an establishment that provides paid lodging, usually on a short-term basis. Resorts often provide a number of additional guest services such as a restaurant, a swimming pool or childcare. Some resorts have conference services and meeting rooms and encourage groups to hold conventions and meetings at their location.

Resorts differ from motels in that most motels have drive-up, exterior entrances to the rooms, while resorts tend to have interior entrances to the rooms, which may increase guests' safety and present a more upmarket image. A comfortable room, good food, and a helpful staff can make being away from home an enjoyable experience for both vacationing families and business travellers. While most lodging managers work in traditional resorts and motels, some work in other lodging establishments, such as camps, inns, boardinghouses, dude ranches, and recreational resorts.

In full-service resorts, lodging managers help their guests have a pleasant stay by providing many of the comforts of home, including cable television, fitness equipment, and voice mail, as well as specialized services such as health spas. For business travellers, lodging managers often schedule available meeting rooms and electronic equipment, including slide projectors and fax machines.

Lodging managers are responsible for keeping their establishments efficient and profitable. In a small establishment with a limited staff, the manager may oversee all aspects of operations. However, large resorts may employ hundreds of workers, and the general manager usually is aided by a number of assistant managers assigned to the various departments of the operation. In resorts of every size, managerial duties vary significantly by job title.

It is an honour to provide a commentary to the JIBS 2005 Decade Award-winning article 'Revisiting Multinational Firms' Tolerance for Joint Ventures: A Trust-Based Approach' by Anoop Madhok, a truly international scholar by background, training, spirit and vocation, and a prolific author who has enriched the field of international business (IB). Madhok's trust-based approach shifted the attention from ownership as a means for multinational companies to control their international ventures to trust as a source of long-term resilience of the partnership. By building a bridge between Stopford and Wells (1972) and Franko's (1971) mainstream IB theories of ownership and the literature on trust, including earlier work on international joint ventures (IJVs) by Beamish (1985) and Parkhe (1993) among other insights, Madhok changed the discourse in the field of IB.

Furthermore, his award-winning article is a manifestation of a fruitful cross-disciplinary exchange: on the one hand, it brought into IB insights from disciplines such as sociology and anthropology, and on the other hand, it successfully exported IB contributions to other domains, through the universal appeal of the proposed framework. A decade after the article's publication, both the questions it poses and its integrative approach appear remarkably contemporary. The issue of what makes alliances persistently popular despite the challenges in achieving resilience and success continues to draw attention and re-kindle vigorous debates in the field.

This provides some reflections on the significance and implications of Madhok's (1995) article. It is structured as follows. First, I review a number of aspects of the original paper, high-lighting their contribution to the field of IB. Second, I trace the diffusion of some of the article's core ideas in subsequent scholarly publications in IB and other related domains. Lastly, revisiting Madhok's claim that trust matters, I pose some questions for further research.

Albeit Madhok's award-wining article is full of insights, I have chosen to focus on two main contributions: first, the shift in perspective from ownership to relationship, suggesting that trust matters in making IJVs resilient and successful; and, second, the integration rather than substitution of perspectives, using the relationship-centred approach in conjunction with the ownership-based approach in order to better understand the tolerance of multinational firms for IJVs with local partners.

The gist of Madhok's (1995) article is that trust is critical for cooperation. That trust-centred perspective focused attention on those aspects of the relationship that have been overlooked in the mainstream structural concern with control through ownership. In elaborating the framework for a trust-based approach, Madhok distinguished two mutually reinforcing components of trust, a 'yin and yang' of a kind, which he labelled 'structural' and 'social' trust.

The so-called structural component captured the synergic complementarities of the partners' resources and capabilities and, hence, their potential to create more value together than separately. The social component of trust, which Madhok himself has labelled 'social glue', kept the parties together, allowing the value-creating potential of their collaboration to be realised. In that sense, Madhok's trust-based approach appears to me to be concerned not so much with the multinational firm's tolerance for JVs but, rather, with its ability to create and capture value by paying attention to the social aspects of its partnerships.

This distinction between value-attainment potential and value realisation has been further elaborated by Madhok and Tallman (1998), who defined the inter-firm relationship as a productive resource in need of specific expenditures.

In addition to value, another essential element of Madhok's trust-based approach is the notion of trust-building expenses, which the parties of the IJV incur over time. Drawing on extant studies, Madhok posited that the building of a trusting relationship is a lengthy process demanding relational investment and 'various forms of hard and soft commitments'.

In his framework, he argued that this investment was more likely to be made by partners in a relationship characterised by both strong structural and social components of trust — that is, a relationship that counts with strategically complementary resource bundles and with willingness to operate jointly in an efficient and flexible manner.

In addition, Madhok arteculated that investment requirements for trust-building depended on the life cycle of the relationship, with larger investment expected in the beginning, so that shared commitment can be established. Once there is a sound shared foundation, he hypothesised, maintaining the relationship usually becomes less investment-intensive. In the application of his trust-based framework to the case of multinational firms engaged in collaboration with local partners, Madhok argued that the investment in trust-building would differ depending on the strategy and structure chosen by the multinational firms. Madhok sustained that above-normal return would give a multinational firm the slack resources necessary for making what he called 'trust-building gestures' to its local partners. In my interpretation, this view of trust-building investment is rather instrumental and associates trust with payoff.

A related contribution is Madhok's attempt to elaborate on and clarify the dynamic nature of trust. Trust needs time to emerge. In addition, it requires repeated successful interactions as well as ongoing perception of equity. The nature and pattern of these interactions, Madhok posited, are influenced by the combination of structural and social trust. The stickiness of the relationship through the investment in trust allows for conflicts to be addressed and transitory states of inequity endured.

This dynamic assumes that the increased flexibility of the relationship resulting from its relational quality will in turn enable greater adaptability to changes in the environment, and will ultimately lead to improved performance of the alliance. Yet, this is but an assumption, and a recent study by Carson et al. (2003) reveals that the performance of trust-based governance is contingent on the ability of partners to read each other's behaviour in the process.

Madhok did not position his trust-based view as an alternative to the ownership-centred perspective. Rather, he argued that the two approaches were compatible and complementary, and demanded an integration of insights that could advance the understanding of IJVs' success and resilience. Such integration was possible because the two approaches had a common objective of achieving flexibility and efficiency in the way a relationship operates. In addition, they had different orientations, which allowed different aspects of the joint venture to be revealed.

For the ownership-centred perspective, flexibility and efficiency are achieved through hierarchical relations, that is, through control based on ownership. For the trust- or relationship-centred approach, they are attained through the management of the social relationship. By investigating cooperative phenomena, such as JVs, within a structural framework, the ownership-centred approach is outcome-oriented and relatively static. It fails to address the critical role of social context in inter-organisational relationships.

The so-called relationship- or trust-based approach is dynamic, process-oriented and concerned with issues such as reciprocity, commitment and forbearance, rather than control. Another distinction is that the ownership-centred perspective is a macro-approach, which connects strategy-structure-ownership levels of the MNCs with JV's tolerance. The relationship-centred approach is a micro-approach in that it pays attention to the dynamic processes underlying a relationship. Taken together, the two approaches overcome their respective limitations and provide a more balanced and refined understanding of what makes IJVs tick.

One final distinction is that, in addition to flexibility and efficiency, a trust-based approach is attentive to the coordination aspects of the partnership and the need for resolution of conflicts triggered by differential contribution and/or learning by the partners, temporary inequity, as well as exogenous events that can change the partners' strategic priorities.

Beyond its direct contribution to a field, a published piece of scholarly work gains a life of its own in those studies that build on its ideas and the articles that cite it in their theoretical and empirical developments. In this, seek to identify some of the influences of Madhok's article upon studies of IB and the related domain of interorganisational relationships. Also, I trace the article's diffusion to other fields and scholarly discourses.

A decade since its coming into print, Madhok's (1995) article in JIBS is alive and oft-cited. It has served as a building block or inspiration for studies on international JVs and cross-cultural collaboration, as well on strategic alliances in general. Moreover, its ideas have travelled to fields such as marketing, supply chain management, engineering, psychology and law, thus proving their universal appeal and usefulness.

There are two main areas in which Madhok's ideas have been most visible and have exercised the most significant impact — international JVs and strategic alliances. In the first theme — IJVs — scholars who have delved into the issues of control and collaboration with particular interest in trust have found Madhok's framework relevant. Their work has centred on the effectiveness of the JVs, the processes of trust-building, the multi-levelled nature and meaning of trust or the partnering skills needed for success.

The second theme, that of strategic alliances, represents a phenomenon much broader than the original scope of Madhok's framework, centred on IJVs of multinational companies with local partners. Beyond that, Madhok's trust-based framework has become part of a fruitful stream of research into alliances. Scholars dealing with issues of inter-firm relationships have taken on Madhok's ideas when examining formation of strategic alliances or their co-evolution, establishment of commitment through bonding and trust, sources of alliance success or failure, or the link between trust and risk.

Understandably, the biggest diffusion and impact of Madhok's (1995) article has taken place on the pages of JIBS, with numerous scholars drawing inspiration from it. However, the seeds of Madhok's (1995) framework have been planted in a wealth of other journals in the field of strategy, management == and organisation, which place the issues of alliances, relational advantage and inter-organisational relationships at the heart of their editorial agendas.

Thus, the article has been referenced in publications in the following journals (listed alphabetically) including: Academy of Management Review; Accounting, Organization, and Society; Group and Organization Management; International Journal of Management Reviews; Journal of Business Research; Journal of Management; Journal of Management Studies; Journal of Organizational Change Management; Journal of World Business; Long Range Planning; Organizational Science; Organizational Studies; Research Policy; Strategic Management Society.

Furthermore, scholars from various fields and domains have built upon Madhok's ideas. Some examples of diffusion, infrequent in academic circles that tend to operate as silos, include Batt's (2003) article on supply chain performance, Farrelly and Quester's (2005) work on relationship quality in sponsorship exchanges, Robson and Dunk's (1999) article on co-marketing alliances, Salbu's (1997) contribution to business law with work on contracts as device for flexible coordination and control, and Tjosvold's (1998) work in psychology, with focus on cooperative and competitive approach to conflict.

Hence, it is not surprising that journals from other disciplinary domains have also published articles that acknowledged Madhok's (1995) original ideas, including: American Business Law Journal; Applied Psychology — An International Review; Industrial Marketing Management; International Marketing Review; Journal of Engineering and Technology Management; Journal of International Marketing; Journal of the Academy of Marketing Science; and Supply Chain Management — An International Journal. This diffusion of IB ideas to fields of strategy, management and organisation, as well as to other, not necessarily adjacent, areas and disciplines, signals with optimism that IB research is capable of inspiring and informing scholarly conversations in other domains.

Future Research

Madhok (1995) suggested broadening the scope of his trust-based approach beyond the particular case of a multinational firm and its local partners. Madhok proposed a potential extension in the direction of partnerships between two multinational companies, in which the geographical, product and activity scope of the partnership is much broader and the dynamics much more complex. In my view, another fruitful avenue for further exploration, for which the JIBS 2004 Decade Award-winning article by Oviatt and McDougall (1994) has paved the way, is the perspective of the entrepreneurial firms forming the alliance and the dynamics of the partnerships these international new ventures form.

They are distinctive types of player in the IB arena and lack the resources that multinational companies possess to invest in trust-building gestures. In addition, as a variety of new alliance forms have come into being in the decade following the publication of Madhok's award-winning article, the nature of their dynamics is also worthy of further investigation. In that sense, thinking in network rather than dyadic terms can be insightful and informative.

Madhok (1995) employed trust, relationship and cooperation as interchangeable descriptors of his trust-based perspective. Upon reviewing the developments in the trust literature and the cumulative contribution to the field of alliances in the last decade, in my interpretation these three terms are not interchangeable, as they evoke different emphases in understanding the stability of interfirm partnerships. For example, cooperation is not necessarily sustained by trust, and a relationship can be glued by shared social norms and sanctions instead of trust as a 'social lubricant'.

Hence, there is a risk of trust becoming 'a residual term for the complex socio-psychological processes necessary for social action to occur'. Special issues of the Academy of Management Journal (1998), Organization Studies (2000) and Organization Science (2003) have furthered knowledge of the levels, types and effects of trust. Despite their collective contributions, however, trust continues to be an unresolved concern and a rather fragmented and diverse theme.

Doubts continue to be raised 'about the universality of the effect of trust on business transactions'. In this sense, the focus and, in some cases, over-reliance on trust in the alliance literature has obscured a more general treatment of the nature and role of enforcement mechanisms. It may have also confounded the most interesting sources of variation in safeguarding inter-firm relationships and their stability.

Concluding his 1995 JIBS article, Madhok admitted that '[i]t would be naive to overemphasize trust'. In subsequent articles, he continuously and vigorously sought to clarify or deepen understanding of certain aspects and terminology of his trust-based framework. For example, he and Tallman proposed 'a non-trust explanation of why firms might knowingly forgo opportunities to take advantage of their partners'. Recently, Carson et al. (forth-coming) raised doubts on whether social sanctions suffice in stopping opportunism in situations of high ambiguity.

They sought to clarify the contingency nature of formal and relational contracting in conditions of volatility and uncertainty. Furthermore, they went beyond merely assuming opportunism to directly testing its relationship with uncertainty. All these efforts enriched and expanded the scholarly conversation on alliances. Yet, they also signalled the need to consider approaches that provide alternative, integrative and more nuanced explanations of why inter-firm relationships continue experiencing high rates of both foundings and failures, and how their stability can be enhanced.

Svejenova et al. (2005) argue that, in order to improve understanding of the issue of stability in international alliances, attention should be paid to enforcement. Enforcement ensures that behaviours are enacted or that individuals would act in a particular way. Enforcement mechanisms differ from deterrence mechanisms in that the latter rely on avoidance and preclusion of particular types of behaviour, whereas the former enable collaboration and ensure partners' actions are consistent with expectations. They are also likely to evolve with the strategic intent of partners. The sources and certainty of enforcement remain a relatively little explored theme. There is a lack of agreement in the literature on when trust is the enforcement mechanism and when other mechanisms create an enforcement environment that results in trust-like outcomes.

Svejenova et al. (2005) proposed a framework of enforcement. (1) With it they seek to clarify the role of trust in safeguarding inter-firm collaboration and identify other mechanisms that could generate trust-like outcomes of the kind of reliability or predictability of partners' cooperative behaviour. In elaborating their enforcement perspective, they do not allege that trust is unwarranted or unlikely to emerge in a process of productive cooperation; only that its many roles may have been overstated.

The theoretical perspective advanced by Svejenova et al. (2005) defines an enforcement space that takes shape along ownership, legal and social dimensions. Legal enforcement is manifested in the existence of a reliable legal system, with its codification and transparency of laws (*e.g.*, property, contract and commercial law), and a realistic expectation for fair and relatively speedy legal adjudication in the courts. The agreement can be formal, informal, written, oral or just plain 'taken-for-granted'.

The creative complexity and variety of alliance forms has outpaced the legal arena and the analytical tools used by antitrust enforcement agencies to assess their legality. Hence, mechanisms other than contracts have been used as complements to or substitutes for legal enforcement. Social embeddedness has been considered another source of enforcement of cooperation through mechanisms such as friendship (enforcement by the strength of the interpersonal relationship), reputation (enforcement by an open network of third parties) and social norms and sanctions (enforcement by a closed, cohesive network such as kinship relations).

A third source of enforcement is the ownership dimension. To its traditional depiction, understood and conceptualised in terms of financial equity, Svejenova et al. (2005) added two other ownership-related mechanisms: revenue-sharing and brand equity. Revenue-sharing agreements do not involve equity participation of the partners in their respective companies or in their joint venture.

Brand equity is another enforcement mechanism, particularly relevant in franchising and licensing relationships and especially in those cases in which the intellectual property of technology included as the basis of the alliance is proprietary and difficult to imitate. For example, Contractor and Kundu (1998) found that, in the resort business, registered brand names are a potent source of control, and the threat of withdrawing permission to use the brand moderates the opportunistic behaviour of the firm's international partners.

Taking into account mechanisms with different nature, the framework advanced by Svejenova et al. (2005) seeks to identify when trust is a requisite for the alliance and when it may not be essential. This is especially useful in the cases of cross-border alliances, when local partners can occupy enforcement spaces different from those of the multinational company that seeks to partner with them. While each of the three dimensions — legal, social and ownership enforcement — has important individual implications for the enforcement of a partnership, they may act as complements rather than substitutes.

There is a range of intermediary cases shaped by different combinations of the three enforcement mechanisms. For example, within this framework, trust is a requisite enforcement mechanism in the case of friends who cooperate on the basis of a handshake or an oral agreement and share revenues. Trust is dispensable when there is some kind of assurance, that is,

> *"expectations of benign behaviour from an exchange partner based on knowledge of an incentive structure that encourages such behaviour rather than exploitation. Mechanisms that provide assurance include legal or normative authorities that impose sanctions for violations of agreements or failure to fulfil one's obligations, guarantees such as collateral that protect against loss, warranties that assure certain standards of quality, and so forth."*

For example, assurance rather than trust can enforce cooperation in the case of a partnership embedded in a closed, cohesive network, based on a detailed contract and exchange of financial equity.

Further understanding of, and empirical work on when trust matters remains to be done. Future research should consider a broader range of dimensions for the enforcement of stability in a partnership. It should seek to identify what factors may influence the parties in an alliance to seek certain types of enforcement.

In his analysis of the smaller economies of Pacific Asia and their business systems, Redding (2005) described how their social and legal embeddedness differs owing to differences in culture, religion, legacies of the former colonial powers (the English, Dutch or the French), etc. Using the enforcement framework, Svejenova et al. (2005) hypothesise that firms that have been historically and spatially embedded in cultures where institutions are weak or underdeveloped will tend to favour relations, as opposed to contracts, in safeguarding the exchange.

In the case of China, for example, 'Personal networks are... particularly significant modes of economic transacting in China because of the weak institutional sanctions against reneging on commitments'. However, those personal networks can be of little use to a foreign company without access to these networks or previous history of collaboration, when considering a partnership with a Chinese firm.

In that sense, a focus on the dynamics of nation-institutional configurations rather than on culture may be more meaningful in capturing differences along the enforcement dimensions. Importing and integrating insights from political-institutional approaches to sociology into the field of IB could contribute to a more comprehensive view of inter-firm collaborations. How do adjustments in nation-state institutional arrangements affect inter-firm relationships and choices of alliance partners?

How are differences in institutional contexts imprinted on management decisions about initiating and maintaining international alliances? There is a need for studies into alliances being established in developing countries, not only from the perspective of the foreign organisation but also from the point of view of the local partners, which has been largely unaccounted for.

A better understanding is needed of the role played by interlocked business and state elites in purporting their impact on alliances not only as a source of reputation but also as matchmakers. A range of well-known Italian, French and Asian cases illustrate the importance of powerful, well-connected individuals in the business and political elite in triggering and guaranteeing inter-organisational collaboration. Bank managers are in a position to identify from among the portfolio of their clients potential partners whose interests could match theirs. Further attention is needed to the strategies that firms pursue not only to safeguard a partnership by securing partners who behave according to expectations but also to convey an image of a reliable partner. This is especially true for entrepreneurial firms in need of a partner with incumbents to enhance their legitimacy and reputation.

In addition, given that alliances usually have proponents and detractors in the partnering organisations, more studies on the role of organisational politics in developing or detracting from the realisation of the value potential of a partnership over time could enhance understanding and better management of the alliance dynamics.

Expected contribution of comparative sociology to understanding alliance differences across nation-states, along with the accentuated role of political behaviour, individual cognition and attachments in maintaining inter-organisational relationships, raise the issue of the need for multi-level studies and co-evolutionary perspectives. They also suggest that IB literature can benefit from insights coming from other domains, which in turn would allow it to advance knowledge that can be inspirational for scholars from those domains.

Another element in an agenda on inter-firm relationships may encompass their dysfunctional consequences and negative effects. Here, a critical issue that future studies could clarify is the concept of failure in a strategic alliance. Furthermore, research on the dysfunctional outcomes of alliances and networks could help in understanding how and why firms get locked into and sustain unproductive partnerships that could hinder opportunities to collaborate with other viable firms.

International alliances continue to be a vast and vibrant scholarly domain in IB studies in need of further clarification and integration of disparate contributions. In order for future research to result in a better understanding of the enforcement of stability in alliances, studies must incorporate approaches from comparative sociology and economic geography, which can provide a broader and better foundation than merely the culture-based one for understanding alliance differences. In addition, researchers must strive to separate trust from trust-like mechanisms for initiating and maintaining a partnership, which would afford an explanation of how firms who are 'strangers' can initiate a potentially profitable relationship in the absence of a common relational history.

Since its publication, Madhok's award-winning article has enriched and expanded the IB discourse and opened up numerous avenues for theoretical and empirical work on inter-firm relationships. With the extent of its diffusion and influence, it has also revealed that the IB literature could successfully integrate insights from other domains and, in turn, serve as a source of inspiration to scholarship in other disciplines.

By considering the benefits from change in assumptions from opportunism to trust 'till proven otherwise', Madhok (2006) poses yet another challenge to researchers in IB and inter-firm relationships. I am convinced that he will continue planting the seeds of his ideas in numerous forthcoming publications and igniting the imagination of scholars to come.

Staffing Policies and Strategic Control

While the effective management of human resources is increasingly being recognized as a major determinant of success or failure in international business, in practice many organizations are still coming to terms with the human resources issues associated with international operations.

In the international arena, the quality of management seems to be even more critical than in domestic operations. This is primarily because the nature of international business operations involves the complexities of operating in different countries and employing different national categories of workers. Yet, while it is recognized that HRM problems become more complex in the international arena, there is evidence to suggest that many companies underestimate the complexities involved in international operations. The field of international human resource management, however, is only slowly developing as a field of academic study and has been described by one authority as being in the infancy stage. Moreover, there is relatively little empirical research that documents the international HRM strategies and practices of international firm - particularly firms that have their headquarters outside North America.

This reports some of the findings from a recent study of international human resource management in Britain- and Ireland-based international firms. One particular feature of the study was the exclusive focus on "managing managers." Particular attention is given to three key issues in the area of international human resource management: international staffing, international recruitment, and the variety of issues surrounding the problem of shortages of international managers. I will also briefly consider the nature of the human resource management challenges facing companies in the light of the Single European

Market. A study of how companies deal with the international human resource management issues outlined above is particularly appropriate for the reasons enumerated below.

First, the international staffing process is of considerable importance to an international firm: "Virtually any type of international problem, in the final analysis, is either created by people or must be solved by people. Hence, having the right people in the right place at the right time emerges as the key to a company's international growth. If we are successful in solving this problem, I am confident we can cope with all others".

The staffing problems facing international firms are more complex than in domestic firms, and inappropriate staffing policies may lead to difficulties in managing overseas operations. The international literature indicates that expatriate failure is a persistent and recurring problem, particularly for U.S. multinationals. Frequently, the human and financial costs of failure in the international business arena are more severe than in domestic business. In particular, indirect costs such as loss of market share and damage to overseas customer relationships may be considerable.

Second, the shortage of international managers is becoming an increasing problem for international firms. A survey of 440 executives in European firms claimed that a shortage of international managers was the single most important factor constraining corporate efforts to expand abroad. Almost one-third of the executives surveyed had experienced difficulties in finding managers with the necessary international experience and orientation. The findings of the survey suggest that the successful implementation of global strategies depends, to a large extent, on the existence of an adequate supply of internationally experienced managers.

Third, there is little empirical research on the international human resource management issues associated with the management of managers in British and Irish international firms, especially in comparison to the considerable literature on international human resource management in U.S. firms.

Fourth, the advent of the Single European Market and the rapid growth of British direct investment abroad since the early 1980s mean that issues of international staffing, recruitment, and development are increasingly important concerns in a far wider range of organizations than the traditional giant multinationals. International HRM problems are becoming increasingly important for a growing number of smaller and medium-sized companies that have significantly internationalized their operations in recent years.

Research Methodology and Sample

The principal research method was structured interviews with each company's corporate personnel or human resources director, or with a senior corporate HR executive. The majority of interviews were conducted in 1990, the remainder in 1991. The duration of interviews varied from two hours to three and a half hours. During each interview, information was sought on company structure and international operations. The interviewer also asked questions concerning international staffing, expatriate performance, international HRM policies, and international management development.

These questions were adapted from a study by Tung (1981) and through consultation with a number of international HRM practitioners. The purpose of the questions was to provide a structured basis for each interview, and responses to questions were noted by the interviewer since interviewees were not asked to fill in a questionnaire. Additional information was obtained from company reports, company documents such as international personnel policies, and newspaper articles.

Forty-five international companies participated in the study. Forty companies were British-owned and five were Irish-owned international firms. The sample was specifically chosen to include companies from both the manufacturing and the service sectors. Twenty-six companies in the study were primarily manufacturing firms and sixteen were service sector firms. Two oil companies and one mining company also participated.

The size of the companies in this international firm sample ranges from medium to very large, with the total number of employees worldwide ranging from 9,500 to 240,000. The smaller size of the Irish international firms and their relatively recent internationalization were two principal reasons for their inclusion in the study. For the sample as a whole, there was a wide range in the number of countries the companies operated in, and in the length of experience in international operations.

International Staffing Policies and Practices

International firms face three alternatives with respect to the staffing of management positions abroad - namely, the employment of parent-country nationals, host-country nationals, or third-country nationals. Much of the existing research focuses on the advantages and disadvantages of using expatriates as opposed to local managers and it identifies a range of host-country, company, and individual factors as important considerations in international staffing decisions. Most studies are, however, largely inconclusive on the question of when parent-country nationals should be sent abroad.

The findings of the present study on staffing practices in British and Irish international firms reveal that a majority of the companies continued to rely heavily on parent country nationals to run their foreign operations. The research findings showed that, while almost 50 per cent of companies had formal policies favouring the use of host-country managers to run their foreign operations, in practice just over one-third operated with host-country nationals in senior management positions in their foreign operations.

In other words, two-thirds of the companies relied primarily on expatriates to run their foreign operations. Furthermore, the trend has moved in the direction of greater use of expatriates. Half of the companies in the sample (22 out of 45) reported an increase in the use of expatriates over the previous decade and only 20 per cent indicated that they had reduced their use of expatriates. The remainder reported no significant change.

These findings raise serious questions about the ability and commitment of some British multinationals to identify and develop host-country managers effectively in their foreign operations. Therefore, the recruitment, selection, and development of host-country managers emerges as a vital issue for British and Irish multinationals, given the need to develop global teams with a variety of different perspectives and competences.

The findings of the present study on staffing practices in British and Irish firms reveal sharp differences with U.S. experience. Indeed, recent work by Kobrin suggested that the tendency of U.S. multinationals to reduce the numbers of expatriates had gone too far. He argued that U.S. firms have tended to substitute host-country nationals to replace expatriates primarily in response to the difficulties U.S. managers have experienced in adjusting to other cultural environments.

Kobrin recognized that the increased use of host country managers may in part reflect the cost of maintaining expatriates abroad, the greater sensitivity of local managers to local culture, and local market needs and the growing international maturity of some multinationals. It is suggested, however, that expatriate reduction may result in U.S. multinationals facing reduced identification with the worldwide organization and its objectives, difficulties in exercising control, and a lack of opportunities for U.S. managers to gain international experience abroad. The principal concern is that U.S. multinationals could face major strategic management control problems where managers identify with local units rather than with global corporate objectives.

The present study identified a number of principal reasons for employing expatriates. The first was the lack of availability of management and technical skills in some countries. There was a greater tendency for companies to use expatriates in less developed countries due to the weak pool of available local management talent. This was also true for those companies that used host-country managers to run their foreign operations in advanced countries.

The second major reason cited for using expatriates was the objective of control of local operations. Thirty-three out of forty-five firms in the present study identified control as a key reason for their use of expatriates. Expatriates were felt to be more familiar with the corporate culture and the control system of headquarters, and this was felt to result in more effective communication and coordination. Indeed, a key role for senior expatriates was to train local managers to understand corporate financial and control systems.

This point is illustrated by a comment by the human resource director of a financial services company: "The main advantage of using expatriates is that they understand our [corporate] culture and reporting systems and they teach the locals how to relate to the centre. This is vital when you are establishing a new foreign business."

This finding on the importance of control is consistent with previous research on European multinationals which shows control to be an important reason for expatriate transfers. Yet, in previous research, only rarely has control been identified as an important aim of expatriate assignments. This probably reflects the North American origin of much previous research and the tendency of some managers and researchers to view control as a rather disreputable rationale for using expatriates.

A further key reason for using senior expatriates was to maintain trust in key foreign businesses, following large international acquisitions. This finding is particularly interesting because previous research has suggested that the employment of expatriates will be lower in acquisitions by comparison with greenfield sites. The emergence of trust as a major factor is related to the rapid growth in the number and scale of foreign acquisitions by British companies in the 1980s.

For example, in the late 1980s, a U.K. brewing and leisure company emerged as one of the world's leading resort groups, following a massive [pounds]2 billion acquisition of a global resort chain. In this example, a major reason given for using expatriates to run the acquisition was "the need to have the peace of mind which comes from having our people running such a large and strategically important investment."

There was often an unwillingness to allow newly acquired foreign businesses to be run by the existing host-country national management, primarily because they were not known well enough and their loyalty to the business was not proven.

The research also found that using expatriates for management development purposes was important and was increasing in significance for British multinationals. Thirty-four out of forty-five companies reported that expatriates were used for development purposes, and twenty-five of these firms claimed that use of expatriates for this purpose was becoming more important. This reflects the tendency of British companies to see expatriation as part of the career-development process. In this context, it is interesting to note that, in most cases, the management of expatriates was the responsibility of the corporate human resource function. This was the case even in some highly decentralized organizations (*e.g.*, engineering companies) where the corporate human resource role was rather limited.

One very recent trend identified by the research was the tendency for companies to give younger managers international experience much earlier in their career than previously. Over half of the companies in the sample (26 out of 45 companies) reported significant changes in this respect. This was linked to the growing problems of mobility (spouse's job, children's education, etc.) for older managers. This also reflects the strategy of some companies to broaden the opportunities for international development, and the growing recognition in some quarters that the payback on the investment of a developmental assignment may well be greater with a younger manager.

The performance of foreign subsidiaries also emerged as a significant factor influencing the use of expatriates. There was a greater tendency for the companies in the sample to use senior expatriates where the acquired business had been underperforming before the foreign acquisition. Similarly, poor performance by host-country managers in the post acquisition phase was cited as an important reason for replacing them with expatriates. This finding is well supported in the literature, which has frequently reported that crisis accentuates headquarters control.

This is well illustrated by the case of a major British food and drinks company that made two very large acquisitions in the United States in the late 1980s. The first acquisition was a global drinks business with its headquarters in the United States, and the second was a large U.S. food business. The staffing policy differed sharply in the two acquisitions. In the former case, the existing management team (composed entirely of host-country managers) continued to run the business. "In this case," said a corporate HR executive, "we inherited an excellent management team who were achieving first-class results. Why change a winning team and upset morale by introducing expatriates?" In the second case, by contrast, the entire U.S. management team was replaced by expatriates, "mainly due to poor financial results and weak managerial performance."

Another factor influencing the approach adopted by companies was a strong expectation on the part of major foreign customers (and sometimes foreign governments) that the top managers in their country should be parent-country nationals.

Thirteen of the sixteen international firms in the service sector and a minority of manufacturing firms (6 out of 26) said they had taken this into account in deciding their policy. Public relations and marketing were usually the key roles in this context. Previous research has largely ignored this factor because it has concentrated on the very largest multinationals and tended to neglect the service sector.

For example, two Irish banks operating in the United States felt that there were considerable marketing and public relations advantages in using expatriates, given their marketing strategy of targeting the ethnic Irish population. In the banking, insurance, and finance areas, British companies reported that, in many countries, major foreign customers frequently had a strong preference for their senior executives to be British expatriates.

There is also strong evidence from the present research that expatriates are more likely to be used in the early stages of new foreign operations. This is consistent with previous research that shows this practice is common in the early stages of internationalization where a company is setting up a new business, process, or product in another country, and prior experience is considered essential. A majority of firms indicated that control and trust were particularly important in the early stages of internationalization. In the present study, this factor had become more significant due to the rapid growth of international business in the last decade.

Nearly half of the companies (21 out of 45) also cited weaknesses in their training and development of host-country national and third-country national managers to explain their continued use of expatriates, despite a formal policy to replace expatriates with host-country managers after the startup phase. A typical comment in this respect came from a pharmaceutical company: "The training and development of host-country nationals and third-country nationals is a major weakness in achieving our objective of localising management in our operating companies."

Shortages of International Managers

It was argued above that the successful implementation of global strategies depends, to a large extent, on the existence of an adequate supply of internationally experienced mangers. In the present study, two-thirds of the companies (30 out of 45) said that they had experienced shortages of international managers and over 70 per cent indicated that future shortages were anticipated.

While the faster pace of internationalization was cited as the primary reason for shortages by thirty-four of forty-five firms in the sample, the findings suggest that over half the firms (24 out of 45) reported that failures to recruit, retain, and develop host-country managers effectively were another key reason why shortages exist. A number of factors make the recruitment of host-country managers more difficult and costly compared with recruiting in the home country. These include: lack of knowledge of local labour markets; ignorance of the local education system and the status of qualifications; language and cultural problems at interviews and trying to transfer recruitment methods that work well in the United Kingdom to foreign countries.

Many international firms have tended to neglect the training and development needs of their host-country managers and focus virtually all of their managerial development efforts on their parent-country nationals' managers. Twenty-six of the forty-five firms in the sample reported that weaknesses in their training and development in respect of host-country managers had contributed to shortages of international managers. The failure to develop local managers effectively was frequently given by British multinationals as a reason for continuing to use U.K. expatriates in similar management positions rather than using local managers. Alternatively, this could be interpreted as something of an excuse for their preference to use expatriates beyond the development phase of international operations.

The present research highlighted three important lessons for those international firms that are seriously attempting to provide management training and development for host-country nationals and third-country nationals. First is the need to avoid the mistake of simply exporting parent-country training and development programmes to other countries. This point is illustrated by the following comment from the personnel director of a large chemical firm: "We have learned from some tough experiences that training and development programmes for local managers must be culturally adapted to local conditions."

Second, the management development programmes for host-country and third-country nationals need to be linked to the strategic situation in each country, as well as to the overall strategy of the firm. This need to take into account a variety of foreign product-market situations superimposed upon the overall strategic thrust of the firm adds considerably to the complexity of devising appropriate management development programmes.

The third lesson is the need to utilize much further the practice of developing host-country managers through developmental transfers to corporate headquarters. It has been argued that this type of international transfer exposes host-country nationals and third-country nationals to the headquarters' corporate culture and facilitates their developing a corporate perspective, rather than simply reflecting their own local interests.

It has also been argued that this approach to development can be very effective in helping to develop global management teams and is a necessary part of successfully operating a truly global firm. The present research indicated, however, that a majority of British companies still failed to recognize the need to develop high-potential host-country national managers to senior positions that exist outside their own countries, and this exacerbates the problem of attracting and retaining high-potential young managers in the host countries.

The Shortages of International Managers

Nineteen of the forty-five companies had responded to the shortage of international managers by attempting to identify parent-country managers of high potential at an earlier stage in their career, and by giving them international experience at a much younger age. Over one-third of the companies reported that they were sending young managers of high potential on international assignments partly for developmental purposes.

This was in sharp contrast to the previous practice when many MNCs relied on developing a cadre of career expatriates who moved from one international position to the next. The trend towards giving younger managers from the parent country the opportunity for international experience earlier in their careers was often part of a more general trend to give international experience to a wider range of managers, and not just to a relatively small group of expatriates. Increasing numbers of international firms were also using short-term developmental assignments in order to develop larger pools of employees with international experience.

Another significant response to the shortage of international managers was the rapid growth in importance of external recruitment to fill management positions abroad. Until a few years ago, the majority of firms had relied almost exclusively on internal recruitment for foreign management positions. British MNCs traditionally had a strong preference for well-known internal managers for expatriate management positions, as they had established track records and their loyalty to the company was proven. Over one-quarter of the firms in the study had, in the past five years, introduced external recruitment to fill management positions abroad, and several others were planning to do so. Financial services companies were a good example of this: some of these companies had rapidly internationalized relatively recently and felt they had to recruit externally at the senior level to establish their foreign operations.

A third response to the shortages of international managers by fourteen of the forty-five companies was to attempt to sell themselves more effectively to graduates through various types of marketing designed to highlight the international nature of their activities (*e.g.*, in graduate recruitment brochures and in national press advertising). This type of marketing highlighted the prospects of early international experience to attract graduates seeking an international career. This can be illustrated by the example of the two textile companies that had a policy of sending young graduates on international assignments within three or six months of joining the firm.

This policy was very effective and was designed specifically to recruit high-potential young graduates who were particularly interested in an international career. The corporate human resources director of one of the textile companies commented: "Textiles is not a particularly fashionable industry. We are competing for the best graduates with companies that enjoy a more glamorous image. The fact that we can offer the opportunity of very early international experience is the main reason we can attract some high potential graduates when the big guns, such as Shell, BP, and ICI, are fishing in the same pool."

A minority of companies were also broadening their sources of graduate recruitment to include some continental European countries, and this reflected their anticipation of a growth in the competition for high-potential graduates following the advent of the Single European Market. Two computer companies had recently introduced Euro-graduate management development programmes.

A feature of these programmes was that graduates were recruited from several European countries for a two-year period of training and development in the United Kingdom. On completion of their training, graduates were transferred to a management position in a third country. The need to develop more flexible succession planning systems to support the development of Euro-graduates was identified as an important issue by both firms operating this type of programme.

There was also growing recognition of the importance of developing effective international management development programmes to help secure an adequate supply of international managers. The majority of firms reported that they were spending more money and more time on international management education, particularly for top and senior management. These firms were using a combination of internal and external international management development programmes. One interesting feature of these programmes was that teachers frequently came from prestigious foreign business schools in Europe and the United States, as well as from internal sources. However, only three of the forty-five firms claimed they had effective systems for evaluating their international management development programmes.

The introduction of language training for top, senior, and middle levels of management by the majority of companies in the study was seen as an important development in light of the acute shortages of international managers with language skills. This suggests that the importance of language training is increasingly being recognized by British multinationals. This finding is in sharp contrast with studies of U.S. MNCs, which found that only a minority of U.S. MNCs felt that knowledge of foreign languages was necessary for conducting business abroad.

Increasingly, it was recognized that language training increased the effectiveness of staff working abroad and helped them relate more easily to a foreign culture. There was also a growing awareness that language training promoted a better image of the MNC in the host country.

There were two areas, however, where the companies were clearly failing to take effective action to ease the acute shortage of international managers. First, there was no evidence that British multinationals were taking serious steps to increase the proportion of women in international management.

International management has long been a masculine preserve in Europe and the United States. Adler's study estimates that under 3 per cent of North American expatriates are female.

In the present study, no company claimed to have more than 3 per cent of female expatriates. Indeed, the evidence suggests that women in British multinationals are not making as much progress in international management as women in U.S. multinationals. For example, in the U.S. banking and financial sector, there has been a significant increase in female expatriates.

The under representation of women in international management is illustrated by a quote from a woman HR executive of a U.K. pharmaceutical company: "In the UK, the majority of marketing staff are women. By contrast, in our foreign operations, the vast majority of marketing staff are male. Companies still tend to shy away from using female expatriates because of fears that women will not be accepted in some countries and the major problem of disrupting the career of their partner." The lack of willingness to recruit and develop women as international managers is worrying as recent research suggests that, in many ways, women are well suited to international management.

The second area that impacts on the supply of internationalists is the failure by many companies to adequately address repatriation problems. The repatriation of managers has been identified as a major problem for multinational companies in the United Kingdom and North America. Over 70 per cent of the firms (33 of 45) in the present study said they faced significant problems regarding reentry. Further, it was generally recognized that this may lead to low morale and a higher turnover of expatriates.

For example, only three of the firms claimed that repatriates had no difficulty reintegrating into the U.K. organization. A key problem for the majority of companies was finding suitable posts for repatriates of similar status and responsibility to those they held abroad. For many British MNCs, this problem had become more acute in recent years because, for many of the companies, expansion of overseas operations had taken place at the same time as the rationalization of U.K. operations, thereby reducing the number of senior posts in the United Kingdom.

Other problems associated with reintegrating into the United Kingdom are loss of status, loss of autonomy, loss of career direction, and a feeling that international experience is undervalued by the company. Further, there was growing recognition that where companies are seen to deal unsympathetically with the problems faced by expatriates on reentry, managers will be more reluctant to accept the offer of international assignments.

Research in North America indicates that 20 per cent of all managers who complete foreign assignments wish to leave their company on return. This was a growing problem for British multinationals, particularly when many companies are willing to pay a premium to attract the experienced international manager. Yet, while it is widely accepted that the costs of expatriate turnover are considerable, very few firms had introduced formal repatriation programmes to assist managers and their families with repatriation difficulties.

Similarly, very few companies had introduced mentor systems to check the career progression of the international manager. Many expatriate managers were concerned about losing out on opportunities at home, and, in some companies, this was a constraint on their willingness to go abroad. Clearly, British companies need to give a higher priority to the issue of repatriation in order to encourage international mobility and to help secure an adequate future supply of international managers.

Barriers to International Mobility

This briefly considers the reasons why shortages of international managers are expected to continue. In particular, it examines the growing restrictions on international mobility and their significance for the international capability of the firm.

Over 70 per cent of the firms (34 out of 45) reported that they anticipated shortages of international managers over the next five years. There was a growing concern on the part of many firms that the pace of internationalization would further outstrip the supply of international managers. The growing internationalization of European firms and the advent of the Single European Market in 1993 led firms to expect a more international and competitive market for managers and graduates.

For example, one financial services corporate HR executive expressed the problem like this: "Attracting and retaining high potential graduates and managers with international experience is vital if we are going to implement our corporate objective of achieving a much stronger presence in Europe. The problem is that the pool of available talent is not growing fast enough to meet demand." The same executive commented: "In the short run, we have to ensure that our reward package becomes internationally competitive, but this will not be enough. We need to look at new sources of labour supply such as women, host-country managers, third-country nationals and reduce our dependency on expatriates."

The problem of ensuring an adequate supply of international managers is further exacerbated by growing resistance to international mobility. Indeed, it was suggested by twenty-six of the forty-five firms in the sample that individuals were becoming less internationally mobile just when there was a growing need for international managers because of expansion abroad. The reduction in international mobility was attributed to several factors, including continued rationalization in the United Kingdom, which created uncertainties regarding reentry; the growing unwillingness to disrupt the education of children; the growing importance of quality of life considerations; and finally, continued uncertainty regarding international terrorism and political unrest.

Concerns about dual-career problems and disruption to children's education were seen as major barriers to future international mobility by many companies. In the past, working spouses were less common, generally female, and were prepared to follow their partners' career transfers. More frequently now, however, spouses must also leave a job or career in order to follow their partner to the foreign country.

The growing significance of the dual-career problem is well illustrated by a quote from the HR corporate executive of a large oil company: "Nowadays families are less willing to disrupt personal and social lives even where they accept that international experience will enhance the manager's career prospects."

And a banking HR executive described the problem in these words: "More and more women have careers and not just jobs. For many it would be impossible to continue their careers in a foreign country. Increasingly international mobility is limited by the dual-career factor. Also we need to recognise that dual-career problems can seriously affect career development plans for our international managers."

Two further restrictions on international mobility are illustrated by the following quote from an HR executive in a chemical firm: "It's becoming more common for offers of foreign assignments to be rejected because the location does not appeal to the family, and when managers are willing to go abroad, they are much more demanding about all aspects of the remuneration package."

The above discussion would suggest that restrictions on international mobility appear to be growing just at the time when the need for international mobility is becoming vital for the internationalization of U.K. business. Indeed, the problem of international mobility could emerge as a key factor in determining the international capability of a firm.

In the present study, companies were asked to identify the main HRM challenges they faced arising from the advent of the Single European Market. Eighty per cent (36 out of 45) of firms felt that the main challenge was to secure an adequate supply of international managers. A majority of firms said they needed to upgrade management skills and competences in order to compete effectively in Europe, and many companies were concerned about the poaching of graduates and managers by firms based in continental Europe.

Over 70 per cent of companies identified recruitment as a priority area. It was felt that the Single European Market would intensify competition for labour, increase the mobility of labour, and augment pressure on U.K. salaries. While some companies identified a number of positive opportunities presented by 1992 - namely, an increase in opportunity to recruit labour and management from other European countries - the majority of firms felt there would be a net loss of staff to continental Europe.

A small minority of companies were seeking to develop a pan-European approach to recruitment, but they were facing many practical problems such as which journals to advertise in and which qualifications to seek. In addition, there is a problem of the profile of a company abroad, because a company that is well known in the United Kingdom may be much less well known in other countries.

The need to develop a more international top management team to reflect the growing international nature of the business was increasingly recognized as a major challenge because, at the present time, very few British companies can claim to have a truly international top management team. Similarly, a growing concern was the need to assess what new knowledge, skills, and competencies are required to operate effectively in the internal European market.

There was also growing anxiety about the managerial skills and competencies needed to deal with the complex HRM issues and problems associated with the growth of international joint ventures (*e.g.*, the evaluation and promotion of managers and the problem of conflict of loyalty of managers to the joint venture or to the parent companies.

There was also a growing recognition by the companies of the need to understand the importance of cultural differences within Europe. This is particularly interesting in the light of the finding that only a very small minority (3 out of 45) of companies currently use cross-cultural training to help prepare managers for international transfer within Europe. By contrast, it was much more common for firms to provide cultural training for transfers to countries in the Far and Middle East, where the culture gap was seen to be greater. Specialist external courses were often used but not for international transfers within Europe.

The above discussion suggests that the most formidable task facing British companies wishing to operate across Europe is the recruitment and development of a cadre of managers and executives who understand and can operate effectively in the international environment. In practice, the impact of the Single European Market on human resource management strategy varied according to the stage of internationalization and the overall strategy of the firm. Most multinational firms traditionally pass through various stages of internationalization between the evolution from a domestic to a truly global organization.

For some well-established international firms, the Single European Market intensifies and sharpens the focus of problems associated with internationalization, rather than creating new problems. A small number of highly internationalized businesses that regarded themselves as transnationals (companies with the ability to manage across national boundaries, retaining local flexibility while achieving global integration) felt the nature of the HR challenge of 1992 would be marginal rather than central.

Such companies (*e.g.*, the oil companies) tended to see pan-European recruitment and language training initiatives as a response to the single market, but they stressed that fundamental issues such as the supply of managers and management development should be related to the broader international strategy of the business rather than to the Single European Market alone.

The single market did, however, represent a major HR challenge for "new" international firms that had internationalized in the recent past, and for firms that were significantly shifting the focus of their international activities towards Europe. International human resource management strategy, like human resource management strategy generally, must be linked to the strategic evolution of the firm.

This has highlighted some of the HRM issues and challenges that such firms will face as they undergo the internationalization process. It also suggests that, for British international firms, the recruitment and development of international managers will be the key challenge of the 1990s.

Competitive Advantage

An impressive body of literature on the management of service companies has emerged since 1977' that services "break free". The unique characteristics of services have received acceptance, while related issues of service design and production, services marketing, and services management have been given an impressive amount of attention in books and leading journals.

Despite this progress, a number of issues mandate continued scrutiny. There is the growing recognition that the boundaries between goods and services have become increasingly blurred and that the majorities of goods contain significant service components and vice versa. For example, some commentators have noted the potential for competitive advantage that is inherent in correctly leveraging the service components of products. This fluidity is perhaps best captured in Shostack's (1977) molecular model, which views all market entities as containing some tangible and intangible elements with services being defined as intangible-dominant entities.

The outcome of this dialogue has been an increase in the number of services management perspectives that are applicable in what were traditionally considered manufacturing domains and, conversely, an increase in the level of attention given to the strategic management of service firms. Central to this debate is the issue of how service companies can attain a sustainable competitive advantage."

Service businesses generally are noted for their high level of mimetic or imitative behaviour. Innovations, such as new types of bank accounts or investment vehicles, are invariably quickly imitated by competitors. Innovative airlines, which sought to use frequent flyer programmes to build switching costs for customers, found that, very quickly, many other major airlines were offering similar incentives. This level of imitation has focused attention on what kinds of resources and capabilities a service firm might leverage in order to gain a competitive advantage.

Gaining positions of competitive strength has become more important in an environment that has become increasingly global and competitive. Competition in industries such as air travel and transportation is inherently more global than in many manufacturing businesses. Deregulation in the likes of financial services has ushered in a new era of global competition and quick competitive reactions. The size and importance of the service sector has grown considerably. This sector accounted for 74 per cent of gross domestic product and about 79 per cent of national employment in the United States in 1992. In addition. almost 60 per cent of total value added in the U.S. economy in 1992 came from private (non-government) services.

This responds to these developments by proposing a model of competitive advantage in the international services sector, which is designed to help managers evaluate the potential sources of such advantage. It draws heavily on an existing foundation of literature spanning the disparate fields of services marketing, strategic management, international business, and industrial organization economics. At the intersection of these strands of thought is the resource-based view (RBV), which is the conceptual premise of this paper.

The next outlines the perspectives provided by the RBV for international services firms. Subsequently, a conceptual model is presented, and selected sources of international competitive advantage are outlined. Finally, conclusions are drawn and implications discussed.

Competition in international business: Insights from the resource-based view.

Organizational strategy has long been viewed as the challenge of matching internal resources and strengths with the opportunities existing in the environment. This is perhaps best summarized in the seminal framework of Learned, Christensen, Andrews, and Guth. Thus, the task of strategic management is viewed in terms of the interplay of the personal values of management with the firms' skills and resources, and of how these are matched to environmental opportunities/threats and broader societal expectations.

Throughout the early 1980s, the broad thrust of strategy research focused on the second quadrant. This research is best demonstrated by the work of Porter (1980, 1981). It posited that a firm's performance was largely a function of the structure of the industry and the firm's position in the industry. However, empirical research towards the end of the decade increasingly began to show greater performance differences among firms in the same industry than across industry boundaries.

Allied to this was a conceptual swing towards the end of the decade back to a forgotten portion of the LCAG framework, namely quadrant 1. Building on earlier work by Penrose (1959) and Nelson and Winter (1982), what has become known as the resource-based view is illustrated by the work of Barney (1986, 1991), Conner (1991), Dierickx and Cool (1989), Grant (1991), Mahoney and Pandian (1992), and Peteraf (1993), to name but a few.

The resource-based view focuses on heterogeneity among firms in the same industry. It views firms in terms of unique bundles of resources and capabilities that provide the basis upon which a competitive advantage can be pursued. The normative implication of this view is that the firm should base its strategy on its own resources and capabilities. Irrespective of the markets or combination of markets served, firms should seek to leverage the resources best suited to those markets.

This may even lead to a situation where the firm will choose to compete in inherently less structurally attractive markets if it possesses resources that are valuable in serving those markets. Of course, in an international context, there may be other motives for competing in structurally unattractive markets, most notably defensive foreign direct investment or cross-subsidization, where firms try to pre-empt the strategic moves of international rivals.

Conditions Necessary for Competitive Advantage

The potential to confer a competitive advantage is not inherent in all resources but, rather, in only those that meet a rigorous set of conditions. The first condition is that the resource must be valuable — it must provide the opportunity to exploit some environmental opportunity or neutralize some threat. Resources are considered valuable when they enable a firm to conceive of or implement strategies that improve the firm's efficiency or effectiveness. Some authors construe value in terms of meeting a key buyer need.

In addition, resources must have the characteristic of rareness. If valuable resources are possessed by a large number of competitors or potential competitors, they no longer represent a source of competitive advantage.

This is the key issue of heterogeneity underlying the resource-based view — firms possessing unique bundles of skills and resources can attain a sustainable competitive advantage. Third, there must be the condition of imperfect mobility of resources. Where resources are easily traded between competitors, no competitive advantage can be maintained.

Imperfectly mobile resources include those that are idiosyncratic to the firm, those for which property rights arc not well defined, or those that are co-specialized assets.(2) The imperfect mobility of assets is a critical factor in service businesses as people are the key assets in many cases, and their high mobility frequently results in the loss of accounts and the emergence of new competitive threats as in the case, for example, with personnel employed by advertising agencies and moving to other ones.

Finally, for an advantage to be sustained, resources must be imperfectly imitable or provide some ex-post limits to competition: That is, subsequent to a firm gaining a superior position and earning rents, forces must exist that limit competition for those rents. It was noted above that innovations such as the development of a new type of account by a retail bank or a new advertising style by a creative department frequently results in a host of imitations from competitors.

For a firm to be in a position to exploit a valuable and rare resource, there must be a resource position barrier preventing imitation by other firms. Sustaining a competitive advantage over a period of time requires the presence of isolating mechanisms that prevent imitation. Several such barriers that have been cited in the literature include causal ambiguity and uncertain imitability, where the drivers of success are difficult to identify. Imitation may also be prevented by the process of asset stock accumulation within the firm.

Where these stocks possess the characteristics of time compression diseconomies (accumulation has taken place over a long period of time), asset mass efficiencies (a critical mass of stocks has been developed), and interconnectedness (stocks are interrelated), then imitation is difficult. Indeed, the significance of asset stock accumulation in the services sector has been demonstrated elsewhere, when the "reservoir of organizational and managerial expertise that has been built up over the years can provide branch offices with information at a cost very much lower than a de novo indigenous firm would have to incur" — in other words, an ownership advantage in international competition.

Thus, service firms must seek to identify the skills and resources they possess and that meet the above criteria, and to leverage such resources to attain a competitive advantage. For service firms trading internationally, there is the added dimension of the location of such resources, which may be in the home or host country, or both.

The traditional international-business literature and the more recent global strategic management literature have identified that the success of a multinational firm is likely to be based on some combination of three sets of advantages, namely, firm-specific advantages, country-specific advantages, and internalization advantages. In resource terms, this effectively amounts to the combination of country-specific and firm-specific resources since internalization or coordination can be viewed as a managerial capability and hence a firm-specific resource.

The conceptual lens of the RBV demonstrates important differences between these two sets of resources. Country-specific resources derive from the resource endowments of countries or, in neo-classical economics terms, its comparative advantages. Country-specific resources are available on equal terms to all firms competing in an industry. Therefore, there are no barriers to prevent competing firms from imitating a given firm's portfolio of country-specific advantages. It is recognized, however, that a given firm's ability to gain access to these resources or to pre-empt their usage may be dependent on firm-specific political competences.

In addition, some authors suggest that country-specific advantages are dynamic and change over time — for example, Japan's move from a low-labour-cost country to a high-labour-cost country. However, firm-specific resources are considered unique to the firm, and, therefore, are likely to possess greater barriers to imitation, which suggests that they will be a more important source of competitive advantage.

Resources Versus Capabilities

Authors have recently sought to distinguish between the potential rent-generating assets of an organization. A variety of distinctions have been suggested, including assets and core competences, resources and capabilities, intellectual assets and non-intellectual assets, tangible and intangible resources, and assets and skills. Despite the range of nomenclature, the issue being addressed by the various authors is similar, namely, that the rent-generating assets of an organization can be broadly classified in terms of two basic types.

On the one hand, there are the organization's resources, which are tangible, can be either inputs or outputs, and possess two key attributes: ownership and value. Ownership can be legal in terms of title deeds to land, property, or equipment, or in intellectual property such as patents, trademarks, licenses, or trade secrets. In addition, the firm may own assets that are not legal in nature, such as reputation with customers, organizational or personal networks, and databases. The most acceptable measure of value from an accounting perspective is exchange value. Thus, resources in the main are viewed as relatively easy to trade between firms.

On the other hand, organizations also possess capabilities or competences — that is, the capacity to deploy resources, usually in combination, in order to effect a desired end. The key characteristics of capabilities are that they are firm-specific and developed over time, but, unlike resources, they are not easily tradable between firms. In general, capabilities are information-based or intellectual assets.

In addition, they tend to be cross-functional or arise from the integration of individual functional capabilities and thus are sometimes referred to as "intermediate goods" in the production process. Therefore, by definition, capabilities meet the requirements of rareness and inimitability and are a strong basis for competitive advantage. The normative implication of this logic is that service-firm capabilities are likely to be the most sustainable source of competitive advantage.

The issue of potential synergies between home- and host-country firm-specific advantages has been a central issue in the vast body of work that broadly falls within the gambit of globalization. The globalization debate began in the early 1980s and has continued with intensity ever since. One of the primary hypotheses of globalization was that markets were converging. Reaching back to the marketing-standardization literature of the 1960s, this meant that companies could be successful by selling standardized products throughout a global market at low prices due to the resulting economies of scale, in effect utilizing only home-country firm-specific advantages.

This was in sharp contrast to the earlier view of the multinational corporation as a collection of autonomous subsidiaries tailoring resource use and strategy to particular local market needs. However, even some of the early proponents of globalization conceded that this hypothesis might be a little simplistic, and began to suggest that standardization was a matter of degree.

From this recognition of complexity emerged the view that, to be successful in the global marketplace. the firm must organize itself to achieve the benefits of global integration, national responsiveness, and learning. In resource terms, this meant that the firm should not rely solely on the resources of the parent company (global integration) or the subsidiary (national responsiveness), but must seek to emphasize both and successfully transfer learning in both directions (*i.e.*, from the home-country headquarters to the subsidiary and vice versa). So, while several authors contend that a company should pursue a global strategy on the basis of the globalization potential of the industry, there is a contrasting view that firms need to combine both global and local dimensions, sometimes known crudely as “"localization".

Stated in resource terms, this "transnational solution" suggests that superior performers in international business will combine both home- and host-country firm-specific resources and capabilities. This suggests that service firms must consider extensive foreign direct investment and create an opportunity for the successful combination of home- and host-country firm-specific resources and capabilities.

However, other "non-equity" forms of organization, with origins largely in the services sector, such as licensing, franchising, and management contracts, equally present an opportunity for the successful integration of home-and host-country resources. Their effectiveness in achieving such integration seems to be greater in consumer services than in industrial or business services.

Firm-specific Resources

Porter (1990) highlighted that many firm-specific resources were rooted in the firm's country of origin. This is illustrated by the strength of German companies in engineering, of U.S. companies in consumer goods and services, and of Italian companies in craft-based industries. Kogut (1991) extended this analysis to show that long cycles of country leadership in international competition can be explained by differences in country capabilities embodied in the firms in these countries.

In addition, many of these capabilities are sticky and diffuse slowly across borders due to four factors: technological opportunities, selection forces, identifiability, and institutional lock-in. In terms of technology, many firms have established relationships with country-specific research centres, trade associations, educational institutions, and skilled individuals. These relationships are built up over a long time and are not easy to replicate in other countries. In many cases, these are the clusters of organizations identified in Porter's "diamond" framework.

Equally, selection pressures are analogous to Porter's concept of domestic rivalry, an essential requirement to the development of globally competitive firms. Identifiability refers to domestic firms having a better understanding of the sources of success of domestic competitors than do international competitors.

This understanding can have numerous reasons and results in a greater propensity to imitate domestic competitors that leads to greater national rather than international diffusion of management capabilities. Institutional lock-in is analagous to the notions of administrative heritage or strategic commitment at a national level where the change and adoption of new techniques are impeded by previous investment, past practices, and perceived wisdom. The immediate implication of this analysis is that the firm-specific advantages underlying service-firm strategy are likely to vary from country to country, reflecting the fact that such advantages derive largely from the country of origin and diffuse slowly across borders.

Kogut (1991), however, noted that long cycles of country leadership are driven not only by technological investments (resources) but also by the efficiency of the dominant organizing principles (capabilities).

Foreign direct investment is the extension of the organizing principles of domestic firms to foreign markets. Organizational types, such as the global firm, provide a vehicle for the diffusion of capabilities across borders due to the high level of integration or coordination of its activities. Close interaction between parents and subsidiaries is also a central aspect of the transnational firm, which has been advocated as the organizational type most suitable, given the current complexity of international business. though not necessarily in every industry.

Most major multinational firms have at various times experimented with increasing the integration of their operations. The learning that has accrued from these integration efforts suggests that the firm-specific advantages underlying the strategy of leading international competitors will not vary from one host country to another, thereby reflecting the diffusion of management capability.

Towards a resource-based model of competitive advantage in international business. The process by which resources and capabilities are translated into a competitive advantage for the multinational firm is outlined, which demonstrates that superior performance is likely to be attained through the adoption of strategies based on a combination of home- and host-country firm-specific resources with host-country location-specific resources.

It highlights that management plays an essential role in leveraging this resource pool in ways that enable the firm to gain advantage. Management must make choices regarding which product markets to compete in, whether to try to attain a position of low-cost leadership or differentiation, or both, and which resources and capabilities to use in order to attain these positions of competitive leadership. Superior performance, which can be measured in the conventional terms of market share leadership or return on investment, accrues to firms achieving a competitive advantage. Sustaining the advantage over time requires reinvestment on the basis of competitive strength.

This model is an extension of the model of competitive advantage that can be found in the strategic-management literature, but it clearly sits very comfortably with the extant international business literature, as well as the "transnational solution" proposed by Bartlett and Ghoshal (1989) to help managers deal with the complexity of international business.

The model presented is designed to assist managers of service firms in building a sustainable competitive advantage on the foundation of the resources and capabilities inherent in the company. It also helps managers identify which skills and resources are most likely to be an important source of advantage and to realize the importance of being able to combine potential advantages from both home- and host-country locations. In specific cases, the actual skills and resources underlying competitive advantage are likely to be contingent on the characteristics of the service itself, the service firm, and the service industry as well as of the country of origin of the firm. However, sources of advantage in service industries identified elsewhere can be seen to meet the requirements outlined in the model. For example, Stalk, Evans, and Schulman (1992) contend that the growth and subsequent market dominance of WalMart resides in the company's unique logistics capability, which confirms the importance of capabilities as a potential source of competitive advantage. The logistics system known as "cross-docking" ensures that goods are simply moved from one loading dock to another in forty-eight hours or less, resulting in minimal inventories and shaving between 2 per cent and 3 per cent off the cost of sales.

The system is a source of competitive advantage because it meets all of the criteria outlined earlier. It is used in a value-generating way — creating cost savings in a business where tight margins are critical and low costs are a key success factor. It is a rare system, and, because it combines people, delivery vehicles, and communication systems, it is clearly immobile. But it is its inherent barriers to imitation that help to confer a competitive advantage on WalMart. It is extremely difficult to duplicate the required constant communication between suppliers, distribution centres, and sales outlets achieved through the company's investment in a private satellite communications system.

Similarly, Pleval, Nellis, Lane, and Schuler (1994) attribute the success of AT&T's Global Business Communication Systems (GBCS) division to its unique human resource capability. Its human resource strategy is linked to overall business strategy, and review and reward mechanisms are designed to increase personal motivation while simultaneously achieving company goals. The company views its employees as "its only sustainable competitive advantage."

Again, this division of AT&T has been successful because it utilizes a set of resources/capabilities that meet the criteria necessary for competitive advantage. GBCS uses people in a value-generating way by explicitly connecting their efforts with key company goals. such as using a total quality management approach, being a leader in customer-led applications of technology, and being the best value supplier.

People can always leave an organization, so why do many firms contend that their people are their only sustainable advantage? In the ease of GCBS, mobility of personnel is not a major concern, as its success resides not in individuals but rather in a complex set of relationships among individuals reflected in performance management, recognition, compensation practices, and communication programmes. Furthermore, even though individuals who are hired away by competitors are able to describe them, these systems prove difficult to imitate because of the levels of reaming that occur while these "asset stocks" are being accumulated.

The key role of people, as a source of competitive advantage in internationally traded services, is demonstrated by the high level of foreign direct investment by firms in industries like financial and management services in order to maintain control over this resource.

This paper contends that competitive advantage for service firms lies in the unique resources and capabilities possessed by the firm. Not all resources or capabilities are a source of competitive advantage-only those that meet the stringent conditions of value, rareness. The actual sources of competitive advantage are likely to vary depending on the nature of the service, the particular traits of the firm, the nature of the industry, and the country of origin.

The normative implication of this analysis is that service managers conduct a rigorous analysis of internal resources and capabilities. What eve resources and capabilities does the firm have, and which of any of these strengths are unique? What scope is there for making investments to develop unique resources and capabilities that would yield competitive advantages in the future? The analysis also raises the question of control of key sources of competitive advantage.

Foreign direct investment arguably creates the greatest potential not only for control but also for the effective integration of resources across national boundaries. More traditional forms of organization in the services sector, such as licensing, franchising, and management contracts, have been shown to be effective control mechanisms in consumer, though not in business, services. Their effectiveness as a means for integrating resources may represent a fruitful area for further research.

4

Orientation and Training

EMPLOYEE EDUCATION, TRAINING AND DEVELOPMENT

In general, education is 'mind preparation' and is carried out remote from the actual work area, training is the systematic development of the attitude, knowledge, skill pattern required by a person to perform a given task or job adequately and development is 'the growth of the individual in terms of ability, understanding and awareness'.

Within an organization all three are necessary in order to:

- Develop workers to undertake higher-grade tasks;
- Provide the conventional training of new and young workers (*e.g.* as apprentices, clerks, etc.);
- Raise efficiency and standards of performance;
- Meet legislative requirements (*e.g.* health and safety);
- Inform people (induction training, pre-retirement courses, etc.);

From time to time meet special needs arising from technical, legislative, and knowledge need changes. Meeting these needs is achieved via the 'training loop'. (Schematic available in PDF version.) The diagnosis of other than conventional needs is complex and often depends upon the intuition or personal experience of managers and needs revealed by deficiencies. Sources of inspiration include:

- Common sense - it is often obvious that new machines, work systems, task requirements and changes in job content will require workers to be prepared;
- Shortcomings revealed by statistics of output per head, performance indices, unit costs, etc. and behavioural failures revealed by absentee figures, lateness, sickness etc. records;
- Recommendations of government and industry training organizations;
- Inspiration and innovations of individual managers and supervisors;
- Forecasts and predictions about staffing needs;
- Inspirations prompted by the technical press, training journals, reports of the experience of others;

- The suggestions made by specialist (*e.g.* education and training officers, safety engineers, work-study staff and management services personnel).

Designing training is far more than devising courses; it can include activities such as:

- Learning from observation of trained workers;
- Receiving coaching from seniors;
- Discovery as the result of working party, project team membership or attendance at meetings;
- Job swaps within and without the organization;
- Undertaking planned reading, or follow from the use of self–teaching texts and video tapes;
- Learning via involvement in research, report writing and visiting other works or organizations.

So far as group training is concerned in addition to formal courses there are:

- Lectures and talks by senior or specialist managers;
- Discussion group (conference and meeting) activities;
- Briefing by senior staffs;
- Role-playing exercises and simulation of actual conditions;
- Video and computer teaching activities;
- Case studies (and discussion) tests, quizzes, panel 'games', group forums, observation exercises and inspection and reporting techniques.

Evaluation of the effectiveness of training is done to ensure that it is cost effective, to identify needs to modify or extend what is being provided, to reveal new needs and redefine priorities and most of all to ensure that the objectives of the training are being met.

The latter may not be easy to ascertain where results cannot be measured mathematically. In the case of attitude and behavioural changes sought, leadership abilities, drive and ambition fostered, etc., achievement is a matter of the judgement of senior staffs. Exact validation might be impossible but unless on the whole the judgements are favourable the cooperation of managers in identifying needs, releasing personnel and assisting in training ventures will cease.

In making their judgements senior managers will question whether the efforts expended have produced:

- More effective, efficient, flexible employees;
- Faster results in making newcomers knowledgeable and effective than would follow from experience;

- More effective or efficient use of machinery, equipment and work procedures;
- Fewer requirements to implement redundancy (by retraining);
- Fewer accidents both personal and to property;
- Improvements in the qualifications of staff and their ability to take on tougher roles;
- Better employee loyalty to the organization with more willingness to innovate and accept change.

DIFFERENCE BETWEEN ORIENTATION AND TRAINING

Training constitutes a third set of practice modifications for effective team implementation. There is often a mistaken belief that people who are highly educated have the basic skills to work effectively in team settings. In fact, highly specialized individuals are often used to working alone and may lack some of the basic interpersonal skills necessary for collaboration. Training programmes designed for interpersonal skills in teams take one of two approaches: traditional classroom instruction in which a lecturer delivers material about techniques or strategies for working in teams and creative off-site team-building sessions in which teams participate in athletic, artistic, or competitive activities unrelated to their actual day-to-day responsibilities.

What is generally missing is the development of hands-on team capabilities, which is best accomplished by treating the team as a whole and applying the training as the team performs its actual tasks. In this way, the value of the training is established in the context of the work that the team does. In addition to teaching interpersonal skills, training must focus on establishing the skills necessary for self-management. First, considerable attention must be given to determining an optimal degree of autonomy. Self-managing teams are an appropriate response to situations where performance can be enhanced by taking decisions closer to the organization's environment. In contrast, self-management is not appropriate when the team is particularly large, when there is a high degree of functional diversity, or when the team is newly formed. In these situations, the team is faced with a high level of complexity, information-processing requirements are extensive, and managerial tasks are particularly challenging.

Having an external leader provide direction in these instances can improve team effectiveness. Perhaps the most substantial costs associated with increasing self-direction in teams are associated with the level of training and development needed to ensure that all or most of the members have the KSAs required to perform what were previously managerial responsibilities. In addition, on some teams employees are asked actually to carry out the training and development of their fellow members. Another training focus pertains to learning. In a team-based system, multidirectional learning is required across functions, levels, and organizations. This requires norms that are far different from those that prevailed in the traditional organization.

For example, learning requires the willingness to surface bad news and act on it. But that will not happen unless the traditional reaction— negatively evaluating the messengers of bad news—changes. Organizations that encourage experimentation and innovation and set up mechanisms for shared reflection can capitalize on this learning potential. Lateral learning must occur through dialogue and collaboration, and vertical learning must occur between teams at different levels in the organization. Local learning and innovation occurs through trial and error, but broader learning depends on whether organizations establish mechanisms for reflecting on and capturing learning from a variety of experiences.

If organizations wish to motivate teamwork, they must incorporate teamwork KSAs into their appraisal systems. It is important that the appraisal system not only reward good team players but also discourage behaviours that are not conducive to team effectiveness. An organization-specific job analysis should be conducted to determine the precise nature of the behavioural and performance measures to be included in the appraisal form for each individual team member.

Categories of teamwork KSAs such as conflict resolution, collaborative problem solving, communication, goal setting, performance management, planning, and task coordination could be translated into critical work behaviours or performance dimensions and incorporated into such an appraisal form. Equally important, however, is that team behaviours then be assessed. Imagine four teams, each performing the same task.

In the first team, each team member is given an individual goal. In the second, a goal is set for the team as a whole only. The third team is given both individual and team goals. The fourth is given no specific goal at all. Which team will do the poorest work? In an experiment that replicated this situation, the team with individual goals only was the poorest performer among all four teams. The team with both individual and team goals performed the best.

Most organizations might claim they have both individual and team goals if they have profit sharing or gain sharing. However, psychologically, these types of "team goals" are often overshadowed by individual goals, because the personal sense of control over performance lessens as one focuses on larger and larger groups, such as the entire organization. Each team should identify a set of critical measures representing a combination of results and process-oriented outcomes. Focusing only on results (for example, return on sales, revenue growth, and so on) does not help inform the team about which behaviours should be adjusted. Process measures (time spent per call, days before call returned, and so on) identify key behaviours that the team can change in order to improve results. Teams should avoid developing too many measures. If a measure is not critical in guiding the team's behaviour, then discard it. Most experts recommend that teams track six to ten performance areas.

Finally, in team-based organizations, people are responsible for collective performance at multiple levels. Individual, team, and business unit performance must be evaluated. Optimizing performance at any one level may hurt performance at other levels. The link between behaviour at one level and performance at another may be uncertain. People are often concerned that they will not get adequate feedback on how they are performing when the focus is on collective performance. Therefore, appraisal systems should assess behaviours that contribute to performance of other units or other levels within the organization. Team members should receive feedback from multiple sources, not just a manager. In small teams, each person can receive peer feedback, that is, feedback from all other team members and, where appropriate, feedback from customers.

Customers may be external to the organization (for example, a person who purchases a product or service) or internal (a person downstream in the process who receives the work of the team). It is also critical that feedback be given on multiple levels.

It should be provided on individual performance, individual contributions to the team, team performance, and the team's contribution to the organization as a whole. Especially for the latter, feedback from customers and about competitors is critical. Whenever possible, it is best for teams themselves to document their own performance. This documentation should be developed and then discussed regularly at team meetings.

A final set of HR practices that should be examined when implementing teams pertains to compensation. Good practices for rewarding team performance require good processes for defining what the performance should be and for measuring and evaluating the performance. Some researchers have advocated that rewards should be the last component put in place in the transition to teams. This argument is made because team rewards are difficult to develop and have to be tailored to the organization.

Individual compensation should then be based on the accomplishment of these objectives. This is an intermediary step on the path towards team-based rewards; it allows recognition for teamwork and allows time for the organization to adjust other systems. Next, HR professionals can work to change the organizational compensation and reward practices. For example, team awards and team bonuses help team members focus on the performance of their own team. Profit sharing and gain sharing help team members focus on unit wide performance and orient employees to the larger performing unit by making it in everyone's interest to improve the performance of the enterprise as a whole.

This combination ensures that performance at each level is recognized and encouraged, in turn ensuring that individual behaviour is in the best interest of the team and that team behaviour is in the best interest of the organization. HR professionals may face several additional impediments. We see four challenges in particular: the inability of work teams to make a dramatic improvement in organizational performance quickly; the inevitable inter team conflict inherent in team-based organizations; resistance to work teams in foreign affiliates; and North American cultural barriers to working in teams. An unwillingness to communicate between teams destroys one of the reasons that organizations implement teams in the first place: to create a higher level of integration in a complex organizational environment.

Inwardly focused teams that fail to collaborate with others or communicate with external customers perform more poorly than externally focused teams. Several strategies are available to the HR professional for overcoming problematic inwardly focused teams. First, managers should keep teams focused on a higher level, or super ordinate, goal. Such a goal can be organization-, plant, or unitwide. A super ordinate goal keeps teams focused on the big picture, lowers competition between teams, and ties everything that all do more closely to overall organizational success.

A second strategy is to implement rewards (possibly based on goals) that are tied to the success of a set of teams as whole (a work unit, for example). Unit-level rewards are tricky in that all team members have to know how their contribution affects their rewards (also known as line of sight). A final strategy is to create linking or integrating teams composed of members from each of the competitive teams. Integrating teams tend to dilute original team member loyalties and ensure that each team's concerns are heard. Regardless of the strategy chosen, ignoring the problem of combative teams will inevitably erode any potential gains to be realized from the implementation of work teams.

HR professionals should take a proactive stand by designing strategies to reduce competition before the teams are allowed to become inwardly focused. A third impediment may arise when multinational organizations use work teams in their foreign affiliates.

Organizations often wish to "export" their management practices because having similar HR practices in each country streamlines operations and reduces costs. For example, the Goodyear Tire and Rubber Company has begun using work teams in Europe, Latin America, and Asia; Sara Lee Corporation currently uses teams in Puerto Rico and Mexico; and Texas Instruments Malaysia has organized its entire workforce into teams.

Organizational scholars have pointed to national culture as a determinant of the success or failure of management initiatives that are developed in one culture and implemented in another. Some employees may resist management initiatives or react angrily when those initiatives clash with their deeply held cultural values.

HR professionals should learn about the cultures in which the company's work teams will operate. Through better understanding of cultural differences comes the knowledge of potential stumbling blocks to successful implementation before attempts are made to export work teams. Success stories about work teams in foreign affiliates exist, but that success depends on an understanding of the cultural forces that shape employee reaction to teams.

Just as some cultures are more individualistic or more collectivistic than others, individuals within cultures also vary on this dimension—even though there is, on average, more variation across cultures than within cultures. For example, when faced with the prospect of moving to a team-based work environment, some employees in a study conducted in the United States expressed concerns that reflected their individualistic values. Their comments included these: "Why should someone else's performance affect my pay?" "Will the team get credit for what I do?" "Individual achievement won't count anymore." "My achievement will be diluted by overall team success." These comments suggest that some employees may resist work teams because they are not compatible with their own work-related values.

Tests exist for measuring individualistic and collectivistic values at the individual level. Other measures such as preference for teams could be used as selection tools to evaluate prospective team members before they are placed on a team. If the teams are self-managing or autonomous, measures such as need for growth or need for achievement could be used to assess prospective member preferences for increased autonomy and responsibility. Whatever the measures used, HR professionals need to be aware of the role of individual differences in a team's success or failure in order to select more carefully individuals who are suited to working in a team. Barring the availability of such individuals, training must attempt to enhance employee receptivity to work teams.

Facilitators

First, in the years during which Total Quality Management enjoyed its heyday (the 1980s), many companies began a practice that had previously seemed contradictory to maintaining competitive advantage: benchmarking HR practices in other organizations. In years past companies viewed their internal operations as sources of extreme value.

But with the growth in international competition—especially in automobiles, electronics, and textiles—some businesses in the United States have realized the benefits of sharing information more openly to increase the global competitiveness of entire industries. This realization coupled with the work team success stories in the popular press have fueled an unprecedented exchange of both ideas and visits between companies and even competitors interested in adopting or improving work teams. For example, companies such as General Electric have looked to other seemingly unrelated businesses, such as Southwest Airlines, in order to adapt team-based practices. The benchmarking of HR practices also occurs within industries.

Several major semiconductor manufacturers (for example, Intel, DEC, Texas Instruments) have benchmarking agreements that allow for information exchange around HR best practices. Second, in many industries, organizational environments are becoming exceedingly dynamic and complex. Scholars and practitioners alike have long realized the importance of aligning organizational structures with environmental characteristics. For example, the rapid changes witnessed in the computer industry forced companies such as IBM to restructure to achieve a better organizational structure-environment fit. There is general consensus that increasing environmental complexity will continue for the foreseeable future for organizations in many industries.

As these changes continue, the use of work teams will continue to serve as an integrated and flexible means of responding to organizational environments. Finally, regarding cultural change, researchers have suggested that there may be a substantial amount of cross-national convergence of management practices, values, and beliefs as a result of the interactions between organizations across cultures. As cultural convergence continues, a common set of values and assumptions may develop across national boundaries. This implies that eventually it may be possible to develop a universal set of best practices that will be appropriate no matter the cultural setting. In other words, less cultural adaptation may be necessary. Thus, HR practitioners in multinational corporations may gradually have an easier time dealing with cultural impediments.

We caution, however, that although some convergence is likely to take place, there are fundamental cultural values within nations that will remain stable. Researchers have referred to this phenomenon as the distinction between peripheral and core values. Therefore, it will always be necessary to adapt HR practices to some degree to fit the cultural context if the effectiveness of those practices across national boundaries is to be enhanced.

The Prospect of Teams Work

First, as the environment grows increasingly complex, temporary team structures will supplant more permanent work teams. As the forces outside organizations continue to change, the structures inside organizations will become more fluid. Rather than permanently assigning people to work teams, team composition will shift as projects, problems, or customers demand. Ad hoc teams or project teams will be more prevalent, placing extraordinary demands on employees to be flexible and demonstrate their value to organizations consistently through their team efforts. The challenge for HR managers will certainly involve compensation and evaluation for employees who may be constantly moving from one project team to another without a regular supervisor or team members with whom they have any long-term contact.

Second, the use of multicultural teams and globalized teams is likely to rise as trade barriers continue to fall. National culture plays a strong role in determining employee attitudes and behaviour. If a significant rise in these more culturally diverse teams occurs—and we feel strongly that it will—then HR managers must familiarize themselves with the cultures in which their organization operates. For example, if peer evaluations are part of the performance appraisal process on a multicultural team, HR managers must identify the key cultural characteristics that may serve as stumbling blocks to these evaluations.

If globalized teams are used, it is likely that entirely different compensation systems will be needed depending on the dominant cultural values of the areas in which an organization has business. Finally, with more telecommuting and flextime there will be less face-to-face time in work teams. We predict that traditional work teams will be replaced by virtual teams, whose members may seldom or never meet in person. Also referred to as "mobile, " these teams have no geographic centre. The members work out of their homes, automobiles, and clients' facilities and communicate via e-mail, fax, telephone, and videoconference. Team meetings may take place only once each quarter. The challenge for HR professionals is to assist managers in integrating team members, building cohesive teams, and facilitating communication and information exchange without having team members together in one place.

Teams are a powerful design option for organizations that hope to meet the challenges of increased global competition, improve output quality, and address the social needs of the ever-changing global workforce. However, the success or failure of work teams in multinational organizations will depend largely on the HR professional. Effective implementation of teams requires that HR practitioners adapt key assumptions about motivation, structure, and accountability. Adapted assumptions must support lateral thinking, collaboration, interdependence, a focus on process, permeable boundaries, and mutual responsibility. At the same time, HR practices must evolve to support teambased systems. Modifications in recruitment and selection, task design, training, evaluation, and compensation are all key to the effective use of teams in multinational organizations. Key to effective selection and recruitment for teams is the identification of teamwork KSAs.

Critical for task design is the development of teams around task processes and the integration of functional areas. Developing interpersonal, managerial, and learning skills are important training needs in team-based organizations. Finally, effective evaluation and compensation for teams requires a multilevel perspective and a balance between individual and team-based systems. Numerous impediments will challenge the effective implementation of teams across national contexts, including the inherent time lag between implementation and results, the often tenuous relationships between teams, cultural differences that require adaptations in practices to fit the context, and increasing domestic demographic diversity within nations.

To address these potential impediments, HR practitioners can encourage sharing practices within and between organizations, observe and adapt to organizational environmental trends, and maintain awareness of cultural convergence.

HR professionals who can change their assumptions and are adept at modifying basic HR practices will be better poised to face future trends in the use of teams that are just on the horizon. As temporary team structures, multicultural teams, and virtual teams proliferate, these team-savvy practitioners will be able to lead their organizations through successful implementation and use of teams in multinational contexts.

DEVELOPING A HRM STRATEGY

Faced with rapid change organizations need to develop a more focused and coherent approach to managing people. In just the same way a business requires a marketing or information technology strategy it also requires a human resource or people strategy.

In developing such a strategy two critical questions must be addressed.

- What kinds of people do you need to manage and run your business to meet your strategic business objectives?
- What people programmes and initiatives must be designed and implemented to attract, develop and retain staff to compete effectively?

In order to answer these questions four key dimensions of an organization must be addressed. These are:

- Culture: the beliefs, values, norms and management style of the organization

- Organization: the structure, job roles and reporting lines of the organization
- People: the skill levels, staff potential and management capability
- Human resources systems: the people focused mechanisms which deliver the strategy - employee selection, communications, training, rewards, career development, etc.

Frequently in managing the people element of their business senior managers will only focus on one or two dimensions and neglect to deal with the others. Typically, companies reorganize their structures to free managers from bureaucracy and drive for more entrepreneurial flair but then fail to adjust their training or reward systems.

When the desired entrepreneurial behaviour does not emerge managers frequently look confused at the apparent failure of the changes to deliver results. The fact is that seldom can you focus on only one area. What is required is a strategic perspective aimed at identifying the relationship between all four dimensions. If you require an organization which really values quality and service you not only have to retrain staff, you must also review the organization, reward, appraisal and communications systems.

The pay and reward system is a classic problem in this area. Frequently organizations have payment systems which are designed around the volume of output produced. If you then seek to develop a company which emphasizes the product's quality you must change the pay systems. Otherwise you have a contradiction between what the chief executive is saying about quality and what your payment system is encouraging staff to do.

There are seven steps to developing a human resource strategy and the active involvement of senior line managers should be sought throughout the approach.

Steps in developing HRM strategy

Get the 'Big Picture'

Understand your business strategy.

- Highlight the key driving forces of your business. What are they? *e.g.* technology, distribution, competition, the markets.
- What are the implications of the driving forces for the people side of your business?
- What is the fundamental people contribution to bottom line business performance?

Develop a Mission Statement or Statement of Intent

That relates to the people side of the business. Do not be put off by negative reactions to the words or references to idealistic statements - it is the actual process of thinking through the issues in a formal and explicit manner that is important.

- What do your people contribute?

Conduct a SWOT Analysis of the Organization

Focus on the internal strengths and weaknesses of the people side of the business.

- Consider the current skill and capability issues.

Vigorously research the external business and market environment. High light the opportunities and threats relating to the people side of the business.

- What impact will/ might they have on business performance?
- Consider skill shortages?
- The impact of new technology on staffing levels?

From this analysis you then need to review the capability of your personnel department. Complete a SWOT analysis of the department - consider in detail the department's current areas of operation, the service levels and competences of your personnel staff.

Conduct a Detailed Human Resources Analysis

Concentrate on the organization's COPS (culture, organization, people, HR systems)

- Consider: Where you are now? Where do you want to be?
- What gaps exists between the reality of where you are now and where you want to be?

Exhaust your analysis of the four dimensions.

Determine Critical People Issues

Go back to the business strategy and examine it against your SWOT and COPS Analysis

- Identify the critical people issues namely those people issues that you must address. Those which have a key impact on the delivery of your business strategy.
- Prioritize the critical people issues. What will happen if you fail to address them?

Remember you are trying to identify where you should be focusing your efforts and resources.

Develop Consequences and Solutions

For each critical issue highlight the options for managerial action generate, elaborate and create - don't go for the obvious. This is an important step as frequently people jump for the known rather than challenge existing assumptions about the way things have been done in the past. Think about the consequences of taking various courses of action.

Consider the mix of HR systems needed to address the issues. Do you need to improve communications, training or pay?

What are the implications for the business and the personnel function?

Once you have worked through the process it should then be possible to translate the action plan into broad objectives. These will need to be broken down into the specialist HR Systems areas of:

- Employee training and development
- Management development
- Organization development
- Performance appraisal
- Employee reward
- Employee selection and recruitment
- Manpower planning
- Communication

Develop your action plan around the critical issues. Set targets and dates for the accomplishment of the key objectives.

Implementation and Evaluation of the Action Plans

The ultimate purpose of developing a human resource strategy is to ensure that the objectives set are mutually supportive so that the reward and payment systems are integrated with employee training and career development plans.

There is very little value or benefit in training people only to then frustrate them through a failure to provide ample career and development opportunities.

DEVELOPING AND DESIGNING A TRAINING PROGRAMME

Attracting the most qualified employees and matching them to the jobs for which they are best suited is significant for the success of any organization. However, many enterprises are too large to permit close contact between top management and employees.

Human resources, training, and labour relations managers and specialists provide this connection. In the past, these workers have been associated with performing the administrative function of an organization, such as handling employee benefits questions or recruiting, interviewing, and hiring new staff in accordance with policies and requirements that have been established in conjunction with top management.

Today's human resources workers manage these tasks and, increasingly, consult top executives regarding strategic planning. They have moved from behind-the-scenes staff work to leading the company in suggesting and changing policies. Senior management is recognizing the significance of the human resources department to their financial success. In an effort to enhance morale and productivity, limit job turnover, and help organizations increase performance and improve business results, they also help their firms effectively use employee skills, provide training and development opportunities to improve those skills, and increase employees' satisfaction with their jobs and working conditions. Although some jobs in the human resources field require only limited contact with people outside the office, dealing with people is an important part of the job.

In a small organization, a human resources generalist may handle all aspects of human resources work, and thus require an extensive range of knowledge. The responsibilities of human resources generalists can vary widely, depending on their employer's needs. In a large corporation, the top human resources executive usually develops and manages human resources programmes and policies. (Executives are included in the Handbook statement on top executives.) These policies usually are implemented by a director or manager of human resources and, in some cases, a director of industrial relations.

The director of human resources may supervise several departments, each headed by an experienced manager who most likely specializes in one human resources activity, such as employment, compensation, benefits, training and development, or employee relations.

Employment and placement managers supervise the hiring and separation of employees and supervise various workers, including equal employment opportunity specialists and recruitment specialists. Employment, recruitment, and placement specialists recruit and place workers.

Recruiters maintain contacts within the community and may travel considerably, often to college campuses, to search for promising job applicants. Recruiters screen, interview, and occasionally test applicants. They also may check references and extend job offers. These workers must be thoroughly familiar with the organization and its human resources policies in order to discuss wages, working conditions, and promotional opportunities with prospective employees. They also must keep informed about equal employment opportunity (EEO) and affirmative action guidelines and laws, such as the Americans with Disabilities Act.

EEO officers, representatives, or affirmative action coordinators handle EEO matters in large organizations. They investigate and resolve EEO grievances, examine corporate practices for possible violations, and compile and submit EEO statistical reports.

Employer relations representatives, who usually work in government agencies, maintain working relationships with local employers and promote the use of public employment programmes and services. Similarly, employment interviewers—whose many job titles include human resources consultants, human resources development specialists, and human resources coordinators—help to match employers with qualified jobseekers.

Compensation, benefits, and job analysis specialists conduct programmes for employers and may specialize in specific areas such as position classifications or pensions. Job analysts, occasionally called position classifiers, collect and examine detailed information about job duties in order to prepare job descriptions. These descriptions explain the duties, training, and skills that each job requires. Whenever a large organization introduces a new job or reviews existing jobs, it calls upon the expert knowledge of the job analyst.

Occupational analysts conduct research, usually in large firms. They are concerned with occupational classification systems and study the effects of industry and occupational trends upon worker relationships. They may serve as technical liaison between the firm and other firms, government, and labour unions.

Establishing and maintaining a firm's pay system is the principal job of the compensation manager. Assisted by staff specialists, compensation managers devise ways to ensure fair and equitable pay rates. They may conduct surveys to see how their firm's rates compare with others and to see that the firm's pay scale complies with changing laws and regulations. In addition, compensation managers often manage their firm's performance evaluation system, and they may design reward systems such as pay-for-performance plans.

Employee benefits managers and specialists manage the company's employee benefits programme, notably its health insurance and pension plans. Expertise in designing and administering benefits programmes continues to take on importance as employer-provided benefits account for a growing proportion of overall compensation costs, and as benefit plans increase in number and complexity.

For example, pension benefits might include savings and thrift, profit-sharing, and stock ownership plans; health benefits might include long-term catastrophic illness insurance and dental insurance. Familiarity with health benefits is a top priority for employee benefits managers and specialists, as more firms struggle to cope with the rising cost of health care for employees and retirees.

In addition to health insurance and pension coverage, some firms offer employees life and accidental death and dismemberment insurance, disability insurance, and relatively new benefits designed to meet the needs of a changing workforce, such as parental leave, child and elder care, long-term nursing home care insurance, employee assistance and wellness programmes, and flexible benefits plans. Benefits managers must keep abreast of changing Federal and State regulations and legislation that may affect employee benefits.

Employee assistance plan managers, also called employee welfare managers, are responsible for a wide array of programmes covering occupational safety and health standards and practices; health promotion and physical fitness, medical examinations, and minor health treatment, such as first aid; plant security; publications; food service and recreation activities; carpooling and transportation programmes, such as transit subsidies; employee suggestion systems; child care and elder care; and counseling services. Child care and elder care are increasingly significant because of growth in the number of dual-income households and the elderly population.

Counseling may help employees deal with emotional disorders, alcoholism, or marital, family, consumer, legal, and financial problems. Some employers offer career counseling as well. In large firms, certain programmes, such as those dealing with security and safety, may be in separate departments headed by other managers.

Training and development managers and specialists conduct and supervise training and development programmes for employees. Increasingly, management recognizes that training offers a way of developing skills, enhancing productivity and quality of work, and building worker loyalty to the firm, and most importantly, increasing individual and organizational performance to achieve business results. While training is widely accepted as an employee benefit and a method of improving employee morale, enhancing employee skills has become a business imperative. Increasingly, managers and leaders realize that the key to business growth and success is through developing the skills and knowledge of its workforce.

Other factors involved in determining whether training is needed include the complexity of the work environment, the rapid pace of organizational and technological change, and the growing number of jobs in fields that constantly generate new knowledge, and thus, require new skills. In addition, advances in learning theory have provided insights into how adults learn, and how training can be organized most effectively for them.

Training managers provide worker training either in the classroom or onsite. This includes setting up teaching materials prior to the class, involving the class, and issuing completion certificates at the end of the class. They have the responsibility for the entire learning process, and its environment, to ensure that the course meets its objectives and is measured and evaluated to understand how learning impacts business results.

Training specialists plan, organize, and direct a wide range of training activities. Trainers respond to corporate and worker service requests. They consult with onsite supervisors regarding available performance improvement services and conduct orientation sessions and arrange on-the-job training for new employees. They help all employees maintain and improve their job skills, and possibly prepare for jobs requiring greater skill. They help supervisors improve their interpersonal skills in order to deal effectively with employees. They may set up individualized training plans to strengthen an employee's existing skills or teach new ones.

Training specialists in some companies set up leadership or executive development programmes among employees in lower level positions. These programmes are designed to develop leaders to replace those leaving the organization and as part of a succession plan. Trainers also lead programmes to assist employees with job transitions as a result of mergers and acquisitions, as well as technological changes. In government-supported training programmes, training specialists function as case managers. They first assess the training needs of clients and then guide them through the most appropriate training method. After training, clients may either be referred to employer relations representatives or receive job placement assistance.

Planning and programme development is an essential part of the training specialist's job. In order to identify and assess training needs within the firm, trainers may confer with managers and supervisors or conduct surveys. They also evaluate training effectiveness to ensure that the training employees receive, helps the organization meet its strategic business goals and achieve results.

Depending on the size, goals, and nature of the organization, trainers may differ considerably in their responsibilities and in the methods they use. Training methods include on-the-job training; operating schools that duplicate shop conditions for trainees prior to putting them on the shop floor; apprenticeship training; classroom training; and electronic learning, which may involve interactive Internet-based training, multimedia programmes, distance learning, satellite training, other computer-aided instructional technologies, videos, simulators, conferences, and workshops.

An organization's director of industrial relations forms labour policy, oversees industrial labour relations, negotiates collective bargaining agreements, and coordinates grievance procedures to handle complaints resulting from management disputes with unionized employees. The director of industrial relations also advises and collaborates with the director of human resources, other managers, and members of their staff, because all aspects of human resources policy—such as wages, benefits, pensions, and work practices—may be involved in drawing up a new or revised union contract.

Labour relations managers and their staffs implement industrial labour relations programmes. Labour relations specialists prepare information for management to use during collective bargaining agreement negotiations, a process that requires the specialist to be familiar with economic and wage data and to have extensive knowledge of labour law and collective bargaining trends. The labour relations staff interprets and administers the contract with respect to grievances, wages and salaries, employee welfare, health care, pensions, union and management practices, and other contractual stipulations. As union membership continues to decline in most industries, industrial relations personnel are working more often with employees who are not members of a labour union.

Dispute resolution—attaining tacit or contractual agreements—has become increasingly significant as parties to a dispute attempt to avoid costly litigation, strikes, or other disruptions. Dispute resolution also has become more complex, involving employees, management, unions, other firms, and government agencies. Specialists involved in dispute resolution must be highly knowledgeable and experienced, and often report to the director of industrial relations. Conciliators, or mediators, advise and counsel labour and management to prevent and, when necessary, resolve disputes over labour agreements or other labour relations issues. Arbitrators, occasionally called umpires or referees, decide disputes that bind both labour and management to specific terms and conditions of labour contracts. Labour relations specialists who work for unions perform many of the same functions on behalf of the union and its members.

Other emerging specialties include international human resources managers, who handle human resources issues related to a company's foreign operations; and human resources information system specialists, who develop and apply computer programmes to process human resources information, match job seekers with job openings, and handle other human resources matters.

CREATING TRAINING SESSIONS

Human resources play a critical role in developing and implementing organizational strategies and structures. Successful HR professionals will be those who can align their organizational HR practices with the unique demands of team-based organizational structures.

First, we provide HR professionals with a brief history of the use of teams in the United States, reviewing definitions and types of teams, evidence regarding the impact of teams, and the factors that led to their proliferation. Second, we aim to provide the HR professional with tools to increase the effectiveness of teams, discussing the key assumptions underlying supportive conditions for teams.

Third, we review modifications in HR practices that are necessary to implement teams effectively. Finally, we discuss potential challenges that HR practitioners may face in implementing teams in multinational organizations; looking to the future, we present guidelines for meeting these challenges. We conclude with some predictions about the use of teams that will likely develop as our team-based organizations continue to evolve.

What Teams Are

In general, a work team can be defined as a group of individuals working interdependently to solve problems or accomplish tasks. However, a single definition is not sufficient to capture the key differences that exist between the various types of teams being used in organizations. A number of key differences between these types of teams will determine the efficacy of HR practices designed to enhance their effectiveness. For example, compensation structures are normally altered for self-managing work teams to include team-based rewards to encourage cooperation between members and motivate them to reach team goals.

Because self-managing members are working on permanent teams, the effort and expense involved in changing compensation structures is often justified. However, in more temporary teams, such as cross-functional or problem solving teams, other types of HR policy changes (for example, altering an evaluation system to include team behaviours) may be more appropriate to encourage positive behaviours.

Our point here is not to review all of the appropriate HR policies for each type of team but rather to acknowledge that our use of the term work team includes several different types of teams.

Contrary to popular belief, teams are not a new phenomenon. The origins of teams can be traced to the Tavistock studies of post–World War II and the Swedish socio technical movement generally associated with the Volvo Corporation. The first work teams in the United States were found in the Procter and Gamble Company in the early 1960s, the Topeka work system at a General Foods pet food plant in the late 1960s, and the Rushton Quality of Work Project in Pennsylvania in the mid–1970s. Given that teams were identified as a mechanism for improving employee performance as early as the 1960s, why has it taken over thirty years to implement work teams on a large scale in the United States?

We attribute the recent rise in the interest in and use of teams over the last ten years to three factors: a higher concern for the social component of work; the globalization of the U.S. economy and resulting downsizing; and the early adoption of work teams by highly visible companies such as General Motors, AT&T, General Electric, Xerox, and Motorola. Although many believe that organizations have adopted work teams to improve employee morale or productivity, the forces behind their adoption have been much larger in scale and much more connected to global patterns of international business. Organizations have adopted work teams because many had no choice.

Dramatically reduced numbers of managers could not keep up with employee activities on a day-today basis.

Furthermore, the increased use of teams can be attributed, in part, to evidence of their success. Work teams have been associated with higher levels of productivity. It should be noted, however, that most of these studies have been conducted with self-managing work teams that have considerable control over their own structure and process. For traditional work teams, much of the evidence of impact has been collected on a case-by-case basis. Wellins, Byham, and Dixon (1994), for example, chronicle the pervasive positive impact teams have had in twenty companies. These companies claim that implementing teams resulted in improvements in bottom-line indicators such as cost savings, quality and service improvement, speed, absenteeism, and turnover.

This is not to say that teams are a panacea. Several studies on the impact of teams have failed to find effects for performance on more quantitative measures, such as productivity; others report only modest findings for productivity. Smaller effect sizes for productivity may be the result of using work teams in contexts where they are not appropriate. Clearly, work teams are not ideal for every task (even if you have a hammer, not every problem is a nail). Work teams are more effective under the right circumstances and situations.

For example, work teams are most effective when there is high task interdependence or a high degree of coordination and collaboration required between team members to accomplish tasks. Thus, a group of insurance sales agents who are geographically dispersed and have little interaction with one another to carry out their tasks would most likely be an inappropriate context in which to implement teams. The agents would probably see such an effort as an empty, poorly developed strategy designed to capitalize on a management fad.

Work teams are also more appropriate when the tasks that their members carry out are complex and well designed. If a group's work is routine and unchallenging, of dubious importance, and wholly preprogrammed with no opportunity for feedback, teams will probably not make much difference in productivity. As Johns (1996) has stated, "Taking a bunch of olive stuffers on a food processing assembly line, putting them in distinctive jumpsuits, calling them the Olive Squad, and telling them to self-manage will be unlikely to yield dividends in terms of effort expended or brainpower employed". Work teams, especially those that increase autonomy and responsibility, are most effective when members are given complex tasks that capitalize on their diverse knowledge and skills. Thus, teams should view their tasks as significant, the tasks should require the use of a variety of skills, and members should, where possible, assemble an entire product or deliver a complete service.

The effectiveness of work teams also depends on whether an organization has high integration needs as a result of operating in a complex environment. Complex environments usually force organizations to serve a wide variety of customers, deal with rapidly changing technology, and satisfy large numbers of different stakeholders. IBM, for example, faces a much more complex environment than McDonald's (compare the rate of change in PCs with that of Big Macs over the last fifteen years). Organizations must simultaneously deal with all of these issues—in other words, differentiate into smaller, more responsive units—and then integrate these widely dispersed efforts and units back into one cohesive organization. Teams will be most effective when a team structure is the best solution to obtaining the integration required to accomplish goals in a complex organizational environment. Without effective integration, the benefits attributed to work teams (increased productivity, higher quality, better job satisfaction) will not be realized.

Thus, companies implementing teams from a "bandwagon" perspective will not realize the benefits to be had from an appropriate fit between teams and context. In fact, many organizations are currently struggling with team effectiveness. We argue that this is the result, in part, of traditional assumptions about work that still prevail. In order to implement teams effectively, assumptions must change. We next discuss these adaptations.

Adapt Our Assumptions

We discuss the assumptions that shaped the decisions made by HR professionals in traditional hierarchical organizations in three areas: motivation; structure of work; and accountability. Traditional assumptions must be adapted in order to support effective implementation of teams.

Motivation

The first set of assumptions that must be examined pertain to motivation. National culture helps determine what motivates people. For example, some cultures can be classified as individualistic, where people tend to value their own self-interest and welfare over the interests of groups or societies; other cultures are known as collectivistic, where people tend to value the welfare of groups more than their own. Individualists are motivated by the opportunity to gain personal recognition.

They resist working in teams more than people from collectivistic cultures. Such resistance lowers team effectiveness on outcomes such as productivity, job satisfaction, cooperativeness, and organizational commitment. It takes time and experience for people to adjust their notions of fairness and equity to include collective accountability. Taking a longer-term focus and understanding the eventual payoffs for early investments in team-based systems is essential for harnessing the motivational power of teams. In understanding motivational assumptions, it is also important to consider expectations. Research attests to the importance of collective expectations in determining our level of motivation and subsequently our performance. When we believe we can accomplish objectives as a team, we are motivated to stick with our work tasks and prevail. But sometimes these high expectations get out of hand, to the point that teams hold unrealistic expectations. Cohesive teams often fall prey to this phenomenon, which is referred to as groupthink. Coinciding with extremely high expectations, teams suffering from groupthink also hold illusions of invulnerability.

They ignore important external information sources that might help them adjust their performance to fit the needs of customers better. Teams in individualistic cultures appear to be particularly susceptible to overconfidence. This may be because individualists view their team as an entity in and of itself rather than one that is connected to the external context and are therefore even less apt to use external sources of information to make corrections in their behaviour and improve their performance.

Particularly in individualistic cultures, team-based organizations need to have systems that help teams set realistic expectations. This allows them to stay motivated while at the same time remaining open to learning from feedback and mistakes.

Work Structure

A second domain of assumptions concerns the structure of work. Traditional work groups were generally formed around common technical or functional skills and areas of expertise (for example, accounting, finance, or production). In recent years, it has become apparent that organizing work around a process (for example, new product development) rather than around a specific task or function is more effective. Doing so often requires extending team members' task skills. Multi skilled teamwork involves teams made up of individuals with multiple and overlapping skills that are deployed around the performance of a whole task, which represents a significant part of a larger work flow. Members are multi skilled so that work can be flexibly allocated among them.

In organizing work around processes, organizational boundaries must often be renegotiated. Increasingly, work teams include external customers and suppliers. For example, General Electric Medical Systems invites representatives from leading health maintenance organizations (HMOs) to serve on its sales and service teams. The American Red Cross has members of communities serving on key committees that set organizational objectives. Eastman Kodak allies itself with key competitors to form market segment task forces. These types of work structures require a whole new notion of collaboration—collaboration with external constituencies. Those who were previously viewed as "them" are now viewed as "us."

The reorganization of work around processes and across boundaries has numerous benefits. For example, multi skilling (the learning of new skills in addition to functional expertise) can result in reduced staffing as fewer workers can perform the same range of tasks. It can create efficiencies through more flexible task assignment.

Multi skilling also often leads to lower inventories because there is more effective work flow coordination. It also makes the team more flexible in meeting fluctuating market demand through operational flexibility. Finally, it can lead to a more differentiated response to the needs of particular customer segments and so contribute to strategic flexibility. Multi skilling leads to greater awareness of the whole task and enables the team member to take part in problem solving, innovation, and strategic thinking. These same benefits do not accrue when tasks and organizations are structured under traditional assumptions of static, independent jobs.

Accountability

A third domain of assumptions that shape team effectiveness pertain to accountability. The focus of most HR departments has been on the individual. Individual accountability and responsibility have been the foundation on which all of the business practices in the United States have been built. Furthermore, accountability in traditional work organizations was vested in those with formal positions—the managers and supervisors. Individual employees showed deference to people in these positions. Reporting structures were vertical and a command-and-control philosophy reigned. Skills such as planning, coordination, personnel functions, quality management, health and safety, and boundary management were the domain of managers. But increasingly, these duties are becoming the domain of teams.

Managerial responsibility is shifting from individual accountability to collective, mutual accountability. As this has occurred, the notion of self-management has gained acceptance. Self-management grows as the team's operational tasks are delegated to the team itself. Many different terms have evolved to describe and distinguish varying degrees of autonomy, including self-directed work teams, empowered teams, and superior work teams. The common distinguishing characteristic of such teams is that they operate with some degree of autonomy.

As non-managers become collectively responsible for managerial duties, basic assumptions about the legitimacy of authority are challenged. Team members may begin to question what gives peers the right to set rules for others. They may have difficulty dealing with authority that does not stem from position. Rather than depending on a job description and direction from the manager, people work jointly with coworkers to determine what they do. Because personal success depends on collective success, an individual's fate is tied to coworkers. Feelings of mutual trust and partnership must develop. The organization must help people learn to deal with greater ambiguity, uncertainty, continual change, and collaborative relationships. Both managers and employees in the team-based organization need to adjust to this shift in accountability and responsibility. We discuss the HR systems that increase team effectiveness in the next section.

Modify HR Practices to Support Teams

In addition to recognizing and adapting the assumptions on which they base their practices, HR professionals must also modify those practices to support teams. The practices to be modified cluster in five areas: recruitment and selection; task design; training; evaluation; and compensation. In the following sections, we summarize the modifications and provide references for practitioners interested in exploring them in greater depth.

Recruitment and Selection

Working effectively in a team requires a particular set of knowledge, skills, and abilities (KSAs) that were not as critical in traditional organizations. Proficiency is needed in at least five areas: conflict resolution, collaborative problem solving, communication, goal setting and performance management, and planning and task coordination. During recruitment, organizations aspiring to create a workforce of effective team members should clearly communicate the importance of these proficiencies. Doing so provides a realistic job preview and can therefore help to reduce turnover. Recruiting individuals who prefer these activities also makes sense because team members' preferences for teamwork are related to team effectiveness.

It is also important to consider teamwork KSAs in the selection process. It might seem easy to include measures of KSAs in most selection systems, but most selection instruments focus on basic learning abilities (for example, math, language, perceptual skills) or specific technical abilities (for example, mechanical, electrical, and so on). In the last few years, employment tests designed to measure teamwork KSAs have been under development.

Early results suggest that the tests can predict subsequent performance beyond the level of prediction from a large battery of traditional employment aptitude tests. These initial findings offer encouraging support for such instruments. Interviews might also be a viable method of assessing social and interpersonal attributes that contribute to teamwork. There is evidence that a structured interview designed to measure social KSAs can predict future team effectiveness. Finally, selection techniques that involve collecting biographical information may be another way to assess teamwork KSAs.

Task Design

The second set of practices that must be modified relate to task design. Effective teams are designed around the tasks they perform. Two key considerations are that teams should be relatively self contained and handle many aspects of their own functioning.

First, teams should be collectively responsible for an identifiable and substantial part of the work of the organization. To the extent possible, support services should be included in the team so that it has the resources necessary to accomplish its goals. Members should be multi skilled and dedicated to the team so that they do not have to split priorities. Finally, the team should report as a unit so that members do not have conflicting directions from different managers.

Second, the team should be responsible for many aspects of its own functioning. For example, it should be able to determine how to apply the team's resources, strategies for completion of work, and quality monitoring. It should also be responsible for working with internal and external customers. Finally, part of the team's task should be performance evaluation. Whenever appropriate skill levels and task conditions exist, team members should be involved in reviewing their own performance and determining their own rewards.

Beyond these two fundamental design principles, a third issue is whether teams should be functional or cross-functional. Functional organizations group people by common specialties and break work down into functional packets that translate into individual assignment. Project organizations combine different specialties required to perform the entire project but then break the work down for members of functional groups within the project. Team-based organizations require a shift away from a hierarchical breakdown to focus instead on the lateral distribution and integration of work.

Whether teams should be functional or cross-functional is a choice to be based on an analysis of the work to be accomplished. Process analysis can be used to determine the sets of activities that have to be carried out and integrated to deliver value to customers.

If within an identifiable set of activities coordination must occur across different functional areas, then teams should be cross-functional. In the cross-functional teams members can integrate work across disciplines and make trade-offs that require a multidisciplinary perspective. But if the process analysis indicates that an identifiable set of activities occurs within a functional area, then teams should be functional.

EVALUATING THE TRAINING PROGRAMME

Long-term employment security is no longer promised or implied, and this has changed the degree of mutual commitment that employees and organizations feel towards one another. The consequences are paradoxical for many companies. On the one hand, they want to be freer to shed employees who are not needed; on the other hand, they want to encourage needed employees to stay as long as possible. But employees who know they have no long term security are often busy looking for better opportunities. Instead of a long-term relationship or even a "marriage, " both employees and companies can wind up in a "dating game" as they look for short-term selfish advantage.

As an HRM strategy in tight labour markets or when employees with rare skills are involved, some firms have committed themselves for specific contracted periods or offered stock options and incentive-based schemes to hang on to desired individuals. Nevertheless, at least one organizational survey consortium reports that employee attitudes on job security have become much less favourable in all companies over the last decade, even as other attitudes have remained relatively constant Corporation, private communication with the authors, January 1998).

As several commentators have noted and as the chapters by Noer and others in this volume note, the psychological contract has changed. One noticeable effect of this change is in college recruiting, where companies no longer promise long-term careers and actually use "signing bonuses" to get the most talented graduates to join them. In other words, short-term payoffs are being used to make up for long-term inducements.

Non-work Obligations

Most companies now see family responsibilities as a more acceptable counterpoint to work obligations. Many employees desire flexible work schedules and supervisor support for emergencies and use these criteria to select employers when there is a choice. Some books have become best-sellers because they rate and describe "the best places to work". Underlying realities that have helped give voice to such concerns include changes in marriage patterns.

Divorce rates have gone up substantially during recent decades, leaving many women dependent on their own efforts for economic well-being and creating many more single parents than in the past. For single parents, work is an economic necessity but it also competes with family for time and energy. In a related phenomenon, age at first marriage has increased by almost a year per decade for the last half century, so that it is now about twenty-four for women and twenty-six for men.

With this shift, many couples now live together without benefit of the clergy's blessing. Their concerns include many mutual career decisions, which may affect accepting a job or relocating. In recent years, this concern has sometimes emerged as a desire for company benefits to be extended to domestic partners. This has been especially noted when homosexual partners, who do not have the option of legal marriage, want such coverage. The open expression of such living arrangements and sexual orientations by workers represents another major shift in attitudes and values.

Assumptions

This review of the environmental forces affecting industry and HRM indicates that many of the assumptions made in the past about people in the work setting are no longer valid. If the assumptions are no longer valid, then the concepts and practices based on them may also be invalid. As we indicated in our opening discussion, many of these assumptions arose in the 1950s, and it is these beliefs that need to be reexamined and reevaluated.

Current Assumptions

The changes in the environment we have noted, which most companies operate in today, have required a new set of assumptions that are more appropriate for the times and that generate new HRM concepts and practices. These new assumptions may be subdivided according to their application to organizations and to individuals.

Organizations today contrast in several respects with those of the past. The shifts are evident in corporate forms and dynamics:

- More than ever, organizations are likely to be fluid, continually changing, and have many new relationships, from joint ventures, alliances, and partnerships to use of vendors and subcontractors.
- Embattled organizations are continually under pressure to increase outputs, improve cycle time, enhance competitiveness.
- A focus on short-term achievements is an imperative. Corporate acquisitions may often be seen as a better bet than undertaking long-term product development.
- Important skills and talent are to be hired as needed rather than developed internally over a long period. Conversely, unneeded employees should be quickly converted or disposed of.

HRM concepts and practices arise from a complex set of forces that form the operating environment for the organizations HRM serves. When the environment is stable, many of the changes are determined by the organization itself, often in a desire to give itself a competitive advantage in attracting, retaining, and motivating employees. Sometimes the concepts and practices arise out of the company founder's personal philosophy and preferences. But the environment has not been very stable during the last two decades.

Many of the operating assumptions on which HRM operates have been severely but gradually challenged in the last two decades in a series of inexorable changes. As a story popular in some management circles puts it, a frog dropped into a pot of boiling water will instantly jump out. But if the frog is placed in a pot of cool water that is gradually brought to a boil, the frog will simply grow warmer and doze off until it is too late. It is the suddenness of change that makes it vivid for people as well.

Many of the shifts noted have taken place gradually and in different spheres, and they may not have been given sufficient notice at the time of their occurrence. But when we look back over the last twenty-five years, it is obvious that many principles that were simply taken for granted are no longer true. This is as dangerous for us as the slowly warming pot is for the frog. To be effective, it is necessary for HRM concepts and practices to be lined up with assumptions that are based on the reality of our environments.

For organizations to assess their environments accurately it is useful periodically to go through a disciplined scan of their current and expected environments. In fact, many large firms and some consortia conduct environmental scans on a regular basis. This certainly seems like a healthy practice. We believe that a useful framework for doing environmental scans is one that looks at the DELTA forces around us, that is, the demographics, economics, legal and regulatory issues, technology, and attitudes and values. These are the forces that have greatly affected us in the past and seem the right places to look to for future change.

Employers and Employees

Most knowledgeable observers in the field of human resource management (HRM) would agree that its major development as a profession came during the half century or so between the end of World War II and the early 1990s. As organizations employing as many as hundreds of thousands became dominant influences in the world of work and as questions about selection, training, work motivation, and compensation practices became more challenging in a growing, dynamic society, the need for professionally trained, skilled personnel became great. Also, despite occasional downturns in the economy, the professional growth of HRM took place against a general culture of prosperity, a belief that such good patterns would continue and even improve, and an assumption that work organizations should and would share in such growth.

Important too as HRM developed during this era was that the policies and practices developed and implemented were based in large part on the assumption that a desire for personal growth was the most important motivational characteristic of the workforce, along with the belief that more of everything (particularly economic outcomes) is better. Korman (forthcoming) has referred to this pattern as self-enhancing motivation and has cited as illustrative of this type of motivation such actions as making choices that match and fulfill one's personal needs, engaging in activities that foster self-growth, attempting to attain high levels of work performance, and working for goals that legitimately enhance oneself in one's own eyes and those of others. Given the cultural context and the assumption of the dominance of this type of motivational pattern, it was a relatively short step for HRM professionals during this era to develop a perspective that reflected them.

Characteristic programmes of this type included job enrichment, career management and career development, self-appraisals and peer performance appraisals, and income incentives of various kinds. Less significant as an influence on HRM during this era but still of some importance were programmes based on what Korman (forthcoming) has called self-protective motivation, defined as the desire to defend oneself from perceived threatening environmental and personal forces that might affect one's sense of identity. Korman suggests that it is this motivational force that underlies the need for personal and job security.

Despite its importance, however, this need was generally viewed as less important than employee needs for growth, development, and achievement during the years of prosperity.

There were several reasons for this difference in emphasis. One factor, certainly, was the prosperity and the continued expectations of same. It was not a climate that generated a sense of anxiety, whether warranted or not. Second, the strength and membership of labour unions—organizations that have traditionally made job security a keystone of their efforts—were declining. With the assumption of continued prosperity and the weakness of labour unions, human resource (HR) managers and their allied professionals, such as industrial-organizational psychologists, worried less about providing job security than about providing the opportunity for growth, development, and achievement.

Third, theorists on motivation in work organizations generally had a low level of interest in such concepts as anxiety, even though important research findings were beginning to be reported on the significance of such related variables as fear of failure in performance settings. Instead, theories were popular if they saw people as growth-oriented, desiring meaningful work achievement, and interested in attaining both intrinsic and extrinsic goals.

Nevertheless, despite these influences, there was some concern even during these years about providing a greater sense of security for employees. Prominent among those expressing such interest was Frederick Herzberg, an important management writer who saw in the reduction of anxiety that came with job security a significant approach to reducing job dissatisfaction. In addition, although their membership continued to decrease, labour unions and their emphasis on job security did not totally disappear from the work scene. Unions remained strong in some areas, particularly the federal, state, and local civil services, and their presence did much to ensure that job security remained on the table as an employee concern, at least in some instances.

There were, then, these two patterns of HR practice. One, the more influential, assumed that the more important motivational patterns were desires for growth, development, achievement, and self-enhancement. The second, less significant as an influence, assumed desires for job security and self-protection. Both were recognized, and both influenced HRM practices. Less recognized was that the disparity in influence of these patterns of practice encouraged another important underlying assumption. This assumption was that HRM policies and practices could be developed in a manner that would enable the attainment of two goals.

The first of these goals was to help organizations obtain their objectives. The second was that HRM could help employees meet their most important needs because the employees' desire to attain positive outcomes (both intrinsic and extrinsic), that is, self-enhancement, and their willingness to work for them were congruent with organizational needs for effective performance. Furthermore, this congruence could be maintained and encouraged because of the continuing expected affluence. In contrast, rarely if ever discussed was that these practices and policies and the assumed congruence between employer and employee depended on these assumptions of continued prosperity and that other approaches would become necessary if the situation changed.

The New World of Work

Now that time has come. A new and different world of work has begun to emerge, one that exists alongside the traditional work setting and that may eventually come to supplant it. It is a world characterized by at least three major trends that have implications for HRM.

- First, downsizing is now a frequent key component of managerial decision making, with all the potential short- and long-term anxiety-inducing effects on employee motivation that we would expect.
- Second, the work-family conflict is an endemic part of the lives of both employers and employees.
- Third, we live in a world marked by the extensive use of temporary workers, part-time employees, and outsourcing.

Workforce Reduction

Downsizing has become so much a part of the world of work during the past decade that it is a term familiar to almost all who work or who wish to. Table lists some of the more dramatic illustrations of downsizing that have occurred in American corporations during the past five years.

Downsizing is a phenomenon that continues to this day. Downsizing is a fact of the world of work that influences the lives, attitudes, and emotions of millions. That other jobs are continually being created—and they are—may not significantly affect those concerned about their long- and short-term job prospects.

Work-Family Conflict

Also part of this new world of work is conflict with the family, an inevitable fact of life as our society is increasingly characterized by women in the workforce, dual-career couples, and single-parent families. The increasing presence of women in the workforce contributes to this conflict, a conflict that is among the most serious facing American families and work organizations as we approach the new millennium. It is a problem, both actual and potential, that is becoming increasingly widespread. It is also one of the characteristics of the new world of work that has had and continues to have a major impact on the motivational and attitudinal characteristics of people in the workforce, both men and women.

Non-core Workers

We now also have a work setting marked increasingly by outsourcing agreements between companies, relocation of companies from high- to low-wage areas, globalization, a desire for individuals to develop multiskill capability rather than job specialization, and explosive growth in the use of temporary and contingent employees.

Feelings of ambiguity and conflict have resulted from these changes. On the one hand, there are now new ways for individuals to seek self-enhancement in the world of work, paths that have important implications for the practices and policies HRM may adopt. But on the other hand, the resulting anxiety from these changes has led to a high level of self-protective motivation. The outcome has been a world of work where the two different motivations are assuming equal significance. In other words, it is a world in which the desire and need for security has become as relevant as the need for achievement, growth, and development. It is therefore a world in which both motivational patterns will need to be addressed by HRM, but in different ways than they have been previously.

The New Assumptions

HRM needs new and different assumptions on which to base policy and practice. One necessary change, I believe, is to assume no longer that there is a congruence of interests between employees and employers. Sometimes there may be, but sometimes there may not be. Second, we need to assume that the key interpersonal and intergroup relationships in a particular work setting are as likely to be among individuals from different organizations with different investments as they are to be among individuals within the same organization. The following paragraphs elaborate on these recommendations in greater detail.

Because self-enhancement was assumed to be the dominant work motivation during the years of the growth of the field, it is not surprising that HR professionals operated on the belief that it was both possible and desirable to design and implement policies and practices that could and would integrate the goals of both employees and organizations. In fact, one of the major books of this era, and one which served as a sort of conceptual guideline for many, was titled Integrating the Individual with the Organization. In a similar vein and serving as further illustration of this assumption of congruence between employer and employee was the growth of job enrichment as a management tool, fueled by the belief that individuals would respond to the challenge of enriched jobs.

According to this perspective, the enriched job provided a mechanism for self-enhancement and, in satisfying such desires, the individual would be more highly performance motivated and contribute more to the attainment of organizational goals.

Now, however, we need to change this assumption. More specifically, we need to view the individual and the organization as separate entities who will be able to integrate their efforts and cooperate with one another under certain conditions but not under others. Furthermore, determining what those conditions might be will be an important objective for HRM professionals in the coming years.

A second assumption about people and organizations during the years of growth and prosperity was that the interpersonal and inter group relationships HRM needed most to be concerned with were those that took place within the organization, that is, intra organizational relationships. In other words, the focus was on the relationships between people in different jobs, in different functions, and at different hierarchical levels, but all within the same organization. Although it was recognized that individuals often met with salespeople, suppliers, and others, such meetings with "outsiders" were generally limited to specifically designated occupational groups. Now, however, more attention will have to be paid to relationships between those with primary allegiance to a particular organization and those who may work in that organization but not have primary allegiance to it.

Today, individuals work full-time in an organization to which they have primary loyalty while next to them or with them are individuals on temporary assignments, part-time workers, and people working in joint venture settings and in outsourcing situations. The result may therefore be individuals working together whose allegiances and concerns may involve differences that are highly important to us. Relationships, views, and expectations among those who are all part of one group—or who view themselves as part of the same company or as "insiders"—are different from the types of relationships and communication patterns that develop among those who view themselves as belonging to different groups. For example, Korman (1988) has proposed that in situations in which we find insiders and outsiders, the former are more likely to discriminate and act in a prejudicial manner towards the latter.

The result may be unnecessary conflict and sometimes even "tribalistic" patterns, where each group cares only about itself and not about the other or joint goals. Although cases of severe conflict may be extreme—because there are usually some reasons for these different groups and individuals to at least try to work together— the potential for conflict between groups and individuals exists in this new work setting and there will be a need to take account of such possibilities in developing future HRM programmes. These new assumptions, which I believe to be more appropriate for the emerging work setting, suggest the need for new HRM approaches, techniques, policies, and practices that will allow satisfaction of both the self-enhancing and the self-protective motivational processes.

Some Programme Suggestions

Programmes consistent with the new assumptions need to be developed for HRM as it confronts this new world of work. The remainder outlines four such programmes, with each discussed in greater detail in the following sections.

- Effective self-career management programmes based on the desire for self-enhancement.
- Labour pool associations designed to meet needs for both self enhancement and self-protection.
- Performance incentive programmes that are not based on organizational commitment, including financial rewards providing direct income as well as health, welfare, and pension benefits.
- Insider-outsider training programmes.

Self-Career Management

Self-career management programmes are designed primarily for those individuals who view themselves as relatively independent professionals or "businesses, " rather than as organizationally dependent job holders. These are individuals who can and do make their own decisions about their careers, know their capabilities, and understand where they can find the types of work opportunities where they can "sell" themselves as a business or service. Self-career management is a different way of looking at oneself and one's work capabilities.

It is a mechanism for declaring oneself independent of an organizational control system but at the same time being willing to negotiate mutual terms of acceptability concerning work contributions to that system. Self-career management—thus defined as the giving up of relatively permanent organizational relationships in favour of more self-controlled career decision making—has become increasingly recommended to and by HRM professionals as a possible approach to dealing with challenges presented by the emerging world of work, a world still dominated in great degree by the use of downsizing as a management strategy despite continuing questions about its outcomes.

Clearly, there are reasons for such positive evaluation. Self career management recognizes the tentative nature of a specific employment relationship while also emphasizing the need for employee skills and meaningful contributions and the opportunity to fulfill the desire for self-enhancement that is so important in the work setting. In addition, for the appropriate individual and the appropriate situation, self-career management also provides an approach to meeting the need for self-protection, because this can be negotiated by the individual involved. The key, however, is in the word appropriate. Self-career management is appropriate when the individual has or can develop both meaningful self-knowledge and the types of skills and abilities that are in demand. In addition, self-career management is appropriate when the individual has knowledge of the job market and the freedom to respond to the opportunities available.

A variety of techniques reflect self-career management when it is defined in this manner. Perhaps the most important and first question that needs an answer (for which the HRM professional must provide input) is whether a specific organization should provide financial and other resources for developing and implementing self-career programmes for its employees, particularly programmes emphasizing personal growth. This is not an easy question to answer. At first glance, there are clearly reasons for companies to undertake such programmes.

They provide recognition of the frequently temporary nature of contemporary work settings while at the same time encouraging positive relationships between individuals and organizations over the long run. Both of these outcomes may serve the individual and the organization in good stead at once or at some time in the future. In addition, these programmes may serve to illuminate and develop skills in the participants not previously realized and thus eventually prove beneficial to the individual and the organization. Finally, such programmes help the organization in situations where downsizing may become inevitable. Clearly, preparing individuals to deal with the loss of employment before it happens is to be preferred over sudden notices of termination.

Still, some negative aspects also need to be recognized before a corporate decision is made to undertake a personal growth programme encouraging self-career management. One obvious problem is the cost involved. The cost may be considerable, depending on the number of individuals involved and the type of programmes chosen. Second, there is the continuing reality that all the benefits the programmes may provide to employees may never be of value to the organization that pays for them (and, indeed, may turn out to be of value to competitors).

Third, it needs to be realized right from the beginning that such programmes are not for everyone. They should not be oversold as "the answer" to the problems of the new world of work. Rather, companies need to keep in mind that other programmes will be necessary regardless of what they decide about self-career management programmes (for more on this, see the following section). To be blunt, self-career management is not and cannot be appropriate for those who have neither the personality nor the technical skills, educational levels, or likelihood of developing the skills to the degree needed to make the approach fruitful. For these individuals, other alternatives will be necessary.

Assuming these pros and cons have been considered and the company decides to proceed with such programmes, how might they do so? One possible procedure is to make self-career management programmes a voluntary aspect of the HRM process. Such an approach would increase the probability of successful outcomes by making it likely that the individuals participating in the programmes possess the skills, abilities, interests, or personality that would enable them to benefit from the programmes.

In addition, once the decision to proceed is made, HRM can increase the effectiveness of self-career management programmes by generating and making available as much information as possible about the nature of potential and actual career possibilities in a particular job market for those participating in the programmes. Self career management programmes are much concerned with personal growth but are not aimed at personal growth alone. They also have career and work-oriented goals.

The more work opportunities available that the participant knows about and the more the participant has the time, knowledge, and personal characteristics to carry out a job or career search, the more self-management career programmes will be useful. A further advantage of providing job knowledge to those undergoing self-career management is that doing so will help identify those for whom such programmes might not be useful, that is, those who will not have job opportunities for the skills they have or are likely to develop. For this latter group, other types of programmes will be necessary, perhaps programmes of the type we now turn to.

Labour Pool Associations

HRM also needs to begin to develop mechanisms that are appropriate in assisting the adaptation of current and potential employees for whom the concept of self-career management is inapplicable. Among these are the unskilled and semiskilled, immigrant workers, single parents whose job freedom is limited, and people with little growth potential. Two factors concerning these individuals are crucial. First, there are great numbers of such employees and they may, in fact, be increasing relative to the population at large. Second, despite their numbers, economically they are falling farther and farther behind people with higher skill levels, as evidenced by the findings of an increasing disparity in income between those at the higher and lower levels of our population.

Yet despite their numbers and this disparity, it is fair to say that little attention has been paid to how the new world of work can meet the needs of these people. For these individuals, basic educational training may have been insufficient, job training opportunities may not be available, and financial resources to keep up skill development may not be there. Also, the habit and encouragement of self-reliance in the occupational sphere may be more foreign to these individuals than those who are higher on the occupational hierarchy. Rather, these individuals may have, perhaps, more of a tendency to rely on traditional employment relationships and organizational reward systems as sources of meeting self enhancement and self-protection needs. Because the characteristics of the emerging world of work makes this pattern increasingly unlikely, it is even more important to pay attention to helping these groups adapt to the new and different setting.

Such associations can be conceived of as organizations based on cooperative relations among different companies (and perhaps government agencies) that focus on maximizing the human resources available to all of them. As cooperatively managed HR personnel from different organizations, labour pool associations would have several objectives. First, they would keep a continuing registry of individuals and their skills, thus ensuring a labour supply as needed by member organizations, large or small.

Second, they would serve as training-retraining-counseling centres for occupational entry and upgrading as desired and available. Third, and perhaps most uniquely, they would serve as "permanent employers" who, besides supplying and making available job and training opportunities, would also provide such "security type" benefits as health insurance and pension plans. These benefits would be paid into accounts maintained for each individual by the organizations. They would thus replace the security systems traditionally used by organizations, which are increasingly difficult to maintain in this era of downsizing and rapid corporate change.

One step towards this type of organization is the Talent Alliance (TA), an association of companies that has been operating since spring 1997 and includes such members as AT&T, Du Pont, GTE, Johnson & Johnson, Lucent Technologies, NCR, TRW, Unisys, and UPS. The TA, has several goals. One is to keep individuals employed in companies and settings where they are most needed when they are needed. It is therefore an employee allocation system (or labour pool association) of the type we envision here. A second objective is to increase employee marketability; this is done in a number of ways, including through career growth counselors, training and retraining programmes for employees, and strategic planning seminars for corporate management aimed at adapting HR practices to the new world of work.

The TA is, therefore, a step towards the type of organization suggest here because it has some of the aspects recommend. However, it lacks at this time a focus on the necessity of meeting the needs underlying self-protective motivation, that is, the desire for the security of health and welfare benefits and pensions.

A second possible limitation is that it is designed for the occupational spectrum of relatively big organizations employing large numbers of individuals, a considerable percentage of whom may be at a high technical level. Such organizations are, of course, crucial as major employers and these occupational groups are of legitimate concern. However, believe that labour pool associations need also be concerned with those individuals who, though working for small, sometimes marginal organizations, nevertheless have traditionally looked to organizations as the mechanisms through which they will meet their needs for both enhancement and protection.

One Further Note

Labour pool associations may be of value to those for whom self-career management programmes are appropriate as well as for those for whom it is not.

This is because systems need to be developed to bring individuals and organizations at all levels together for their mutual benefit in this emerging world of short-range assignments as well as long-range jobs and rapidly changing skill and competency demands. Labour pool associations, as we have envisioned them, would satisfy this need.

In sum, we need organizations like the TA and others like it, such as Job Link in Louisville, Kentucky, to meet self-enhancement needs but also to meet the need for self-protection.

It is basically a referral and counseling centre that makes training available as a final resort.) We need organizations such as the TA and Job Link because the two major motivations in work settings—self-enhancement and self-protection—increasingly may not be met by individual companies. For some organizations, self-career management will be an appropriate alternative mechanism.

However, for others, cooperative efforts like labour pool associations will be needed to help them find qualified workers and to help workers find jobs that meet both self-enhancing and self-protective needs. Key here is the need for cooperative activity among different organizations, including accepting the principle of having these associations serving as an "employer" designed to meet self-protective concerns.

This is perhaps a somewhat different perspective from that we are used to, but it is an idea that reflects the new world of work and the needs it has generated.

Non-organizationally Linked Incentive Systems

Financial incentive systems for performance have long been one of the staples of HRM and there is little reason to think they would or should lose their relevance in the new world of work. On the contrary, they may become even more relevant as other types of incentives—those that assume organizational links and commitment, such as promotion and transfer opportunities—will become less relevant to those who see their future as falling into the self-career management pattern or who are attaining employment through "labour pool associations."

Purely financial incentives, on the other hand, are not limited to any specific type of setting. Bonuses tied to individual or unit performance are innately transferable (or fungible) and do not have to be linked to any particular organization.

That is, the value of financial incentives as mechanisms to self-enhancement are not limited to any particular context and will usually hold their meaning regardless of where they are offered. Financial incentives will, then, retain significance in the new world of work and may become even more significant as the ties of organizational loyalty become less common and less relevant. First, direct monetary income in this changing world of fewer commitments will gain increased significance.

Second, incentive programmes that enable individuals to meet their needs for self-protection will have increased value. Such needs might be met by developing and applying incentive payments directly into health, welfare, and pension programmes even though the employees involved may be temporary workers who frequently change employers. Consistent with the logic underlying the labour pool associations described earlier, HR professionals might well consider developing financial incentive programmes using individual "benefit" accounts into which employers (and employees) would contribute based on employment, no matter how temporary or varying that employment might be.

These would be financial incentives for performance designed to satisfy self-protection needs by paying into health, welfare, and pension accounts maintained by the labour pool association. In addition to being of value to the individuals involved, such contributions are likely to increase commitment and loyalty to an organization's needs.

(One might note that the type of account we are referring to here is somewhat analogous to Social Security accounts. However, there are two major differences. First, these accounts are linked to individual work patterns and individual work behaviour in a more immediate manner. Second, these plans focus on health and welfare benefits as much as if not more than pay and pension concerns.)

Insider-Outsider Training Programmes

Training programmes designed to integrate individuals of diverse backgrounds and views into cohesive work teams are not new. They have been a standard part of HRM programmes in recent years as cultural and ethnic diversity has become a major challenge for organizations.

Some of these training programmes have proved fruitful and some have not. However, the challenge to HRM here is somewhat different in that the programmes we refer to have generally made one major assumption that we cannot make in the new context: that the individuals and groups in these programmes, diverse though they may be, all wish to maximize the effectiveness of the same organization, that is, the organization to which they are all committed by reason of employment.

In the new world of work, group members may include permanent employees committed to the same organization and work unit as well as temporarily assigned employees who rotate from assignment to assignment within the same organization and are sent to different units with not always consistent goals.

Even more difficult, however, will be dealing with people who are individual contractors or temporary workers who go to different organizations once a specific job is finished. It is not just that there will be changing memberships and changing interaction patterns in these organizational settings. Rather, there are and will also be individuals working together who have different, perhaps even conflicting loyalties. How does one get these groups to work together for some superordinate goal when some are truly insiders and some outsiders?

It is not clear how one proceeds here. Appeals to superordinate goals may not be appropriate over the long run (although they may be for the short run). In addition, the need for emotional cohesion may not be great because the groups may not be conceived of as even quasi-permanent.

It is also uncertain which type of development programme might be most appropriate and which type of incentive programme might be best. One possibility may be the extensive use of financial incentives to integrate such groups into a common effort because financial benefits are not tied to any particular organization or setting. These incentives may be performance based, perhaps even providing stock options keyed to the length, level, and quality of performance in a particular setting.

We really do not have any answers to these questions at this time, but the potential for conflict between insider-outsider groups within organizations is great, as is the potential for conflict among those with different perspectives who also need to work together, such as suppliers and vendors. Hence, it is in the development of appropriate training and performance incentive programmes to meet this need that HRM may make another significant contribution in the new world of work.

A work setting is beginning to emerge that is radically different from the one that has traditionally provided the context for HRM policies and practices. In this world downsizing is a tool of managerial decision making, work-family conflict is a fact of life for millions and, increasingly, contingent workers, part-time workers, and outsourcing are used.

It is a work setting where opportunities to meet self-enhancement and growth needs exist for some individuals but not for all, and where opportunities for self-protection such as job and benefit security are increasingly difficult to come by.

These changes have made it necessary for HRM as a profession to reevaluate its traditional practices and begin to develop and implement programmes that meet these needs for self-enhancement and self-protection in the new work setting.

This offered illustrations of such programmes, including effective self-career management programmes based on personal growth principles; labour pool associations for those for whom self-career management is inappropriate; performance incentive programmes not based on organizational commitment, including financial rewards of both direct income and health, welfare, and pension benefits; and insider outsider training programmes.

Underlying these recommendations is my view that HRM professionals, regardless of specific training, need to take an active role in meeting the demands of the new world of work. Key to this process is recognizing that the opportunities for meeting and satisfying the primary motivational patterns of self-enhancement and self-protection are no longer what they used to be, whatever level of the occupational spectrum we are focusing on. For the benefit of both organizations and individuals, developing new mechanisms for responding to these changes is a major challenge facing HRM today.

5

Resort Staffing

PRELUDE TO STAFFING

Staffing is the third sequential function of management. Up until now the executive housekeeper has been concerned with planning and organizing the housekeeping department for the impending opening and operations. Now the executive housekeeper must think about hiring employees within sufficient time to ensure that three of the activities of staffing—selection (including interviewing), orientation, and training—may be completed before opening. Staffing will be a major task of the last two weeks before opening.

The development of the Area Responsibility Plan and the House Breakout Plan before opening led to preparation of the Department Staffing Guide, which will be a major tool in determining the need for employees in various categories. The housekeeping manager and laundry manager should now be on board and assisting in the development of various job descriptions. The resort human resources department would also have been preparing for the hiring event.

They would have advertised a mass hiring for all categories of personnel to begin on a certain date about two weeks before opening. Even though this chapter reflects a continuation of the executive housekeeper's planning for opening operations, the techniques described apply to any ongoing operation, except that the magnitude of selection, orientation, and training activities will not be as intense.

Also, the fourth activity—development of existing employees —is normally missing in opening operations but is highly visible in ongoing operations.

Job Specifications

Job specifications should be written as job descriptions are prepared. Job specifications are simple statements of what the various incumbents to positions will be expected to do. An example of a job specification for a section housekeeper is as follows:

Job Specification—Example

Section Housekeeper (resorts) [often Guestroom Attendant —GRA] The incumbent will work as a member of a housekeeping team, cleaning and servicing for occupancy of approximately 18 resort guestrooms each day. Work will generally include the tasks of bed making, vacuuming, dusting, and bathroom cleaning.

Incumbent will also be expected to maintain equipment provided for work and load housekeeper's cart before the end of each day's operation. Section housekeepers must be willing to work their share of weekends and be dependable in coming to work each day scheduled. [Any special qualifications, such as ability to speak a foreign language, might also be listed.]

Employee Requisition

Once job specifications have been developed for every position, employee requisitions are prepared for first hirings (and for any follow-up needs for the human resources department). Note the designation as to whether the requisition is for a new or a replacement position and the number of employees required for a specific requisition number. The human resources department will advertise, take applications, and screen to fill each requisition by number until all positions are filled.

For example, the first requisition for GRAs may be for 20 GRAs. The human resources department will continue to advertise for, take applications, and screen employees for the housekeeping department and will provide candidates for interview by department managers until 20 GRAs are hired. Should any be hired and require replacing, a new employee requisition will be required.

Staffing Housekeeping Positions

There are several activities involved in staffing a housekeeping operation. Executive housekeepers must select and interview employees, participate in an orientation programme, train newly hired employees, and develop employees for future growth. Each of these activities will now be discussed.

Selecting Employees

Each area of the United States has its own demographic situations that affect the availability of suitable employees for involvement in housekeeping or environmental service operations. For example, in one area, an exceptionally high response rate from people seeking food service work may occur and a low response rate from people seeking housekeeping positions may occur. In another area, the reverse may be true, and people interested in housekeeping work may far outnumber those interested in food service.

Surveys among resorts or hospitals in your area will indicate the best source for various classifications of employees. Advertising campaigns that will reach these employees are the best method of locating suitable people. Major classified ads associated with mass hirings will specify the need for food service personnel, front desk clerks, food servers, housekeeping personnel, and maintenance people. Such ads may yield surprising results.

If aliens are hired, the department manager must take great care to ensure that they are legal residents of this country and that their green cards are valid. More than one resort department manager has had an entire staff swept away by the Department of Immigration after hiring people who were illegal aliens. Such unfortunate action has required the immediate assistance of all available employees (including management) to fill in.

Processing Applicants

Whether you are involved in a mass hiring or in the recruiting of a single employee, a systematic and courteous procedure for processing applicants is essential. For example, in the opening of the Los Angeles Airport Marriott, 11,000 applicants were processed to fill approximately 850 positions in a period of about two weeks. The magnitude of such an operation required a near assembly-line technique, but a personable and positive experience for the applicants still had to be maintained.

The efficient handling of lines of employees, courteous attendance, personal concern for employee desires, and reference to suitable departments for those unfamiliar with what the resort or hospital has to offer all become earmarks for how the company will treat its employees. The key to proper handling of applicants is the use of a control system whereby employees are conducted through the steps of application, prescreening, and if qualified, reference to a department for interview.

Note the opportunity for employees to express their desires for a specific type of employment. Even though an employee may desire involvement in one classification of work, he or she may be hired for employment in a different department. Also, employees might not be aware of the possibilities available in a particular department at the time of application or may be unable to locate in desired departments at the time of mass hirings.

Employees who perform well should therefore be given the opportunity to transfer to other departments when the opportunities arise. According to laws regulated by federal and state Fair Employment Practices Agencies (FEPA), no person may be denied the opportunity to submit application for employment for a position of his or her choosing.

Not only is the law strict on this point, but companies in any way benefiting from interstate commerce (such as resorts and hospitals) may not discriminate in the hiring of people based on race, colour, national origin, or religious preference. Although specific hours and days of the week may be specified, it is a generally accepted fact that resorts and hospitals must maintain personnel operations that provide the opportunity for people to submit applications without prejudice.

Prescreening Applicants

The prescreening interview is a staff function normally provided to all resort or hospital departments by the *human resources* section of the organization. Prescreening is a preliminary interview process in which unqualified applicants—those applicants who do not meet the criteria for a job as specified in the job specification–special qualifications—are selected (or screened) out.

For example, an applicant for a secretarial job that requires the incumbent to take shorthand and be able to type 60 words a minute may be screened out if the applicant is not able to pass a relevant typing and shorthand test.

If a candidate is screened out by the personnel section, he or she should be told the reason immediately and thanked for applying for employment. Applicants who are not screened out should either be referred to a specific department for interview or, if all immediate positions are filled, have their applications placed in a department pending file for future reference. All applicants should be told that hiring decisions will be made by individual department managers based on the best qualifications from among those interviewed.

A suggested agenda for a prescreening interview is as follows:

1. The initial contact should be cordial and helpful. Many employees are lost at this stage because of inefficient systems established for handling applicants.
2. During the prescreening interview, try to determine what the employee is seeking, whether such a position is available, or, if not, when such a position might become available.
3. Review the work history as stated on the application to determine whether the applicant meets the obvious physical and mental qualifications, as well as important human qualifications such as emotional stability, personality, honesty, integrity, and reliability.
4. Do not waste time if the applicant is obviously not qualified or if no immediate position is available. When potential vacancies or a backlog of applicants exists, inform the candidate. Be efficient in stating this to the applicant. Always make sure that the applicant gives you a phone number in order that he or she may be called at some future date. Because most applicants seeking employment are actively seeking immediate work, applications more than 30 days old are usually worthless.

5. If at all possible, an immediate interview by the department manager should be held after screening. If this is not possible, a definite appointment should be made for the candidate's interview as soon as possible.

An interview should be conducted by a manager of the department to which the applicant has been referred. In ongoing operations, it is often wise to also allow the supervisor for whom the new employee will work to visit with the candidate in order that the supervisor may gain a feel for how it would be to work together.

The supervisor's view should be considered, since a harmonious relationship at the working level is important. Although the acceptance of an employee remains a prerogative of management, it would be unwise to accept an employee into a position when the supervisor has reservations about the applicant. Certain personal characteristics should be explored when interviewing an employee.

Some of these characteristics are native skills, stability, reliability, experience, attitude towards employment, personality, physical traits, stamina, age, sex, education, previous training, initiative, alertness, appearance, and personal cleanliness.

Although employers may not discriminate against race, sex, age, religion, and nationality, overall considerations may involve the capability to lift heavy objects, enter men's or women's restrooms, and so on. In a housekeeping (or environmental services) department, people should be employed who find enjoyment in housework at home. Remember that character and personality cannot be completely judged from a person's appearance.

Also, it should be expected that a person's appearance will never be better than when that person is applying for a job. Letters of recommendation and references should be carefully considered. Seldom will a letter of recommendation be adverse, whereas a telephone call might be most revealing. If it were necessary to select the most important step in the selection process, interviewing would be it. Interviewing is *the* step that separates those who will be employed from those who will not.

Poor interviewing techniques can make the process more difficult and may produce a result that can be both frustrating and damaging for both parties. In addition, inadequate interviewing will result in gaining incorrect information, being confused about what has been said, suppression of information, and, in some circumstances, complete withdrawal from the process by the candidate.

The following is a well-accepted list of the steps for a successful interview process.

1. *Be prepared*: Have a checklist of significant questions ready to ask the candidate. Such questions may be prepared from the body of the

job description. This preparation will allow the interviewer to assume the initiative in the interview.

2. *Find a proper place to conduct the interview*: The applicant should be made to feel comfortable. The interview should be conducted in a quiet, relaxing atmosphere where there is privacy that will bring about a confidential conversation.
3. *Practice:* People who conduct interviews should practice interviewing skills periodically. Several managers may get together and discuss interviewing techniques that are to be used.
4. *Be tactful and courteous:* Put the applicant at ease, but also control the discussion and lead to important questions.
5. *Be knowledgeable:* Be thoroughly familiar with the position for which the applicant is interviewing in order that all of the applicant's questions may be answered. Also, have a significant background knowledge in order that general information about the company may be given.
6. *Listen:* Encourage the applicant to talk. This may be done by asking questions that are not likely to be answered by a yes or no. If people are comfortable and are asked questions about themselves, they will usually speak freely and give information that specific questions will not always bring out. Applicants will usually talk if there is a feeling that they are not being misunderstood.
7. *Observe*: Much can be learned about an applicant just by observing reactions to questions, attitudes about work, and, specifically, attitudes about providing service to others. Observation is a vital step in the interviewing process.

Perhaps of equal importance to the interviewing technique are the following pitfalls, which should be avoided while interviewing.

1. Having a feeling that the employee will be just right based on a few outstanding characteristics rather than on the sum of all characteristics noted.
2. Being influenced by neatness, grooming, expensive clothes, and an extroverted personality—none of which has much to do with housekeeping competency.
3. Overgeneralizing, whereby interviewers assume too much from a single remark (for instance, an applicant's assurance that he or she "really wants to work").
4. Hiring the "boomer," that is, the person who always wants to work in a new property; unfortunately, this type of person changes jobs whenever a new property opens.
5. Projecting your own background and social status into the job

requirement. Which school the applicant attended or whether the applicant has the "proper look" is beside the point. It is job performance that is going to count.

6. Confusing strengths with weaknesses, and vice versa. What is construed by one person to be overaggressiveness might be interpreted by another as confidence, ambition, and potential for leadership, the last two traits being in chronic short supply in most housekeeping departments. These are the very characteristics that make it possible for management to promote from within and develop new supervisors and managers.
7. Being impressed by a smooth talker—or the reverse: assuming that silence reflects strength and wisdom. The interviewer should concentrate on what the applicant is saying rather than on how it is being said, then decide whether his or her personality will fit into the organization.
8. Being tempted by overqualified applicants. People with experience and education that far exceed the job requirements may be unable for some reason to get jobs commensurate with their backgrounds.

Even if such applicants are not concealing skeletons in the closet, they still tend to become frustrated and dissatisfied with jobs far below their level of abilities. The application of the techniques and avoidance of the pitfalls will be valuable tools in the selection of competent personnel for the housekeeping and environmental service departments.

For many years, the approach of many managers was to write a job description and then fill it by attempting to find the perfect person. This approach may overlook many qualified people, such as disadvantaged people or slow learners. Job descriptions may be analyzed in two ways when filling positions: (1) what is actually required to do the work, and (2) what is desirable. Is the ability to read or write really necessary for the job? Is the ability to learn quickly really necessary?

A person who does not read or write or who is a slow learner can be trained and can make an excellent employee. True, it may take additional time, but the reward will be a loyal employee as well as less turnover. It has been proven many times that those who are disadvantaged or slightly retarded, once trained, will perform consistently well for longer periods. There are agencies who seek out companies that will try to hire such people.

If the results of an interview are negative and rejection is indicated, the candidate should be informed as soon as possible. A pleasant statement, such as "Others interviewed appear to be more qualified," is usually sufficient. This information can be handled in a straightforward and courteous manner and in such a way that the candidate will appreciate the time that has been taken during the interview. When the results of the interview are positive, a statement indicating a favourable impression is most encouraging. However, no commitment should be made until a *reference check* has been conducted.

In many cases, reference checks are made only to verify that what has been said in the application and interview is in fact true. Many times applicants are reluctant to explain in detail why previous employment situations have come to an end. It is more important to hear the actual truth about a prior termination from the applicant than it is to hear that they simply have been terminated.

Reference checks, in order of desirability, are as follows:

1. Personal (face-to-face) meetings with previous employers are the least available but provide the most accurate information when they can be arranged.
2. Telephone discussions are the next best and most often used approach. For all positions, an in-depth conversation by telephone between the potential new manager and the prior manager is most desirable; otherwise a simple verification of data is sufficient to ensure honesty.
3. The least desirable reference is the written recommendation, because managers are extremely reluctant to state a frank and honest opinion that may later be used against them in court.

Applicants who are rated successful at an interview should be told that a check of their references will be conducted, and, pending favourable responses, they will be contacted by the personnel department within two days. Applicants who are currently employed normally ask that their current employer not be contacted for a reference check.

This request should be honored at all times. Applicants who are currently working usually want to give proper notice to their current employers. If the applicant chooses not to give notice, chances are no notice will be given at the time he or she leaves your resort.

In some cases, the applicant gives notice and, upon doing so, is "cut loose" immediately. If such is the case, the applicant should be told to contact the department manager immediately in order that the employee may be put to work as soon as possible.

There is no perfect interviewer, interviewee, or resultant hiring or rejection decision in regard to an applicant. We can only hope to improve our interviewing skills in order that the greatest degree of success in employee retention can be obtained. The executive housekeeper should expect that 25 per cent of initial hires into a housekeeping department will not be employed for more than three months. (This is primarily because the housekeeping skills are easily learned and the position is paid at or near minimum wage.)

Some new housekeeping departments have as much as a 75 per cent turnover rate in the first three months of operation. Certainly this can be improved upon with adequate attention to the interviewing and selection processes. However, regardless of the outcome of the interview, the processing record should be properly endorsed and returned to the personnel department for processing.

A carefully planned, concerned, and informational orientation programme is significant to the first impressions that a new employee will have about the hospital or resort in general and the housekeeping department in particular. Too often, a new employee is told where the work area and restroom are, given a cursory explanation of the job, then put to work. It is not uncommon to find managers putting employees to work who have not even been processed into the organization, an unfortunate situation that is usually discovered on payday when there is no paycheck for the new employee.

Such blatant disregard for the concerns of the employee can only lead to a poor perception of the company. A planned orientation programme will eliminate this type of activity and will bring the employee into the company with personal concern and with a greater possibility for a successful relationship. A good orientation programme is usually made up of four phases: employee acquisition, receipt of an employee's handbook, tour of the facility, and an orientation meeting.

Employee Acquisition

Once a person is accepted for employment, the applicant is told to report for work at a given time and place, and that place should be the personnel department. Pre-employment procedures can take as much as one-half day, and department managers eager to start new employees to work should allow time for a proper employee acquisition into the organization.

At this time it should be ensured that the application is complete and any additional information pertaining to employment history that may be necessary to obtain the necessary work permits and credentials is on hand. Usually the security department records the entry of a new employee into the staff and provides instructions regarding use of employee entrances, removing parcels from the premises, and employee parking areas.

Application for work permits, and drug testing, will be scheduled where applicable. All documents required by the resort's health and welfare insurer should be completed, and instructions should be given about immediately reporting accidents, no matter how slight, to supervisors.

The federal government requires that every employer submit a W-4 (withholding statement) for each employee on the payroll. The employee must complete this document and give it to the company. Mandatory deductions from pay should be explained (federal and state income tax and Social Security FICA), as should other deductions that may be required or desired. At this time, some form of personal action document is usually initiated for the new employee and is placed in the employee's permanent record.

Note the permanent information that will be carried on file. The PAF is serially numbered, is created from data stored on magnetic discs, and is maintained in the employee's personnel file. When a change has to be made, such as job title, marital status, or rate of pay, the PAF is retrieved from the employee's record, changes are made *under* the item to be changed, and the corrected PAF is used to change the data in the computer storage.

Once new information is stored, a new PAF is created and placed in the employee's record to await the next need for processing. A long-time employee might have many PAFs stored in the personnel file.

When either regular or special performance appraisals are given, the last (most current) PAF will be used to record the appraisal. These forms are usually found on the reverse side of the PAF. Since performance appraisals may signify a raise in pay, the appropriate pay increase information would be indicated on the front side of the PAF. All recordings on PAFs, whether on one side or both, require the submission of data, storage of information, and creation of a new PAF to be stored in the employee's record. The PAF and performance appraisal system should be thoroughly explained to the new employee, along with assignment of a payroll number.

The employer should also explain how and when the staff is paid and when the first paycheck may be expected. The new employee should be provided with a copy of the resort or hospital employee's handbook and should be told to read it thoroughly.

Since the new housekeeping employee is not working just for the housekeeping department but is to become integrated as a member of the entire staff, reading this handbook is extremely important to ensure that proper instructions in the rules and regulations of the resort are presented. The handbook should be developed in such a way as to inspire the new employee to become a fully participating member of the organization. Note the tone of the welcoming letter and the manner in which the rules and regulations are presented.

Familiarization Tour of the Facilities

Upon completion of the acquisition phase, a facility tour should be conducted for one or all new employees. For new facilities, access to the property should be gained within about one week before opening, and many new employees can be taken on a tour simultaneously. It is possible for employees to work in the resort housekeeping department for years and never to have visited the showroom, dining rooms, ballrooms, or even the executive office areas. A tour of the complete facility melds employees into the total organization, and a complete informative tour should *never* be neglected.

For ongoing operations, after acquisition, the new employee may be turned over to a department supervisor, who becomes the tour director. An appreciation of the total involvement of each employee is strengthened when a facilities tour is complete and thorough If necessary, the property tour might be postponed until after the orientation meeting; however, the orientation activity of staffing is not complete until a property tour is conducted

The orientation meeting should not be conducted until the employee has had an opportunity to become at least partially familiar with the surroundings. After approximately two weeks, the employee will have many questions about experiences, the new job, training, and the rules and regulations listed in the Property and Department Handbooks. Employee orientation meetings that are scheduled too soon fail to answer many questions that will develop within the first two weeks of employment.

The meeting should be held in a comfortable setting, with refreshments provided. It is usually conducted by the director of human resources and is attended by as many of the facility managers as possible. Most certainly, the general manager or hospital administration members of the executive committee, the security director, and the new employees' department heads should attend. Each of these managers should have an opportunity to welcome the new employees and give them a chance to associate names with faces.

All managers and new employees should wear name tags. In orientation meetings, a brief history of the company and company goals should be presented. A planned orientation meeting should not be concluded without someone stressing the importance of each position. Every position must have a purpose behind it and is therefore important to the overall functioning of the facility.

An excellent statement of this philosophy was once offered by a general manager who said, "The person mopping a floor in the kitchen at 3:00 A.M. is just as valuable to this operation as I am—we just do different things." The orientation meeting should be scheduled to allow for many questions. And there should be someone in attendance who can answer *all of them.*

Although the new employee will be gaining confidence and security in the position as training ends and work is actually performed, informal orientation may continue for quite some time. The formal orientation, however, ends with the orientation meeting (although the facility tour may be conducted after the meeting).

Finally, it should be remembered that good orientation procedures lead to worker satisfaction and help quiet the anxieties and fears that a new employee may have. When a good orientation is neglected, the seeds of dissatisfaction are planted. The efficiency and economy with which any department will operate will depend on the ability of each member of the organization to do his or her job. Such ability will depend in part on past experiences, but more commonly it can be credited to the type and quality of training offered. Employees, regardless of past experiences, always need some degree of training before starting a new job.

Small institutions may try to avoid training by hiring people who are already trained in the general functions with which they will be involved. However, most institutions recognize the need for training that is specifically oriented towards the new experience, and will have a documented training programme. Some employers of housekeeping personnel find it easier to train completely unskilled and untrained personnel. In such cases, bad or undesirable practices do not have to be trained out of an employee.

Previous experience and education should, however, be analyzed and considered in the training of each new employee in order that efficiencies in training can be recognized. If an understanding of department standards and policies can be demonstrated by a new employee, that portion of training may be shortened or modified. However, skill and ability must be demonstrated before training can be altered. Finally, training is the best method to communicate the company's way of doing things, without which the new employee may do work contrary to company policy.

First training of a new employee actually starts with a continuation of *department* orientation. When a new employee is turned over to the housekeeping or environmental services department, orientation usually continues by familiarizing the employee with *department rules and regulations.* Many housekeeping departments have their own department employee handbooks. For an example, which contains the housekeeping department rules and regulations for Bally's Casino Resort in Las Vegas, Nevada? Compare this handbook with that of the generic handbook.

Although these handbooks are for completely different types of organizations, the substance of their publications is essentially the same; both are designed to familiarize each new employee with his or her surroundings. Handbooks should be written in such a way as to inspire employees to become team members, committed to company objectives.

Training may be defined as those activities that are designed to help an employee begin performing tasks for which he or she is hired or to help the employee improve performance in a job already assigned. The purpose of training is to enable an employee to begin an assigned job or to improve upon techniques already in use. In resort or hospital housekeeping operations, there are three basic areas in which training activity should take place: skills, attitudes, and knowledge.

A sample list of skills in which a basic housekeeping employee must be trained follows:

1. *Bed making:* Specific techniques; company policy
2. *Vacuuming:* Techniques; use and care of equipment
3. *Dusting:* Techniques; use of products
4. *Window and mirror cleaning:* Techniques and products
5. *Setup awareness:* Room setups; what a properly serviced room should look like
6. *Bathroom cleaning:* Tub and toilet sanitation; appearance; methods of cleaning and results desired
7. *Daily routine:* An orderly procedure for the conduct of the day's work; daily communications
8. *Caring for and using equipment:* Housekeeper cart; loading
9. *Industrial safety:* Product use; guest safety; fire and other emergencies

The best reference for the skills that require training is the job description for which the person is being trained.

Employees need guidance in their attitudes about the work that must be done. They need to be guided in their thinking about rooms that may present a unique problem in cleaning. Attitudes among section housekeepers need to be such that, occasionally, when rooms require extra effort to be brought back to standard, it is viewed as being a part of rendering service to the guest who paid to enjoy the room. Carol Mondesir, director of housekeeping, Sheraton Centre, Toronto, states that:

A resort is meant to be enjoyed and, occasionally, the rooms are left quite messed up. However, as long as they're not vandalized, it's part of the territory. The whole idea of being in the hospitality business is to make the guest's stay as pleasant as possible. The rooms are there to be enjoyed. Positive relationships with various agencies and people also need to be developed.

The following is a list of areas in which attitude guidance is important:

1. The guest/patient
2. The department manager and immediate supervisor
3. A guestroom that is in a state of great disarray
4. The resort and company
5. The uniform
6. Appearance
7. Personal hygiene

The most important task of the trainer is to prepare new employees to meet standards. With this aim in mind, sequence of performance in cleaning a guestroom is most important in order that efficiency in accomplishing day-to-day tasks may be developed. In addition, the *best method* of accomplishing a task should be presented to the new trainee. Once the task has been learned, the next thing is to meet standards, which may not necessarily mean doing the job the way the person has been trained.

Areas of knowledge in which the employee needs to be trained are as follows:

1. Thorough knowledge of the resort layout; employee must be able to give directions and to tell the guest about the resort, restaurants, and other facilities
2. Knowledge of employee rights and benefits
3. Understanding of grievance procedure
4. Knowing top managers by sight and by name

There is a need to conduct ongoing training for all employees, regardless of how long they have been members of the department. There are two instances when additional training is needed: (1) the purchase of new equipment, and (2) change in or unusual employee behaviour while on the job. When new equipment is purchased, employees need to know how the new equipment differs from present equipment, what new skills or knowledge are required to operate the equipment, who will need this knowledge, and when. New equipment may also require new attitudes about work habits.

Employee behaviour while on the job that is seen as an indicator for additional training may be divided into two categories: events that the manager witnesses and events that the manager is told about by the employees. Events that the manager witnesses that indicate a need for training are frequent employee absence, considerable spoilage of products, carelessness, a high rate of accidents, and resisting direction by supervisors. Events that the manager might be told about that indicate a need for training are that something doesn't work right (product isn't any good), something is dangerous to work with, something is making work harder.

Although training is vital for any organization to function at top efficiency, it is expensive. The money and man-hours expended must therefore be worth the investment. There must be a balance between the dollars spent training employees and the benefits of productivity and high-efficiency performance. A simple method of determining the need for training is to measure performance of workers: Find out what is going on at present on the job, and match this performance with what should be happening. The difference, if any, describes how much training is needed.

In conducting performance analysis, the following question should be asked: Could the employee do the job or task if his or her life depended on the result? If the employee *could not* do the job even if his or her life depended on the outcome, there is a deficiency of knowledge (DK). If the employee could have done the job if his or her life depended on the outcome, but did not, there is a deficiency of execution (DE). Some of the causes of deficiencies of execution include task interference, lack of feedback (employee doesn't know when the job is being performed correctly or incorrectly), and the balance of consequences (some employees like doing certain tasks better than others).

If either deficiency of knowledge or deficiency of execution exists, training must be conducted. The approach or the method of training may differ, however. Deficiencies of knowledge can be corrected by training the employee to do the job, then observing and correcting as necessary until the task is proficiently performed. Deficiency of execution is usually corrected by searching for the underlying cause of lack of performance, not by teaching the actual task.

There are numerous methods or ways to conduct training. Each method has its own advantages and disadvantages, which must be weighed in the light of benefits to be gained. Some methods are more expensive than others but are also more effective in terms of time required for comprehension and proficiency that must be developed. Several useful methods of training housekeeping personnel are listed and discussed.

Using on-the-job training (OJT), a technique in which "learning by doing" is the advantage, the instructor demonstrates the procedure and then watches the students perform it. With this technique, one instructor can handle several students. In housekeeping operations, the instructor is usually a GRA who is doing the instructing in the rooms that have been assigned for cleaning that day. The OJT method is not operationally productive until the student is proficient enough in the training tasks to absorb part of the operational load. With simulation training, a model room (unrented) is set up and used to train several employees.

Whereas OJT requires progress towards daily production of ready rooms, simulation requires that the model room not be rented. In addition, the trainer is not productive in cleaning ready rooms. The advantages of simulation training are that it allows the training process to be stopped, discussed, and repeated if necessary. Simulation is an excellent method, provided the trainer's time is paid for out of training funds, and clean room production is not necessary during the workday.

The coach-pupil method is similar to OJT except that each instructor has only one student (a one-to-one relationship). This method is desired, provided that there are enough qualified instructors to have several training units in progress at the same time.

The lecture method reaches the largest number of students per instructor. Practically all training programmes use this type of instruction for certain segments. Unfortunately, the lecture method can be the dullest training technique, and therefore requires instructors who are gifted in presentation capabilities. In addition, space for lectures may be difficult to obtain and may require special facilities.

The conference method of instruction is often referred to as workshop training. This technique involves a group of students who formulate ideas, do problem solving, and report on projects. The conference or workshop technique is excellent for supervisory training. When new products or equipment are being introduced, demonstrations are excellent. Many demonstrations may be conducted by vendors and purveyors as a part of the sale of equipment and products.

Difficulties may arise when language barriers exist. It is also important that no more information be presented than can be absorbed in a reasonable period of time; otherwise misunderstandings may arise. Many resorts use training aids in a conference room, or post messages on an employee bulletin board. Aside from the usual training aids such as chalkboards, bulletin boards, charts, graphs, and diagrams, photographs can supply clear and accurate references for how rooms should be set up, maids' carts loaded, and routines accomplished. Most housekeeping operations have films on guest contact and courtesy that may also be used in training.

Motion pictures speak directly to many people who may not understand proper procedures from reading about them. Many training techniques may be combined to develop a well-rounded training plan. It is possible to have two students sitting side by side in a classroom, with one being trained and the other being developed. Recall that the definition of training is preparing a person to do a job for which he or she is hired or to improve upon performance of a current job.

Development is preparing a person for advancement or to assume greater responsibility. The techniques are the same, but the end result is quite different.Whereas training begins after orientation of an employee who is hired to do a specific job, upon introduction of new equipment, or upon observation and communication with employees indicating a need for training, development begins with the identification of a specific employee who has shown potential for advancement. Training for promotion or to improve potential is in fact development and must always include a much neglected type of training — supervisory training. Many forms of developmental training may be given on the property; other forms might include sending candidates to schools and seminars.

Developmental training is associated primarily with supervisors and managerial development and may encompass many types of experiences. Note the various developmental tasks that the trainee must perform over a period of 12 months. Development of individuals within the organization looks to future potential and promotion of employees.

Specifically, those employees who demonstrate leadership potential should be developed through supervisory training for advancement to positions of greater responsibility. Unfortunately, many outstanding workers have their performance rewarded by promotion but are given no development training.

The excellent section housekeeper who is advanced to the position of senior housekeeper without the benefit of supervisory training is quickly seen to be unhappy and frustrated and may possibly become a loss to the department. It is therefore most essential that individual potential be developed in an orderly and systematic manner, or else this potential may never be recognized.

While undergoing managerial development student and management alike should not lose sight of the primary aim of the programme, which is the learning and potential development of the trainee, not departmental production. Even though there will be times that the trainee may be given specific responsibilities to oversee operations, clean guestrooms, or service public areas, advantage should not be taken of the trainee or the situation to the detriment of the development function.

Development of new growth in the trainee becomes difficult when the training instructor or coordinator is not only developing a new manager but is also being held responsible for the production of some aspect of housekeeping operations.

Whether you are conducting a training or a development programme, suitable records of training progress should be maintained both by the training supervisor and the student. Periodic evaluations of the student's progress should be conducted, and successful completion of the programme should be recognized. Public recognition of achievement will inspire the newly trained or developed employee to achieve standards of performance and to strive for advancement.

Once an employee is trained or developed and his or her satisfactory performance has been recognized and recorded, the person should perform satisfactorily to standards. Future performance may be based on beginning performance after training. If an employee's performance begins to fall short of standards and expectations, there has to be a reason other than lack of skills. The reason for unsatisfactory performance must then be sought out and addressed.

This type of follow-up is not possible unless suitable records of training and development are maintained and used for comparison. Although evaluation and performance appraisal for employees will occur as work progresses, it is not uncommon to find the design of systems for appraisal as part of organization and staffing functions. This is true because first appraisal and evaluation occurs during training, which is an activity of staffing.

Once trainees begin to have their performance appraised, the methods used will continue throughout employment. As a part of training, new employees should be told how, when, and by whom their performances will be evaluated, and should be advised that questions regarding their performance will be regularly answered. Initial employment should be probationary in nature, allowing the new employee to improve efficiency to where the designated number of rooms cleaned per day can be achieved in a probationary period (about three months).

Should a large number of employees be unable to achieve the standard within that time, the standard should be investigated. Should only one or two employees be unable to meet the standard of rooms cleaned per day, an evaluation of the employee in training should either reveal the reason why or indicate the employee as unsuitable for further retention.

An employee who, after suitable training, cannot meet a reasonable performance standard should not be allowed to continue employment. Similarly, an employee who has met required performance standards in the specified probationary period should be continued into regular employment status and thus achieve a reasonable degree of security in employment. Evaluation of personnel is an attempt to measure selected traits, characteristics, and productivity.

Unfortunately, evaluations are generally objective in nature, and raters are seldom trained in the art of subjective evaluation. Initiative, self-control, and leadership ability do not lend themselves to measurement; therefore such characteristics are estimated. How well they are estimated depends to a great extent on the person doing the estimating. Two raters using the same form and rating the same person will probably arrive at different conclusions.

Certain policies on the use of evaluations should be established so that they are understood by both the person doing the evaluating and the person being evaluated. These policies must be established and disseminated by management. In order to establish such policies, the following questions, among others, must be answered and communicated to all those involved in the evaluation: What will evaluations be used for? Will evaluations influence promotions, become a part of the employee's record, be used as periodic checks, or be used for counseling and guidance? What qualities are going to be evaluated? Who is going to be evaluated? Who will do the evaluating?

Reliable evaluations require careful planning and take considerable time, skill, and work. An evaluation must be understood by the employee. Evaluation should be used at the end of a probationary period, and the employee must understand at the beginning of the period that he or she will be observed and evaluated.

Each item, as well as what impact the evaluation will have on future employment, should be explained to the employee. People undergoing periodic evaluations, such as at the end of one year's employment, should also know why evaluations are being conducted and what may result from the evaluation. In both situations, the evaluation should be used for counseling and guidance so that performance may be improved upon or corrected if necessary.

Certainly, strong points should be pointed out. An employee should be made aware of good as well as not-so-good evaluations. Evaluations should be made for a purpose and not for the sake of an exercise. They should ultimately be used as management tools.

Evaluations should be developed to fit the policies of the particular institution using it and the particular position being evaluated. The same evaluation may not be suitable for every position. In certain locales, such as isolated resorts, resorts are tempted to use contract labour because the local market does not support the necessary number of workers, particularly in housekeeping.

Advocates of outsourcing are quick to point out the advantages of the practice. Scarce workers are provided to the property, and there is no need to provide expensive employee benefits. The entire staffing function is assumed by the contractor. There are no worries regarding recruiting, selecting, hiring, orienting, or even training the employees.

Merely issue them uniforms and send them off to clean rooms. Some employers may even be willing to relax their responsibilities regarding employment law such as immigration and naturalization requirements.

Management should never forget that once a contracted employee dons a company uniform, the guest believes (and has no reason not to) that person is an employee of the resort. The guest also believes the resort has made every reasonable effort to screen that person in the hiring process to ensure that he or she is of good moral character, who has the best interest of the guest at heart.

Unfortunately, there have been several incidents in which the outsourced employees did not quite have the best interest of the guest in their hearts. There have been more than a few cases in which outsourced workers were wanted felons who inflicted considerable bodily harm on guests during the performance of their duties.

A number of these incidents have resulted in lawsuits, with awards against the resort in the millions of dollars. This author does not recommend outsourcing in housekeeping, and cautions operators who ignore this advice to keep their guard up and continue to meet their legal and ethical responsibilities regarding employees and employment law.

Staffing for both hospital and resort housekeeping operations involves the activities of selecting, interviewing, orienting, training, and developing personnel to carry out specific functions in the organization for which they are hired. Each activity should be performed with consistency, dispatch, and individual concern for each employee brought into the organization. Whereas the major presentation of staffing in this text has been developed for the model resort where a mass hiring has been performed, each and every aspect of selecting, orienting, and training new employees applies equally to situations in which replacement employees (perhaps only one) are brought into the organization.

Job specifications are the documents that indicate qualifications, characteristics, and abilities inherently needed in applicants. The Employee Requisition is the instrument by which specific numbers and types of candidates for employment are sought by the personnel department for each of the operating departments.

The next step is interviewing, which should be done by people from various departments. Actual selection, however, should only be performed by the department manager for whom the employee will work. The employee acquisition phase is vital to the successful orientation of a new employee and should not be omitted.

Upon acquisition of the new employee, presentation of an Employee's Handbook is appropriate. This handbook should contain major company rules, procedures, and regulations, along with relevant facts for the employee. Orientation is the basis for allowing the new employee to become accustomed to new surroundings.

The quality of orientation will determine whether the new employee will feel secure in a new setting, and it will set the stage for the relationship that is to follow. As training begins, orientation continues but is now conducted by the specific department in which the new employee will work. There are several methods of training, each of which should be used so as to gain the best effect for the least cost.

Employee performance in training should be evaluated by methods similar to those used in evaluating operational performance that will follow. After new employees receive approximately 24 hours of on-the-job training in the cleaning of rooms, they should become productive and be able to clean a reasonable number of rooms (about 60 per cent efficient).

Continued application of skills will develop greater productivity as the new employee spends each day working at the new skills. As preliminary training ends, orientation should be completed by ensuring that an employee orientation meeting and a tour of the entire facility has taken place.

Failure to complete an orientation or to provide sufficient training can plant the seeds of employee unrest, discontent, and possible failure of the employee's relationship with the company that might well have been prevented.

Whether conducting training or development, adequate records of employee progress should be maintained. Records of training that have been successfully completed establish a base for future performance appraisal. Measurement of growth in skills and promotion potential may not be recalled if training records and evaluations are not initiated and continued. Employees have a right to expect evaluations, and usually consider objectively prepared statements about their performance a mark of management's caring about employees.

6

Front Desk Receptionist

INTRODUCTION

The Front Desk Receptionist is responsible for assisting and directing tenants/guests/owners, monitoring incoming enquiries and ensuring proper check in procedures are followed. This position also provides customer service support to the guests and owners. This ever smiling happy person has administrative skills and needs limited supervision to take the decision in every parties interest.

Front Desk/Concierge Cast Members work in an environment with a high level of Guest interaction. These roles involve the use of computer based systems, resolving challenging Guest situations and cash handling.

Responsibilities may include checking Guests in and out of resorts, assisting Guests with itinerary planning and ticket sales, tagging and delivering luggage, and providing information to Guests. Cast Members receive Theme Park admission and discounts at select dining, merchandise and recreation locations. Full-time Cast Members may be eligible to receive medical, dental and vision benefits, plus paid vacation and sick days.

The purpose of the Front Desk Lead is to handle the daily operation of the Front Desk activities, reservations, and their coordination with other departments. Responsibilities include training and scheduling of Front Desk personnel as directed by the Front Office Manager. Must be willing and able to work any shift as necessary as dictated by the needs of the Resort to insure adequate coverage at all times. Assist in maintaining proper working relationships between the Front Desk, Housekeeping, Maintenance, and Sales departments. Prepare daily reports as directed by Front Office Manager. Track and maintain housekeeping/maintenance reports on a daily basis. Ensure the satisfaction of all guests by implementing and maintaining proper Guest/Owner relation programmes. Respond to Guest/Owner Issues. Assist in maintaining continued training for Front Desk staff. Assist in coaching, counseling, and developing of Front Desk staff as necessary.

The award-winning Nickelodeon Family Suites Resort has welcomed guests to the Orlando area for the past 4 years. With a management team that has always been on the cutting edge with innovative ideas designed to make family travel more enjoyable, they are poised once again to make their mark on the resort industry.

Partnering with the number one kid's television network, Nickelodeon, the first-ever Nickelodeon themed resort premiered in Spring 2005. The Nickelodeon Family Suites showcases a 25 million dollar infusion of water park attractions, Nickelodeon themed suites, banquet space, character breakfasts and a show room hosting Nickelodeon entertainment nightly. The resort is a world class resort destination - a virtual city where "Kids Rule."

At the first-ever Nickelodeon Family Suites, We are seeking positive, energetic employees who desire to be part of an industry leading team, and are prepared to exceed our guest's expectations daily. Our Human Resources Department looks forward to helping you soak up the Nickelodeon Family Suites Values. Become part of our world-class team where we live by the motto: It's a cool place for families, a hot place for kids, where employees make IT happen! The first-ever Nickelodeon Family Suites by Holiday Inn is seeking "A" level talent for our Front Desk Team.

Resort, motel, and resort desk clerks perform a variety of services for guests of resorts, motels, and other lodging establishments. Regardless of the type of accommodation, most desk clerks have similar responsibilities. Primarily, they register arriving guests, assign rooms, and check guests out at the end of their stay. They also keep records of room assignments and other registration information on computers. When guests check out, they prepare and explain the charges, as well as process payments.

Front desk clerks are always in the public eye and, through their attitude and behaviour, greatly influence the public's impressions of the establishment. When answering questions about services, checkout times, the local community, or other matters of public interest, clerks must be courteous and helpful. Should guests report problems with their rooms, clerks contact members of the housekeeping or maintenance staff to correct them.

In some smaller resorts and motels, clerks may have a variety of additional responsibilities usually performed by specialized employees in larger establishments. In these places, the desk clerk is often responsible for all front office operations, information, and services. These clerks, for example, may perform the work of a bookkeeper, advance reservation agent, cashier, laundry attendant, and telephone switchboard operator.

WORKING CONDITIONS

Working conditions vary for different types of information clerks, but most clerks work in areas that are clean, well lit, and relatively quiet. This is especially true for information clerks who greet customers and visitors and usually work in highly visible areas that are furnished to make a good impression. Reservation agents and interviewing clerks who spend much of their day talking on the telephone, however, commonly work away from the public, often in large centralized reservation or phone centres. Because a number of agents or clerks may share the same work space, it may be crowded and noisy. Interviewing clerks may conduct surveys on the street, in shopping malls, or go door to door.

Although most information clerks work a standard 40-hour week, about 3 out of 10 work part time. Some high school and college students work part time as information clerks, after school or during vacations. Some jobs—such as those in the transportation industry, hospitals, and resorts, in particular—may require working evenings, late night shifts, weekends, and holidays. This is also the case for a growing number of new accounts clerks who work for large banks with call centres that are staffed around the clock. Interviewing clerks conducting surveys or other research may mainly work evenings or weekends. In general, employees with the least seniority tend to be assigned the less desirable shifts.

The work performed by information clerks may be repetitious and stressful. For example, many receptionists spend all day answering telephones while performing additional clerical or secretarial tasks. Reservation agents and travel clerks work under stringent time constraints or have quotas on the number of calls answered or reservations made. Additional stress is caused by technology that enables management to electronically monitor use of computer systems, tape record telephone calls, or limit the time spent on each call.

The work of resort, motel, and resort desk clerks and transportation ticket agents also can be stressful when trying to serve the needs of difficult or angry customers.

When flights are canceled, reservations mishandled, or guests are dissatisfied, these clerks must bear the brunt of the customers' anger. Resort desk clerks and ticket agents may be on their feet most of the time, and ticket agents may have to lift heavy baggage. In addition, prolonged exposure to a video display terminal may lead to eye strain for the many information clerks who work with computers.

EMPLOYMENT

Resort, motel, and resort desk clerks held about 159,000 jobs in 1998. This occupation is well suited to flexible work schedules, as over 1 in 4 desk clerks works part time. Because resorts and motels need to be staffed 24 hours a day, evening and weekend work is common.

Although hiring requirements for information clerk jobs vary from industry to industry, a high school diploma or its equivalent is the most common educational requirement. Increasingly, familiarity or experience with computers and good interpersonal skills are often equally important to employers. For new account clerk and airline reservation and ticket agent jobs, some college education may be preferred.

Many information clerks deal directly with the public, so a professional appearance and pleasant personality are important. A clear speaking voice and fluency in the English language also are essential because these employees frequently use the telephone or public address systems. Good spelling and computer literacy are often needed, particularly because most work involves considerable computer use. It also is increasingly helpful for those wishing to enter the lodging or travel industries to speak a foreign language fluently.

With the exception of airline reservation and transportation ticket agents, orientation and training for information clerks usually takes place on the job. For example, orientation for resort and motel desk clerks usually includes an explanation of the job duties and information about the establishment, such as room locations and available services. New employees learn job tasks through on-the-job training under the guidance of a supervisor or an experienced clerk. They often need additional training in how to use the computerized reservation, room assignment, and billing systems and equipment. Most information clerks continue to receive instruction on new procedures and company policies after their initial training ends.

Receptionists usually receive on-the-job training which may include procedures for greeting visitors, operating telephone and computer systems, and distributing mail, fax, and parcel deliveries. Some employers look for applicants who already possess certain skills, such as prior computer and word processing experience, or previous formal education.

Most airline reservation and ticket agents learn their skills through formal company training programmes. In a classroom setting, they learn company and industry policies, computer systems, and ticketing procedures. They also learn to use the airline's computer system to obtain information on schedules, seat availability, and fares; to reserve space for passengers; and to plan passenger itineraries.

They must also become familiar with airport and airline code designations, regulations, and safety procedures, and may be tested on this knowledge. After completing classroom instruction, new agents work on the job with supervisors or experienced agents for a period of time. During this period, supervisors may monitor telephone conversations to improve the quality of customer service. Agents are expected to provide good service while limiting the time spent on each call without being discourteous to customers. In contrast to the airlines, automobile clubs, bus lines, and railroads tend to train their ticket agents or travel clerks on the job through short in-house classes that last several days.

Most banks prefer to hire college graduates for new account clerk positions. Nevertheless, many new accounts clerks without college degrees start out as bank tellers and are promoted by demonstrating excellent communication skills and motivation to learn new skills. If a new accounts clerk has not been a teller before, he or she will often receive such training and work for several months as a teller. In both cases, new accounts clerks undergo formal training regarding the bank's procedures, products, and services.

Advancement for information clerks usually comes about either by transfer to a position with more responsibilities or by promotion to a supervisory position. Most companies fill office and administrative support supervisory and managerial positions by promoting individuals within their organization, so information clerks who acquire additional skills, experience, and training improve their advancement opportunities. Receptionists, interviewers, and new accounts clerks with word processing or other clerical skills may advance to a better paying job as a secretary or administrative assistant. Within the airline industry, a ticket agent may advance to lead worker on the shift.

Additional training is helpful in preparing information clerks for promotion. In the lodging industry, clerks can improve their chances for advancement by taking home or group study courses in lodging management, such as those sponsored by the Educational Institute of the American Resort and Motel Association. In some industries—such as lodging, banking, or the airlines—workers commonly are promoted through the ranks. Positions such as airline reservation agent or resort and motel desk clerk offer good opportunities for qualified workers to get started in the business. In a number of industries, a college degree may be required for advancement to management ranks.

Employment of resort, motel, and resort desk clerks is expected to grow about as fast as the average for all occupations through 2008, as more resorts, motels, and other lodging establishments are built and occupancy rates rise. Job opportunities for resort and motel desk clerks will result from an unusually high turnover rate.

These openings occur each year as thousands of workers transfer to other occupations that offer better pay and advancement opportunities or simply leave the workforce altogether. Opportunities for part-time work should continue to be plentiful, as nearly all front desks are staffed 24 hours a day, 7 days a week.

Employment of resort and motel desk clerks should be favourably affected by an increase in business and leisure travel. Shifts in travel preference away from long vacations and towards long weekends and other, more frequent, shorter trips also should increase demand as this trend increases the total number of nights spent in resorts. The expansion of smaller, budget resorts relative to larger, luxury establishments reflects a change in the composition of the resort and motel industry. As employment shifts from luxury resorts to more "no-frills" operations, the proportion of resort desk clerks should increase in relation to staff such as waiters and waitresses and recreation workers.

However, the growing effort to cut labour costs while moving towards more efficient service is expected to slow the growth of desk clerk employment. The role of the front desk is changing as some of the more traditional duties are automated. New technologies automating check-in and check-out procedures now allow guests to bypass the front desk in many larger establishments, reducing staffing needs. The expansion of other technologies, such as interactive television and computer systems to dispense information, should further impact employment in the future as such services become more widespread.

Employment of desk clerks is sensitive to cyclical swings in the economy. During recessions, vacation and business travel declines and resorts and motels need fewer clerks. Similarly, desk clerk employment is affected by seasonal fluctuations in travel during high and low tourist seasons.

Earnings vary widely by occupation and experience. Annual earnings ranged from less than $11,750 for the lowest paid 10 per cent of resort clerks to over $39,540 for the top 10 per cent of reservation agents in 1998. Salaries of reservation and transportation ticket agents and travel clerks tend to be significantly higher than for other information clerks, while resort, motel, and resort desk clerks tend to earn quite a bit less, as the following tabulation of median annual earnings shows.

Reservation and transportation ticket agents and travel clerks	$22,120
New accounts clerks	21,340
Receptionists	18,620
Interviewing clerks	18,540
Resort, motel, and resort desk clerks	15,160

Earnings of resort and motel desk clerks also vary considerably depending on the location, size, and type of establishment in which they work. For example, clerks at large luxury resorts and those located in metropolitan and resort areas generally pay clerks more than less exclusive or "budget" establishments and those located in less populated areas.

In early 1999, the Federal Government typically paid salaries ranging from $16,400 to $18,100 a year to beginning receptionists with a high school diploma or 6 months of experience. The average annual salary for all receptionists employed by the Federal Government was about $22,700 in 1999. In addition to their hourly wage, full-time information clerks who work evenings, nights, weekends, or holidays may receive shift differential pay. Some employers offer educational assistance to their employees. Reservation and transportation ticket agents and travel clerks receive free or reduced rate travel on their company's carriers for themselves and their immediate family and, in some companies, for friends.

ACCEPTING VISA CARDS AT RESORTS

If you have signed a merchant agreement to accept Visa cards, you should accept all Visa cards, irrespective of which bank issued them. Banks right around the world offer their customers a range of different Visa cards. This includes Classic cards, Gold cards, Infinite cards, Visa Electron cards, Visa Business cards and Visa Purchasing – as well as cards issued in conjunction with other major corporations.

These cards may look different, but they all:

- Have the same basic card elements and security features
- Guarantee payment to you when Visa acceptance procedures are correctly followed

HOW TO IDENTIFY A VISA CARD

There are many different kinds of Visa cards. All share the same essential card elements and security features. The unembossed Visa card is the new Visa product which has the card number and information printed on the front of the card, making the surface of the card smooth instead of being raised. The unembossed Visa card does not share some of the card elements as the normal Visa card. Visa Electron cards also have slightly different features, can only be accepted at an electronic terminal and always require authorization.

- *Visa flag symbol*: Always on the front, right hand side, but can be above or below the hologram.
- *Microprinting:* Should be visible around the Visa flag symbol.
- *Dove hologram:* Always on the front right hand side, and the dove appears to fly when the card is tilted back and forth. The Visa Infinite card, issued by some banks to their very best customers, has a different hologram design.
- *Four-digit number:* Printed above or below the account number. This should always begin with a '4', and should match the first four digits of the account number. If it does not, or if it is missing, the card may be counterfeit.
- *Account number:* Must be even, clear and straight, with all numbers the same size and shape. May be embossed or unembossed.
- *Embossed letter V:* Will be present on embossed Visa cards. On some cards, it may be shown as CV, BV, or PV. For unembossed Visa cards, this feature will not be present.

- *Cardholder name:* Letters must be even and straight. Whenever you are processing a transaction, this should be compared with the cardholder's signature. For unembossed Visa cards and for some prepaid Visa cards, a cardholder name may not be present.
- *Dates:* Whenever you are processing a transaction, you should check the dates are valid. If you are presented with a card where the dates are not valid, you must obtain authorization.
- *Signature Panel*: Look for the signature on the signature panel. You should see the repeated word "Visa" printed diagonally in blue and gold.
- *CVV2*: There should be a unique three-digit code printed after the account number on the signature panel.
- *Chip:* Many Visa cards now have a chip. If you still have a magnetic stripe terminal, these can be accepted in the normal way. If you have a chip-capable terminal, the card should be inserted into the chip reader for the duration of the transaction.

VISA ELECTRON CARD

- *Visa Electron symbol*: Always on the front, right hand side at either the top or bottom of the card. These cards may have a Dove hologram. Occasionally they may also have the Visa flag symbol and well as Visa Electron symbol.
- *Last four digits:* A full account number will not always be printed on the card. Check that the last four digits on the card correspond to the last four digits shown on your terminal.
- *Electronic use only:* Printed on the front of the card to remind you that Visa Electron cards cannot be used with manual systems. This may appear in other languages.
- *Signature panel*: May appear on the front or back of the card. You should see the repeated word "Electron" printed diagonally in blue, red and yellow.

The Visa reservation service helps you to guarantee room reservations and avoids losses from 'No Show' guests.

However, whenever you are using the service, it is important that you correctly follow these simple steps. Failure to do so may result in unnecessary customer queries and complaints.

GUARANTEEING A RESERVATION

While speaking with the guest:

- Ask the guest for:
  - The Visa card account number

- The card expiration date
- The cardholder's name as it appears on the card
- The billing address and phone number.

- Tell the guest:
  - The room rate (plus tax)
  - The resort's address
  - The confirmation code for the guaranteed reservation
    Be sure to keep a record of the code for future reference.
- Be sure to explain:
  - Guaranteed rooms are held until check out time on the day following the scheduled arrival
  - The deadline for cancelling reservations is 6:00pm on the scheduled arrival date
  - If the room is not claimed or cancelled in time, the cardholder will be billed for one night's stay (plus tax).

Note: If your deadline is earlier than 6.00pm on the scheduled arrival date, tell the guest the date and time of your deadline, and send a follow up mailing with the cancellation policy.

- Following up...

If your guest requests a written confirmation, be sure to include:

- The Visa card account number
- The card expiration date
- The cardholder's name as it appears on the card
- The room rate with tax, and any other appropriate details about the accommodation
- The resort's address
- The confirmation code
- The guest's rights and responsibilities under the Visa Reservation Service
- The date and time that the cancellation privileges expire.

HANDLING CANCELLATIONS

While speaking with the guest:

- Provide a cancellation code.
- Advise the guest to keep a record of the code for future reference.
  Following up...
- Write 'cancelled' on the reservation form and record the cancellation code provided to the guest.
- If requested, provide a written cancellation with:
  - The Visa card account number
  - The card expiration date

- The cardholder's name as it appears on the card
- The cancellation code.

HANDLING 'NO SHOW' TRANSACTIONS

If a guest fails to cancel a reservation or claim the room, you may submit a Visa sales draft for one night's accommodation, plus any applicable tax. Simply write 'No Show' on the signature panel of the sales draft and complete all parts of the sales draft normally.

HANDLING OVERBOOKINGS

If the guaranteed accommodation is not available when the guest arrives, you must at least provide the following at your resort's expense:

- Comparable accommodation at a resort of at least equal quality for one night
- Transportation to that establishment
- Forwarding of all messages and calls to the establishment
- A three-minute telephone call

THE VISA ADVANCE DEPOSIT SERVICE

Visa cards may be used when your resort requires an advance deposit to guarantee a reservation. This service also avoids the delay and confusion of handling personal or foreign cheques.

However, whenever you are using the service, it is important that you correctly follow these simple steps. Failure to do so may result in unnecessary customer queries and complaints.

While speaking with a guest:

- Ask the guest for:
  - The Visa card account number
  - The expiration date
  - The cardholder's name as it appears on the card
  - The cardholder's billing address and telephone number
  - The expected arrival date and length of stay.
- Tell the guest:
  - The room rate (including tax)
  - The amount of the advance deposit that will be billed on their Visa card. This must not exceed the cost of 14 nights accommodation
  - That the deposit will be deducted from the final bill
  - That you will hold the accommodation for the period covered by the advance deposit
  - The resort's address

  - The confirmation code of the reservation
  - To keep a record of the confirmation code for their future reference.
- Be sure to explain:
  - Your resort's cancellation requirements
  - That all or part of the deposit may be forfeited if cancellation requirements are not met
  - The date and time the cancellation privileges expire
  - That a written copy of the cancellation policy will be mailed to the guest Following up.
- When filling out the Advance Deposit sales draft, be sure to include:
  - The Visa card account number, expiration date, and the cardholder's name
  - The cardholder's billing address and telephone number
  - The resort identification
  - The words 'Advance Deposit' in the signature panel of the sales draft
  - The scheduled arrival date
  - The reservation confirmation code
  - The transaction date
  - The authorization code, if the transaction is above the floor limit
  - The date and time the cancellation privileges expire
  - The amount of the advance deposit.
- Mail a written reservation confirmation, along with a copy of the sales draft, within three business days.

The confirmation should include:

- The resort's cancellation policy
- The guest's rights and responsibilities under the Advance Deposit Service
- The resort's refund policy, which must allow for a complete refund of the guest's deposit if a reservation is cancelled before the specified deadline.

HANDLING ADVANCE DEPOSIT CANCELLATIONS

While speaking with the guest:

- Provide a cancellation code.
- Advise the guest to keep a record of the code for their future reference. Following...
- Write the word "cancelled" on the reservation form, along with the cancellation code provided to the guest.
- Determine the refund amount and prepare a credit voucher. The voucher should include:

  - The Visa card account number, expiration date, and the cardholder's name
  - The cardholder's billing address
  - The resort identification
  - The cancellation code
  - The words "Advance Deposit" on the signature panel of the sales draft
  - The transaction date
  - The amount of the advance deposit
- Mail the cardholder a copy of the credit vouchers within three business days.
- Include the credit voucher with your daily deposits.

AUTHORIZE THE VISA TRANSACTION

It is important for you to obtain authorization whenever possible, particularly in the following instances:

- If the total transaction amount is above your resort's floor limit
- If the card is not signed
- If the transaction involves suspicious or unusual circumstances
- If the card is a Visa Electron card

Note: the Visa Electron card works like any other Visa card. Procedures at the point of sale do not change except that it must always be authorized through a POS terminal. The authorization will stay valid for the length of the guest's stay. For stays longer than two weeks, we recommend that you close out the guest folio and bill the guests every two weeks.

ESTIMATED AUTHORIZATIONS

The estimated authorization procedure allows you to estimate the final transaction amount and receive the protection of an authorization before the guest checks out. However, whenever you are using the service, it is important that you correctly follow these simple steps. Failure to do so may result in unnecessary customer queries and complaints.

When the guest checks in:

- Estimate the guest's total charges based on:
  - The expected length of stay
  - The room rate including tax
  - Any estimated miscellaneous charges
- Compare the estimate with your floor limit
- Proceed just as to the following procedures

Below the floor limit Check the current Visa Card Recovery Bulletin to ensure it has not been reported lost, stolen or fraud.

Above the floor limit:

- Obtain authorization for the estimated amount do not over-estimate the amount authorized, as this will result in customer complaints
- Record in the guest folio/sales draft the date, amount authorized and approval code. Authorization reversal
- If the authorized amount is higher than the value of the guest's final bill, it is important that you process an authorization reversal for the difference between the authorized amount and the value of the cardholder's final bill.

REVISING ESTIMATED AUTHORIZATIONS

You may want to monitor charges to the guest's account to determine whether you need to revise your estimate. If the revised estimate exceeds the floor limit and:

Do this:

- No previous authorization was obtained
- Authorize the total amount
- Previous authorization was obtained
- Obtain authorization approval for the additional incremental amount(s) separately
- For all revised estimates
- Record on the guest folio/sales draft the date, amount authorized and approval code

When the Guest Checks out:

- When the guest is ready, you should determine the final bill and proceed just as to the following procedures.
- If the estimated amount is:

Do this:

- Below the floor limit
- No need for authorization Above the floor limit and no previous authorization was obtained
- Authorize the total amount

Above the floor limit and previous authorizations have been obtained, you are protected for the sum of the authorized amounts plus 15 per cent of that sum.

To determine whether an additional authorization is required:

- Add up the sum of all authorized amounts
- To that sum add 15 per cent
- Compare this figure to the final transaction amount
- Authorize the total amount

Then do one of these three things:

1. If the final transaction amount is less than the sum of all authorized amounts plus 15 per cent
2. If the final transaction amount is greater than the sum of all authorized amounts plus 15 per cent.
3. No need for authorization

Obtain an additional authorization for the difference between the final transaction amount and the sum of the authorizations already received.

THE VISA PRIORITY CHECK OUT SERVICE

The Visa Priority Check Out Service is a quick and convenient procedure for you and your guests – allowing them and you to avoid delays at peak check-out times.

However, whenever you are using the service, it is important that you correctly follow these simple steps. Failure to do so may result in unnecessary customer queries and complaints.

CHECK OUT PROCEDURES

During the guest's stay:

- Describe the convenience of the Visa Priority Check Out Service. Then, if the guest requests Priority Check Out:
  - Ensure that you have recorded the Visa card account number, expiration date, and cardholder name on a Visa sales draft
  - Give the guest a Visa Priority Check Out agreement
  - Inform the guest of your policy regarding any charges discovered after check out
  - Ask the guest to return the completed signed agreement any time before check out.
- When the guest returns the agreement, verify that:
  - It is signed
  - The mailing address is included so that you can send a copy of the final bill after the guest's departure
  - The cardholder account number on the check out agreement matches the account number of the sales draft.
- After the guest's stay:
  - Complete the sales draft by entering the total charges incurred during the stay, including any restaurant, telephone or miscellaneous charges
  - Consult your authorization procedures to determine whether authorization is required at this time, and if so, obtain an authorization.

- If requested, mail to the guest within three business days after check out:
  - A completed sales draft indicating the final amount with the words "Priority Check Out" on the signature panel, or a printout of the Visa billing
  - The itemized resort bill
  - Another copy of the Visa Priority Check Out agreement.

Retain a copy of the itemized bill and completed check out agreement for at least six months.

ADD CHARGES TO A VISA CARD AFTER CHECK OUT

This procedure allows you to bill Visa cardholders for any additional charges which are discovered after they have checked out – such as room service, telephone or mini bar charges. However, whenever you are billing guests for additional charges, it is important that you correctly follow these simple steps.

AFTER THE GUEST CHECKS OUT

You may deposit a separate sales draft for delayed charges, with the words "Signature on File" on the signature panel of the sales draft. Note: You should only do so if the guest has agreed to be responsible for such charges. You may not submit a separate or amended sales draft for loss, theft or damage to the room. Mail the guest a copy of the sales draft with a detailed explanation of the additional charges. Failure to do so will almost certainly result in customer queries and possible complaints. The cash disbursement service lets your resort offer Visa Gold/Premier cardholders free access to extra cash whenever they need it.

To offer this service to your guests, use a Cash Disbursement sales draft and take the following steps:

- When they check in, the guest must confirm that they will use their Visa card to pay for the resort stay
- The guest may receive a maximum cash disbursement of US$250 during their stay at the resort
- Before disbursement, ask the cardholder for identification that includes an identification number
- Imprint the Visa card
- Verify the expiration date.

TERMS AND CONDITIONS

Brief guide to the terms and conditions of stay at a Resort, and the terms and conditions for the usage of this internet site. Please allow 12 hours notice prior to your expected arrival to process the booking.

Confirmation of a booking by the client is deemed acceptance of these terms:

- *Prices:* All published rates include VAT or local service charges at the current rate. Accommodation rates are per room per night with meal plans as indicated. The Resort reserves the right to alter prices for any reason up to the date of booking or up to 12 weeks prior to arrival, whichever is the later. After such dates, prices may only be altered to reflect a change in the rate of VAT or local service charge and taxes or for any other reason outside of the control of the Resort, in which case the changes will be notified to the Client. In the latter event, the Client may cancel the booking without cost.
- *Availability:* All rooms and rates offered by the Resort are subject to availability and the discretion of the Resort manager. Limited numbers of suitable rooms may be allocated to individual rates, packages or promotions and, when these allocations are taken up, remaining available rooms may be offered to the Client at a higher price.
- *Bookings:* Bookings must be guaranteed for the first night's accommodation by a major credit or debit card, by payment of a deposit or by agreement in writing with a company, travel agent or resort booking agency. At the discretion of the Resort, full pre-payment may be required. At least 3 working days are required to process credit and debit card payments and 5 working days to process cheque payments.
- *Arrival and departure:* Bedrooms are usually available from 2pm local time on the day of arrival. Check out is by 12 noon local time. There may be occasions, at times of high demand, when clients can check in and use the entire resort facilities, but the bedroom is still being prepared.
- *Car parking:* Most Resorts have their own car park, which is usually free to residents. Some Resorts, however, have limited on-site parking and Clients are advised to check with the Resort whether there is a charge for off-site parking. The Resort does not accept responsibility for damage to, or for theft from, or for theft of vehicles parked on Resort premises.
- *Cancellations, amendments and non-arrivals:* When the booking is confirmed, a reservation number and access code will be supplied. This must be retained for access to the booking in the event of the need for cancellation and/or amendment. There is no charge, and any deposit paid will be returned, if a guaranteed reservation is cancelled at any time up to 2pm local time on the day of arrival.

In the event of non-arrival or cancellation after 2pm local time and where the booking has been guaranteed, a charge equivalent to one night's accommodation at the package rate at which the reservation was made will be levied. Normal terms of payment apply to these charges. For this purpose the Resort reserves the right to set-off the amount payable for such cancellation against the Client's credit card without prior notice or approval of the Client, where applicable.

If the Resort cancels before 2pm local time on the scheduled day of arrival, the Resort's liability to the Client will be no greater than the amount paid by the client in respect of any booking.

If the Resort cancels after 2pm local time on the day of arrival, the Resort's liability will be limited to the charge for one night's accommodation. Where possible the Resort may but is not obliged nor will it be liable to find alternative accommodation for the Client in the event that the Resort is unable to accommodate the Client.

A cancellation number will be provided at the time of cancellation and this should be retained for future reference.

PAYMENT

Settlement of the bill in full, less any advance payments must be made prior to departure from the Resort. Upon arrival the Resort reserves the right to request preauthorisation of the Client's credit or debit card or where payment is to be by cash, request the Client to place cash up to an amount of 1.5 times the room rate multiplied by the number of nights booked. All major credit and debit cards are accepted. Company cheques are not accepted without prior clearance.

Please contact the Resort prior to arrival. Accounts may only be forwarded for payment on completion by the Client and formal acceptance by the Resort of an application for credit facilities, which may be withdrawn at any time. Credit facilities are not offered to private individuals. All sums are due for payment on presentation of the invoice. In the event of any query relating to the invoice, the Client must notify the Resort within 7 days of the invoice date and the Client's obligation to pay all outstanding balances immediately will not be affected.

Personal Information and payment details may be used by the system to determine automatically the appropriate way to fulfil your order. In order to process a booking, your Personal Information and payment details may be passed to third party service providers and, where we are lawfully requested to do so, regulatory authorities. Such third party service providers will have access to the Personal Information needed to perform the relevant service. They may not, however, use your Personal Information for any other purposes and are required to process your Personal Information in accordance with the Data Protection Act 1998.

Hospitality is an exciting and multifaceted industry that offers a variety of career opportunities to those who have earned a resort/restaurant management degree. Careers with resort, restaurant, airline, cruise line, gaming, and wine and spirit companies are readily available to such graduates. In addition, careers with service firms that support hospitality companies in the areas of accounting, consulting, real estate development, architecture, interior design, real estate brokerage, resort valuation, investment banking, mortgage brokerage, insurance, advertising, and technology are also available to those with hospitality degrees.

Although dynamic and interesting, the business of hospitality presents many challenges. For example, hospitality businesses operate on low profit margins with fluctuating sales volumes. The ability to forecast revenues and control expenses is critical to achieving budgeted profits and a favourable return on investment for the owners of the company. Also, because hospitality businesses are labour intensive, scheduling employee hours so they are consistent with forecasted revenues and monitoring payroll cost daily are just two major management challenges.

While a hospitality business typically requires a relatively low level of operating inventories, it requires a relatively high level of capital for its real estate component. This component often includes buildings, operating systems, guest room furniture, and restaurant equipment. Securing financing to acquire these assets is a continuing challenge for management.

Finally, hospitality businesses rely heavily on the discretionary income of their customers. During a weak economy, when household discretionary income is low, the hospitality industry usually suffers. High-end establishments, such as resorts and fine dining restaurants, normally feel the effects of a weak economy first, but eventually, the entire industry feels the financial pain. However, as soon as the economy takes a turn for the better, consumers return, discretionary spending increases, and the industry prospers. Accurately predicting these economic fluctuations, and knowing when to buy and sell hospitality assets, can be financially lucrative for the astute hospitality investor. The financial tools utilized by modern-day management to address these challenges and opportunities are the focus of this book. Understanding of these financial tools and applying them to the challenges and opportunities they will soon face when they take jobs in the industry will serve hospitality graduates well throughout their business careers.

Children aged 15 years and under must be accompanied by a responsible adult to ensure that the children's behaviour is appropriate for other guests within the Resort. Subject to the availability of suitable accommodation, children aged 15 years and under stay free when sharing a room with two adults, on the basis of one child per adult. Children sharing with one adult or in their own room pay 50 per cent of the adult rate. At the discretion of the Resort, children may be excluded from certain events or promotions where deemed unsuitable or inappropriate.

Where Resorts have health and leisure facilities, children aged 15 years and under must be accompanied by an adult at all times and they are not permitted to use gymnasium equipment or the sunbed/tanning equipment. Under 5's are excluded from the sauna, spa pools and solaria areas and must be accompanied in the swimming pool by an adult at all times. Clients must read and follow the conditions of use displayed at such facilities.

In the interest and safety of children, some health and leisure clubs may be subject to specific time allocations for use of the facilities by children. Clients are advised to check with the Resort beforehand. The Client is responsible for controlling the pet and will be liable for any damage, soilage or injury however caused by the pet.

The Resort reserves the right to judge acceptable levels of noise or behaviour of Clients, guests or representatives, who must take all steps for corrective action as requested by the Resort. In the event of failure to comply with management requests, the Resort may terminate the booking or stop any event immediately without being liable for any refund or compensation.

It is the policy of the resort not to discriminate on the grounds of race, colour, nationality, creed, sex, marital status, age, ethnic origin or disability. Clients, their employees, guests and all sub-contractors engaged by or on behalf of the Client are expected to adhere to this policy and the Resort may, without incurring any liability to the Client, remove from the Resort any person or persons offending against this policy.

FRONT-OFFICE/BACK OFFICE RELOCATION FRENZY

Restructuring, re-engineering, downsizing, rightsizing, merger mania, unbundling, outsourcing - all of these expressions are 1990s corporate jargon for workplace changes that are sweeping the nation. At the local level, these changes are remapping the regions of growth and decline.

Like the movement of U.S. manufacturing companies overseas during the past 20 years, today's corporate wanderlust is driven by a search for lower operating costs. But unlike the flight of manufacturing, many of today's corporate moves remain on home soil. Today's relocation manager is looking for lower costs but also requires an English speaking, well-educated workforce, advanced technology, excellent telecommunications, stable utility service, and extensive air transport to make a move successful.

State and local incentives to attract footloose companies are part and parcel of the relocation equation. The bidding war has pitted state against state, municipality against municipality, in a game of chicken that no local government alone can afford to give up. Relocation frenzy, makes local tax bases more volatile. The receiving community, is likely to expand infrastructure, increase borrowing, and make some tax changes to accommodate the newcomer.

The losing community is faced with higher unemployment, excess infrastructure capacity fixed costs to finance that infrastructure, and lower revenues. Whichever side of the market we are on, these changes will affect our work, our portfolio, and our decision making. By, taking a walk through the land of relocation, we can get a look at the trends that are out there.

THE FRONT OFFICE

The journey, begins with a comparison of the relocation of Fortune 100 headquarters in 1985 and 1995. Among this group, National Municipal Research found a few moves, mostly from New York City to other locations and mostly, among oil and gas companies. Exxon moved from New York City to Irving, Texas; Mobil moved from New York to Fairfax, Virginia; and Texaco from New York to White Plains, New York.

The Oil and Gas Journal, restructuring ill the oil industry, is far from over. The Quaker State Corporation recently moved its headquarters from Oil City, Pennsylvania, to the Dallas area. Quaker State had been a loyal resident of Pennsylvania since 1931.

Other companies moved their headquarters from urban centres to suburban locations. Sears, for example, moved from downtown Chicago to a huge facility in distant Hoffman Estates, Illinois. JC Penney moved its headquarters from Dallas to the northern suburb of Plano, Texas. And United Parcel Service has moved twice in recent history: from New York City to Greenwich, Connecticut, and later to Atlanta. Companies also are moving their headquarters to smaller metropolitan areas, as did Thrifty, Payless, Inc., which moved from Los Angeles to Wilsonville, Oregon, near Portland.

The New York metropolitan region is home to the highest percentage of large corporate headquarters, followed by Chicago, Los Angeles, Philadelphia, Boston, San Francisco, Dallas, Fort Worth, Houston, Detroit, Minneapolis, Cleveland, and Atlanta, just as to a report in Economic Development Review by Growth Strategies Organization (GSO), Inc. In 1993, Los Angeles, Philadelphia, Boston, and Houston enhanced their shares of corporate headquarters at the expense of New York, Chicago, and Detroit. GSO also found a "modest shift of headquarters from the largest metropolitan areas to MSAS with populations in the 1 to 3 million range." These communities seem to offer the best compromise between lifestyle quality and availability of needed services. Hub airports were cited as one locational advantage for moving to a smaller MSA.

On the whole, large corporate headquarters tend to be loyal to the communities they grew up in. WalMart has stayed in Bentonville, Arkansas, and Coca-Cola in Atlanta. Dennis Donovan, senior manager of the Wadley-Donovan Group, Ltd., has explained why there are so few headquarters moves. "Corporate CEOs" he said, "are looking for specialized locations for their headquarters, and only a few places fit the bill. The location must be part of the global community with extensive international connections. Air service must be excellent and nearby, and which services as banking, courier services, and other support functions help anchor a large corporate headquarters. The image of the location also is important."

Headquarters relocation most commonly occurs within a metropolitan area or when there is a merger, downsizing, or decentralization of functions. More common today is the decentralization trend because it has become easier to locate certain back-office functions in remote locations. Donovan cited Metropolitan Life, which broke up its divisions and moved into six or seven locations.

THE BACK OFFICE

Such back-office functions as accounting, check processing, payroll, data processing, and information management are being spliced and diced and moved around the geographic chess board. Advances in technology and telecommunications also are creating new clusters of back-office functions.

Vast storehouses of information about corporate assets - inventory control, accounting, sales, production, and market conditions - have expanded the potential for corporate data and information centres. Systems for organizing and analysing this information have become standardized to the point at which companies can outsource, or contract with other companies for a service. M. Ross Boyle wrote in Economic Development Review that "until recently, these centres were always found within or near the corporate office building. Some companies now are concluding that this proximity to the corporate decision-makers is unnecessary and may not be cost-effective. They can be located in communities with outstanding telecommunications and mail service, plus at least adequate air service."

Boyle continued: "The justification for shifting these facilities to a location some distance from the corporate headquarters lies in the lower operating costs and greater productivity, that can sometimes be achieved by, such a move." The "help desk" function that grew up with the computer industry is one example of a back-office function that is finding new applications for companies that are willing to implement the technology.

For example, Taco Bell uses a system wide help desk that is available to answer questions about hardware, software, procurement, and asset management for its corporate operations, as well as for its 4,00 restaurants. The help desk is credited with cutting costs so low that the chain is able to continue to offer its 59-cent taco and free drink refills without compromising profitability.

Colleen McCormick, research as sociate at the Gartner Group, specializes in covering 22, large help-desk outsourcers. These companies handle calls from around the world for large international corporations. McCormick cited the South, Midwest, and California as areas for help centres. Texas, she noted, has a lot of call centres. Some hot back-office locations have become so overcrowded that the job market is tight or non-existent. Mark Klender of Deloitte and Touche told the Wall Street Journal last year that Sacramento is one such market. Phoenix, Omaha, suburban San Francisco, Salt Lake City, Tucson, Des Moines, and Seattle are other frequently mentioned back-office locations.

In Florida, Tampa, Orlando, and Jacksonville, as well as newcomers Pensacola and Tallahassee, are strong back-office markets. In February, the Walt Disney Corporation announced that it is looking at Tampa for 500 back-office jobs. Insurance company USF&G chose Tampa for 500 back-office jobs, and American Express Travel Service will be adding 100 jobs there.

In investigating the criteria used to choose new back-office locations, one repeatedly hears "education, education, education." Employees who work computers or toil on a "telephone assembly line,, need to be articulate and to think on their feet in order to provide service to the customers at the other end. Winning locations tend to be those with good schools, colleges, and universities or specialized training programmes. For example, Fitch Investors Service recently moved its corporate and municipal database operations to Powell, Wyoming. Aside from the fact that Chairman Russell Frazer lives a drive away, Fitch had struck a deal with Powell's Northwest College, part of the state University, system. The two organizations will design courses so that students can work at the facility.

Donovan underscored the importance to a successful back-office move of a good supply of well-educated, entry-level labour with solid basic skills and moderate wage levels. Air service is important, although it need not be as extensive as for corporate headquarters. The prestige of the address is less important than other factors. "The nation's urban centres missed the boat in the early 1990s" commented Donovan. That was a time when high office vacancies had shrunk the cost of office space in many localities to levels comparable to those in suburban and exurban locations. However, "nobody stepped up to the plate to address three key ingredients: parking facilities, increasing available floor sizes, and, most important, improving the skills attainment of the workforce." The urban centres lost their advantage to savvier locations.

THE INCENTIVES WAR

The price tag for company moves has increased over the past five to six years, according to Bill Schweke of the Corporation for Enterprise Development. Today, it has become easier to move goods and services around, which has led to companies, playing off one jurisdiction against another. Schweke has attributed the increase in competition to "economic insecurity" on the part of local officials.

"Politicians don't want to be caught napping by not offering the same incentives as their neighbours," he said. Bidding wars have become more press worthy, and the politics of competition in the sweepstakes for corporate moves are more visible than ever before. "Today," he added, "every company that is locationally mobile expects to be given some kind of tax break to make a move."

When Columbia Health care Corporation merged with Nashville based Hospital Corporation of America, it decided to move the new company headquarters to Louisville, Kentucky. Following repeated complaints about Kentucky's provider tax and Tennessee's repeal of its hospital services tax (Tennessee has no provider tax), the company chose in 1994 to move its headquarters to Nashville. Modern Health care commented that Tennessee dropped its antitrust investigation into the company one day, after the company announced its move. The attorney general's office cited the "transaction's pro-competitive effects."

There is a growing trend towards rolling back some of the incentive competition. Factions on both the left and right ends of the political spectrum support limits on tax incentives. Criticisms range from the wastefulness of "corporate welfare" to the desire to keep government entirely of the way of enterprise. Some states have made it harder for local governments within them to use tax incentives to lure companies around the state. Ohio passed SB19 in 1994 to clarify the use of its urban enterprise zones. Ohio's enterprise zones may carry distressed designation," which gives them certain privileges. Bob Stempfer, manager of the tax incentives office of the Ohio Department of Development, there are 319 enterprise zones in the state and about 40 with the "distressed" designation.

At issue in Ohio were a number of communities that essentially were raiding each other's companies using tax incentives. A year ago, Cleveland's Mayor White attempted to block the move of a toolmaking company that was leaving for suburban Solon (he failed). Stempfer, the law generally prohibits movements from a distressed enterprise zone (Cleveland) to a non-distressed enterprise zone (Solon), but waivers may be granted with the director's approval if certain conditions are met.

The lack of control that states have over each other has led some observers to suggest federal constraints on the bidding war. Schweke has commented that today's bidding battles are analogous to those of, an earlier era in this country when the adversarial competition among states served to harm the economy giving rise to the Constitution's interstate commerce clause. Melvin Burstein and Art Rolnick have written a number of reports for the Minneapolis Federal Reserve that have criticize tax incentives as harmful to the overall economy. Burstein and Rolnick have been especially critical of intrastate bidding, in which local communities lure businesses away from each other, often with the help of state dollars. It will not be surprising if the bidding war receives attention in Washington when interstate commerce issues are addressed.

Landing a new corporate headquarters or back-office operation can be the ticket to a community's economic success. Locational changes have created new wealth in communities where little affluence existed before. Losers are faced with tax-base shock and the task of meeting public needs with fewer resources. For the foreseeable future, corporate wanderlust is likely to keep underwriters, analysts, portfolio managers, and public officials on their toes.

7

Catering Management: An Introduction

INTRODUCTION

Hospitality is probably the most diverse but specialized industry in the world. It is certainly one of the largest, employing millions of people in a bewildering array of jobs around the globe.

Sectors range from the glamourous five-star resort to the less fashionable, but arguably more specialised, institutional areas such as hospitals, industrial outfits, schools and colleges. Yet of these many different sectors, catering has to be the most challenging. Whatever the size of the catering operation, the variety of opportunities available is endless. "The sky is the limit with catering".

CATERING INDUSTRY

The food service industry encompasses those places, institutions and companies that provide meals eaten away from home. This industry includes restaurants, schools and hospital cafeterias, catering operations, and many other formats, including 'on-premises' and 'off-premises' caterings. Catering is a multifaceted segment of the food service industry. There is a niche for all types of catering businesses within the segment of catering.

The food service industry is divided into three general classifications: commercial segment, non-commercial segment, and military segment. Catering management may be defined as the task of planning, organizing, controlling a n d executing. Each activity influences the preparation and delivery of food, beverage, and related services at a competitive, yet profitable price. These activities work together to meet and exceed the customer's perception of value for his money.

CATERING SEGMENTS

Catering management is executed in many diverse ways within each of the four segments. The first, commercial segment, traditionally considered the profit generating operation, includes the independent caterer, the restaurant caterer, and the home-based caterer. The food service catering industry is segmented.

The non-commercial segment, or the 'not-forprofit' operations, consists of the following types of catering activities: business/industry accounts, school, college and university catering, health care facilities, recreational food service catering, social organizations and transportation food service catering. The military segment encompasses all catering activities involved in association with the armed forces and/or diplomatic events.

KINDS OF CATERING

There are two main types of catering on-premises and offpremises catering that may be a concern to a large and small caterer. On-premise catering for any function—banquet, reception, or event—that is held on the physical premises of the establishment or facility that is organizing/sponsoring the function.

On-premise catering differs from off-premise catering, whereby the function takes place in a remote location, such as a client's home, a park, an art gallery, or even a parking lot, and the staff, food, and decor must be transported to that location.

Off-premise catering often involves producing food at a central kitchen, with delivery to and service provided at the client's location. Part or all of the production of food may be executed or finished at the location of the event. Catering can also be classified as social catering and corporate catering. Social catering includes such events as weddings, bar and mitzwahs, high school reunions, birthday parties, and charity events.

Business catering includes such events as association conventions and meetings, civic meetings, corporate sales or stockholder meetings, recognition banquets, product launches, educational training sessions, seller-buyer meets, service awards banquets, and entertaining in hospitality suites.

ON-PREMISE CATERING

All of the required functions and services that the caterers execute are done exclusively at their own facility. For instance, a caterer within a resort or banquet hall will prepare and cater all of the requirements without taking any service or food outside the facility. Many restaurants have specialized rooms on-premise to cater to the private-party niche.

A restaurant may have a layout strategically designed with three separate dining rooms attached to a centralized commercial food production kitchen. These separate dining rooms are available at the same time to support the restaurant's operation and for reservation and overflow seating. In addition, any of the three dining rooms may be contracted out for private-event celebrations and may require their own specialized service and menu options. Other examples of on-premise catering include hospital catering, school, University/college catering.

OFF-PREMISE CATERING

Off-premise catering is serving food at a location away from the caterer's food production facility. One example of a food production facility is a freestanding commissary, which is a kitchen facility used exclusively for the preparation of foods to be served at other locations.

Other examples of production facilities include, but are not limited to, resort, restaurant, and club kitchens. In most cases there is no existing kitchen facility at the location where the food is served. Caterers provide single-event foodservice, but not all caterers are created equal. They generally fall into one of three categories:

Party Food Caterers

Party food caterers supply only the food for an event. They drop off cold foods and leave any last-minute preparation, plus service and cleanup, to others.

Hot Buffet Caterers

Hot buffet caterers provide hot foods that are delivered from their commissaries in insulated containers. They sometimes provide serving personnel at an additional charge.

Full-Service Caterers

Full-service caterers not only provide food, but frequently cook it to order on-site. They also provide service personnel at the event, plus all the necessary food-related equipment- china, glassware, flatware, cutleries, tables and chairs, tents, and so forth.

They can arrange for other services, like décor and music, as well. In short, a full-service caterer can plan and execute an entire event, not just the food for it.

TYPES OF CATERING ESTABLISHMENTS

Various catering establishments are categorised by the nature of the demands they meet. The following are some of the catering establishements.

RESTAURANT

A restaurant is an establishment that serves the customers with prepared food and beverages to order, to be consumed on the premises. The term covers a multiplicity of venues and a diversity of styles of cuisine.

Restaurants are sometimes also a feature of a larger complex, typically a resort, where the dining amenities are provided for the convenience of the residents and for the resort to maximize their potential revenue. Such restaurants are often open to non-residents also.

TRANSPORT CATERING

The provision of food and beverages to passengers, before, during and after a journey on trains, aircraft and ships and in buses or private vehicles is termed as transport catering. These services may also be utilised by the general public, who are in the vicinity of a transport catering unit. The major forms of modern day transport catering are airline-catering, railways catering, ship catering and surface catering in coaches or buses which operate on long distance routes.

Airline Catering

Catering to airline passengers on board the air craft, as well as at restaurants situated at airport terminals is termed as airline catering. Modern airports have a variety of food and beverage outlets to cater to the increasing number of air passengers. Catering to passengers en route i s normally contracted out to a flight catering unit of a reputed resort or to a catering contractor or to the catering unit operated by the airline itself as an independent entity.

Railway Catering

Catering to railway passengers both during the journey as well as during halts at different railway stations is called railway catering. Travelling by train for long distances can be very tiring; hence a constant supply of a variety of refreshment choices helps to make the journey less tedious. On-board meal services are also provided on long distance trains.

Ship Catering

Ship catering is catering to cargo crew and passenger ship passengers. Ships have kitchens and restaurants on board. The quality of service and facilities offered depends on the class of the ship and the price the passengers are willing to pay. There are cruises to suit every pocket. They range from room service and cocktail bars to speciality dining restaurants.

Surface Catering

Catering to passengers traveling by surface transport such as buses and private vehicles is called surface catering. These eating establishments are normally located around a bus terminus or on highways. They may be either government run restaurants, or privately owned establishments. Of late there has been a growing popularity of Punjabi style eateries called dhabas on the highways.

OUTDOOR CATERING

This catering includes the provision of food and drink away from home base and suppliers. The venue is left to the peoples' choice. Resorts, restaurants and catering contractors meet this growing demand. The type of food and set up depends entirely on the price agreed upon. Outdoor catering includes catering for functions such as marriages, parties and conventions.

RETAIL STORE CATERING

Some retail stores, apart from carrying on their primary activity of retailing their own wares, provide catering as an additional facility. This type of catering evolved when large departmental stores wished to provide food and beverages to their customers as a part of their retailing concept.

It is inconvenient and time consuming for customers to take a break from shopping, to have some refreshments at a different location. Thus arouse the need for some sort of a dining facility in the retail store itself. This style of catering is becoming more popular and varied nowadays.

CLUB CATERING

Club catering refers to the provision of food and beverages to a restricted member clientele. Some examples of clubs for people with similar interests are turf clubs, golf clubs, cricket clubs etc.

The service and food in these clubs tend to be of a fairly good standard and are economically priced. Night clubs are usually situated in large cities that have an affluent urban population. They offer entertainment with good food and expensive drinks.

WELFARE CATERING

The provision of food and beverages to people to fulfil a social obligation, determined by a recognised authority, is known as welfare catering. This grew out of the welfare state concept, prevalent in western countries. It includes catering in hospitals, schools, colleges, the armed forces and prisons.

INDUSTRIAL CATERING

The provision of food and beverages to 'people at work,' in industries and factories at highly subsidised rates is called industrial catering. It is based on the assumption that better fed employees at concessional rates are happy and more productive.

Catering for a large workforce may be undertaken by the management itself, or may be contracted out to professional caterers. Depending on the choice of the menu suggested by the management, catering contractors undertake to feed the workforce for a fixed period of time at a predetermined price.

LEISURE-LINKED CATERING

This type of catering refers to the provision of food and beverages to people engaged in 'rest and recreation' activities. This includes sale of food and beverages through different stalls and kiosks at exhibitions, theme parks, galleries and theatres. The increase in the availability of leisure time and a large disposable income for leisure activities has made it a very profitable form of catering.

RELATIONSHIP BETWEEN CATERING INDUSTRY AND ALL OTHER INDUSTRIES

Food is the sustainer of life regardless of whether they belong to animal kingdom or plant kingdom. All living beings consume food as they come in nature. Subsequently they may convert the raw natural food into usable form on their own. This transformation never involves the art and science of coking, which is a speciality of human beings alone. Importance of food for the human beings is amply, accurately and appropriately stated in the following age old sayings: "hungry man is an angry man" and "even the army marches on stomach" where stomach implies food Employment of largest number of people in the world in general terms and in commercial terms is in food preparation and servicing. Roughly half the world population is actively engaged in the art and science of food production and then alone comes reproduction.

Food production, simply stated, is the transformation of raw food material into palatable, appetizing and easily palatable tasty food. Unlike all other living organisms, man has to "buy" food by paying money. Where does the money come from? It comes only from industries. Any industry in the world has the primary objective of making money. Money so generated by the industrial activity is shared between the employer and the employee, however disproportionate it may be. Money so shared is used to take care of the three important objectives: food, clothing and residence.

Whatever left after meeting these primary objectives may go towards acquiring wealth. Food is the very basis of existence or survival. To buy food, man needs money. The money comes or must come from industries, all of which have the primary objective of making money and share with those who help generate it. Since the raw food needs to be transformed into palatable food fit for consumption which is achieved, as already stated, through general cooking or commercial cooking.

Therefore, there is no industry in the world which is not directly or indirectly, one way or the other, related to the food industry. Commercial food industry or the catering industry is the only industry that provides food, at a price, away from home. Various types of catering services available would include general or speciality services such as transport catering, welfare catering, industrial catering, etc.

CATERING AND CUSTOMER

CATERING TO DIVERGENT

It sounds rather crass, but when they die, in the next 10-15 years, all of their money-some $10 trillion dollars-is going to another group of people, most of whom don't like banks. They would rather go to Fidelity, play the market, not having lived through a downturn. One of the challenges as we go forward is how the banking industry is going to transform itself, move from the current group who provides the bulk of our earnings, to a second group who will assume society's wealth, and who does not realty like us.

Who likes banks? Those 55 years and older plus those who have lower incomes and less education, according to a 1997 ABA survey-valued customers, but not a group we can solely survive on. Also customer satisfaction is slipping somewhat for banks.

You need to know when you should allocate resources from the group giving you the bulk of your earnings now, to the group that does not like you. You will also get a boost from the federal government's change to electronic benefits transfer on January 1, 1999. Most states will have an EBT environment by the end of 1998.

The people who now get a Social Security check will have to become accustomed to an electronic transaction, and that's in your favour. A lot of the back-office work, you can change through electronic transactions. EBT will provide a large infusion of the infrastructure required for electronic commerce, by increasing the number of point-of-sale terminals.

The ABA asked the Federal Reserve and the Treasury to review the regulations surrounding transaction accounts, because the existing regulations are all in the realm of paper-based accounts. We would really like to get rid of the periodic statement under Regulation E because a purely electronic account will not have any outstanding items so you don't realty need a statement.

Banks will have to do some new things, though-electronic benefits transactions on automated teller machines, and maybe statements on demand. What can you do today on the Internet? You can do consumer education; you can have interactive advertising; you can distribute forms and applications; you can provide account information. You can do some internal transactions, some bill payment and, perhaps, some electronic commerce for the more daring. Electronic commerce, a broader term than electronic banking, better describes what ultimately we might want to do. What customers want today is not necessarily what they are going to want next year. You have to continually reassess.

Reliability on Tomorrow's Systems

Today, most of you keep your real stuff on a mainframe, a rather secure system. On the Internet, how are you going to let people like me hack around in your computer? You are going to be doing the same kinds of things on the Internet that you do today to render service and security to your customers. You will have a lot of the same, concerns. You could have a saboteur on the inside.

You could have a huge virus or software that fails. The new one is the hackers, but then you've got people who forge checks, too; they just attack in a different way. Whatever system you have must be reliable, sound, and secure. What kinds of things will give you these qualities? Well, you have technical standards; you have best practices, and the regulators providing guidance to the industry.

You are going to a much more efficient system and you should have greater margins as you implement it, but meanwhile, many larger institutions have proprietary systems that work very well. Probably nobody here has had a customer question, in the past 50 years, whether her check is going to clear. You are coming off of that kind of reliability. Bankers have systems that, perhaps, can be expanded to an Internet environment.

Determining who has the best products to help you is part of creating a plan. You want, perhaps, to start small, with, say, electronic bill payment, see how secure it is, how your customers accept it, and then go forward. You may lose money, but you are going to do it because your customers want it. There are threats to banks' dominance of the payments system, one of the biggest of which is the post office. You may say that will never happen because it is not an insured depository, but I would submit, for example, that the largest financial institution in Japan is the post office. Financial modernization, after 30 years, seems finally to be coming. Companies with unlimited capital, such as, say, General Electric Corp., will be able to compete very effectively, not for the little old ladies' $50,000 CDs but for their kids' money.

That's why ABA is very concerned. With direct deposit, a customer need never walk into a branch. A customer in Alaska can directly deposit funds into a bank in Alabama and write checks or use his debit card all day long in Alaska. All across the country, community bankers are saying to themselves "Aha!

Maybe I have an opportunity here." This stuff is coming. How are you going to respond? You are concerned about how your customers perceive you. Are you stodgy-as one of ABA's new industry ads shows -or are you out there on roller-blades? Now, you have to be concerned about customer perception beyond the community where you do business.

The Growth of Service Activities

Service sector economics now constitutes a major branch of economic studies although it is a field which no more than a decade ago was variously referred to as the 'poor relation' and the 'Cinderella of academics and politicians alike'.

The explanation of the interest recently evinced in the economics of the service sector is to be found in the extent to which service industries have expanded relative to other economic activities. Whilst the tendency for the tertiary sector to grow in comparison to primary and secondary activities has been identified and commented on for many decades special factors, such as the potential for services to generate new jobs, have helped thrust the sector to the forefront of economic analysis in the last few years.

The relative growth of services in the British economy since 1971, quantified on the basis of official statistics, could well stand as on outline of events in most developed economies during this period. Between 1971 and 1986 the output of the service sector increased by 2.5 per cent a year, or more than twice the rate, 1.1 per cent, achieved by other economic activities. Within the sector commercial services-distribution, catering, financial, business, recreational and personal services-expanded faster than other services, 3.1 per cent compared with 1.7 per cent a year, whilst specific commercial services grew very rapidly indeed-banking and business services by as much as 5.1 per cent per annum.

As a result, by 1985, service activities in Britain accounted for three-fifths of GDP and commercial services themselves were responsible for a third of total output. The importance of service activities is no less when judged by labour force size. On the basis of both numbers of employees, and by numbers of employees plus the self-employed, by 1985 services accounted for 66 per cent of Britain's labour force compared with 53 per cent in 1971. Commercial services alone provided jobs for 37 per cent of all employees in 1985.

The Need for New Measures

At a time when the bases, compilation, accuracy and usefulness of a range of official economic statistics have come under close scrutiny, the measurement of service outputs has not escaped attention. Recently there has been some shift away from a simple acknowledgement that service output measures may be subject to a degree of unreliability towards an apprehension that any errors they contain might lead to a downward bias in the measure of service output, and therefore, GDP growth rates.

It has in fact been suggested that output increases in services may have been underestimated in recent years by as much as 2-1/2 per cent a year implying that annual growth of GDP itself should have been substantially higher. For both conceptual and practical reasons the outputs of many service activities are notoriously difficult to quantify both absolutely and in terms of change over time.

Yet because of their size and growth it is especially important that a reasonable degree of accuracy must attach to service output measures which should reflect current best practice given the data and resources available. If this is not the case then, because of the weight of service activities in the total economy, the accuracy of the registred change in GDP and national productivity, the relative contribution to growth of service and non-service activities, the pattern of structural change within the service sector and the policies to which these various phenomena have given rise, must all be called in question. This assembles some of the principal results which have emerged from a study of alternative output measures for British service industries.

The study reviews the methods currently used by the CSO to measure real output changes in specified services and seeks to devise, develop and implement new measures for these activities. For this purpose an empirical approach has been adopted. Whilst basic conceptual considerations are taken fully into account in that the alternative measures which are compiled can be integrated into the national accounting framework, it is felt that the theoretical complexities associated with service output measurement have received due attention elsewhere whilst very little has been done at the practical level.

When compiling new service output measures the two principal uses for which they are employed must be borne in mind. The original raison d'etre for measuring service sector output is for use, in conjunction with output indicators for industrial activities, to yield a measure of real growth in total GDP. This is the primary role for which the CSO devises and compiles output measures for service sector activities. Increasingly, however, as the weight of services in the economy has grown service output indicators are now used extensively, in conjunction with labour force and other relevant economic series, for the analysis of long-term developments in individual service industries.

Their employment in the latter context accentuates the requirement that they fulfill minimum reliability criteria: it is possible that offsetting errors in individual service industry output measures may modulate their impact on the reliability of overall GDP measurement but this does not apply when attention is focused on the analysis of developments in a specific service industry. The results obtained in the present exercise suggest that official measures of GDP growth may well have been marginally understated as a result of the methods used to track service output changes. Even more significantly, perhaps, the alternative measures which have been compiled portray patterns of development for some individual commercial service industries which are very different from those yielded by official output measures.

When considering alternative output measures attention has been directed first at the strengths and weaknesses of official practice as a prelude to an attempt to improve the rationale and reliability of the resulting output indicators. However in some cases it is necessary to regard the new measure simply as an alternative to the official index: an alternative with a different, rather than superior, base and/or derived from quite separate data sources.

Another feature of the search for alternative indicators is that it has been conducted with an eye to the improved reliability of service output measurement in the future. To some extent this means that data series which are available only for recent years have been drawn upon. Nevertheless a major objective of the study has been to assess the extent to which the official picture of past service sector developments is changed if alternative output measures are used.

The alternative measures have therefore been carried backwards in some cases to 1971, in others to 1973 and for a large number to 1978, using 1985 as the base year. There are three reasons for the latter choice. First data limitations mean that all series cannot be uniformly taken back to a common early date so that a recent year must be adopted as the base. Secondly at the time when the research was initiated 1985 was the latest year for which data-whether values, 'quantities' or 'weights'-were generally available.

Thirdly, the CSO was then in the process of re-basing its output indicators using 1985 GDP weights. The new output measures draw much more extensively on unofficial data sources than do those compiled by the CSO. Broadly such sources can be divided into two types: those which yield data series covering an industry-wide set of activities; and those which contain data relating to individual service industry organisations and firms. Typically the assistance of the latter was enlisted to provide weights with which industry-wide quantity series for different kinds of output can be combined to produce a single output measure for the service sector in question. It is to the credit of the CSO that there has been a continuous attempt to modify service output measures in the light of methodological developments and the emergence of alternative data sources.

Whilst this has had the desired result of improving the reliability of service output measurement inevitably it also introduces inconsistencies and breaks in the time series where-either on practical or other grounds-the new methods have not been carried back to earlier years. A feature of the new measures postulated below is that every effort has been made to ensure temporal consistency in the series which they yield. It has not proved possible to devote to 'quality' aspects of service output the attention they properly merit.

In part this reflects the fact that the incorporation of quality changes in output measures may be even more difficult in services than in goods-producing industries where frequently its assessment is equally neglected. This in turn is due to the consideration that the quality of a given service varies greatly and in many cases is highly subjective. Nevertheless the results do have implications for this aspect of service output measurement, especially in the case of the catering trades. Were quality aspects taken into account more fully, further consideration would need to be given to the relative merits of measures based on deflated value series and service output units.

Coverage of the Measures

The search for alternative output measures has been restricted to the commercial service industries, essentially distribution, catering, financial, business and personal services, for which suggests that output has risen especially rapidly. Within this group of commercial services the CSO distinguishes for output measurement purposes as many as 37 service industries, output changes in which are currently assessed by a total of 114 indicators. These services accounted for some 30 per cent of total GDP in 1985 and about a third of people employed in Great Britain. Given the vast range of service activities which must be covered by official output measures it is natural that the CSO makes use of readily available, relevant, series to yield the required indicators, series which themselves are normally official in the sense that they are compiled by other government departments.

Since the quest for new measures has entailed a search for and detailed examination of, alternative data, involving the identification, location and perusal of non-official sources and also the co-operation of individual firms and organisations it proved necessary to regard the full range of commercial service activities as no more than a frame from which individual service industries could be selected for intensive analysis.

When choosing industries from this list for which alternative measures of output change are identified and implemented, several criteria have been applied. A principal consideration has been to direct efforts to services where, on the face of it, current practice appears to be weak. At one end of the scale this principle tends to divert attention away from activities such as retailing, where the measures are generally regarded as being relatively sound, towards such services as advertising where the official output indicator is based on an employment series.

Secondly some priority was given to activities for which at first blush-sometimes deceptive-alternative measures appeared feasible. Thirdly an attempt has been made to cover the larger service industries such as banking and insurance, and ceteris paribus, attention was focused on service activities which, a priori, are thought to be rapidly expanding, a criterion which points to the inclusion of, especially, financial and business services. Since a systematic attempt has been made to base alternative output measures on numbers of service units produced, such service industries as estate agents, stockbroking and legal services where official output measurement is already founded on numbers of service units-of property transfers, transactions, and court proceedings-have not been considered as candidates for alternative measures. The service industries for which new measures were ultimately compiled fall neatly into three groups.

First, there are ten selected financial and business services: banking, building societies, finance leasing, hire-purchase, insurance, accountants, architects, advertising, computer services and construction plant hire. Secondly eight recreational services have been covered: broadcasting, theatres, libraries, museums, professional sports, participatory sports, local authority leisure centres and betting and gaming. Thirdly, the five catering trades-restaurants, public houses, clubs, catering contractors and resorts-have also been included.

Alternative Output Measures

Continuous CSO action to modify and improve service output measures means that they have developed from year to year in an essentially ad hoc manner with considerable diversity in their conceptual underpinning. Output measures for the commercial service sector rely heavily on deflated value and employment indicators and whilst output measurement for some service activities is based on counting numbers of service units, such practice applies to only a fraction of the output of the commercial service sector.

In fact it has emerged that the use of this type of measure can be extended to a considerable number of commercial services and an attempt has therefore been made to generalise and implement this approach, especially in the case of the financial and recreational services. This method can be summarised as the compilation of [sigma]poqo where q represents the industry's output quantities of the industry's output prices and 0 and 1 refer to the years compared.

This is 'the traditional [measure] used for multi-product industries wherein an index of production is constructed from a weighted sum of various outputs produced by the industry'. Such a deflated value approach to output measurement will yield the required result-as measured by the traditional direct method based on weighted quantities-only if the deflator, the price index, relates specifically to the products or services in question. This condition is not fulfilled in the case of many service output measures where for practical reasons some form of general price index is used.

It is partly to remedy this weakness in service output measurement that, wherever possible, alternative measures have been based in this exercise on the traditional direct methodology using numbers of service output units. A fundamental requirement for the use of this 'traditional' or 'direct' approach is that, for purposes of practical measurement, the outputs of the industry or service in question should be relatively homogeneous.

No economic activity yields a single, identical, product or service so that in practice it is sufficient if the bulk of an industry's activity is represented by a limited range of output types. It is their supposed inability to fulfill this criterion which has discouraged the application of the traditional, direct, measurement methodology to service activities.

Generally it has been assumed that there exists, virtually, an infinite variety and range of outputs in the case of most, especially financial, services: that no two life insurances, mortgages, bank accounts, and the output activities associated with them, are the same. It is argued that this view is based largely on a misconception, associated with what, for want of a better term, we shall call the 'digit illusion', and that in fact many service industries-including betting and gaming-fulfil the basic criterion for the application of the traditional, direct measurement methodology in that the bulk of their output is accounted for by a limited range of essentially homogeneous activities.

For the impression of enormous diversity in the output of most financial services derives from the fact that the values associated with a specific activity-the sums assured by a life company, sizes of mortgages provided by a building society, the amounts loaned under hire-purchase agreements by a finance house, the values of cheques cleared by a commercial bank, the car insurance premiums charged by an insurer etc-do have an infinitely large range. It has been assumed in the search for new output measures that such differences can be essentially ignored. In the case of mortgages, for example, the output associated with writing 500,000 pounds sterling in a deed is, with some relatively minor qualifications, little different from that associated with inscribing 50,000 pounds sterling or even 5,000 pounds sterling; differences in the numbers of digits required in this and other financial instruments-cheques, insurance policies, hire-purchase agreements, betting slips-have relatively little bearing on the amount of output involved.

In brief for a given type of financial activity it is normally legitimate, when measuring output, to ignore the 'digit illusion'. This has the effect of rendering homogeneous a wide range of financial activities, making them amenable, in principle, to the traditional direct, measurement methodology. It means, by way of illustration, that output changes for the life insurance industry can be based on changes in numbers of policies. It must be stressed however that a distinction must be drawn, and numbers counted, for each major type of service/activity provided by the service industry in question where value added per service unit varies significantly between activity types.

This means, for instance, in the case of the life insurance industry, that numbers of policies must be counted separately for ordinary life insurance, industrial life, annuities and personal pensions. It also means that attention needs to be drawn to a feature of this approach which is peculiar to financial service industries: the distinction between stocks and flows. Clearly, the resources devoted to, and therefore the amount of output associated with, the annual 'maintenance' of pre-existing mortgage will be substantially less than required when initiating a new mortgage.

In principle, and where practical, it is as important therefore to draw a distinction when measuring output between numbers of existing mortgages issued in a given year and the numbers of existing mortgages as it is to count separately the numbers of, say, different kinds of policy issued by life insurance companies. Indeed the same distinction needs to be drawn in the case of life insurance-between new policies and policies in force-and in principle at any rate in many other financial service industries: between new and existing contracts for hire-purchase and finance leases for instance.

The practicability of extending the traditional measurement methodology to commercial services thus hinges, in the case of each activity, on the availability of two kinds of data: industry-wide series of numbers of each type of principal product, the series q; and appropriate weights with which these various product series can be combined to yield an aggregate output measure for the service industry in question. To a degree inadequacies in the measurement of service output changes simply reflect the relative lack of interest with which they were regarded in the past and a consequent failure to devote sufficient resources to the collection of basic output data.

Also, it is to some extent, due to the 'insubstantiality' of most services, the fact that they 'pass away' in the moment of production, that a systematic effort has not been made to base their output measurement to a much larger extent on numbers of service units produced. In fact regardless of whether or not a service has any kind of physical embodiment, in the vast majority of cases there exists a physical record or token that a particular service has been performed. The outputs of all kinds of commercial service industries are very well 'documented'-by the ticket required for entrance to Wimbledon, the bill for a meal, the contract which records the finance leasing of a fleet of aircraft-in a form which in principle allows the numbers of each type of service to be recorded.

In this sense, and at this level, the output of service activities is registered at least as well as the products of industrial pursuits. The nig universal existence, at the 'grass roots' level, of this detailed record of service sector outputs, to an ever increasing extent in computerised form, augurs well for the future extension and development of the kind of direct output measurement advocated here.

This comprehensive data base has not yet been properly exploited to yield aggregate series of the numbers of each type of service produced on an industry-wide basis. However research and enquiry have revealed that representative bodies of various kinds at the industry level-especially trade associations-have come to regard the compilation of aggregate numbers of each kind of service produced, using these data bases, as one of their primary tasks, and such sources have been widely drawn upon. That they may not be based on series for numbers of service units which are fully comprehensive for the industry in question should not be regarded as a major weakness of the alternative output measures.

Usually only the major 'products' are counted and in this respect the circumstances are no different from those which exist when the method is applied to industrial activities. For both industrial and service activities so measured the implicit assumption is the same: that real changes in the non-covered outputs parallel the aggregate change measured for the covered operations. Unfortunately, with few exceptions, service industry organisations, do not collect, process or publish, the kind of data which are needed to obtain the 'weights' required for aggregating these various output series into a single measure for the industry in question. In these circumstances it has proved necessary to have recourse inter alia to the goodwill of individual firms in order to derive suitable weights which must be accepted as typical for the service industry in which they operate.

Wherever possible alternative measures have been derived from an application of the traditional, direct methodology based on numbers of service output units. However even when allowance is made for the 'digit illusion' some service industries-such as architecture and accountancy-remain in that class where output units are, in essence, infinitely variable in nature. In these cases an attempt has nevertheless been made to upgrade the output measure, usually by identifying and compiling a more appropriate price deflator. This presents the results of the search for new output measures for the selected commercial activities. Initially the new output series are presented separately for the three major service complexes-financial and business services, recreational services and the catering trades-which have been covered and compared with the official measures. The part concludes with a consideration of the implications of the results for future developments in the measurement of service output.

Financial and Business Services

In 1985 the ten financial and business services for which new output measures have been compiled contributed, in total, about 35 pound sterling billion to GDP and employed approximately a million people. In the case of banking, the largest of the services in this sector, it proved possible to base the new measure wholly on numbers of service units-numbers of accounts, clearings, cash and credit card transactions. This contrasts with official practice in which indicators derived from deflated series for deposits and loans, as well as employment, carry the bulk of the weight.

In life insurance, also, numbers of policies of various types, distinguishing between new policies and policies in force, replace the official series comprising deflated consumer expenditure. Similarly the new building society measure is founded wholly on numbers of service units-shareholders, existing borrowers and new loans-instead of, as is the case with the official measure, a combination of deflated liabilities, employment and numbers of advances. For general insurance, a measure reflecting broadly the stock of insurable assets has been substituted for the official indicator based on deflated premiums.

In the case of two services, architects and advertising, a deflated value series places officla measures based on employment. The primary feature of the new measures used for accountants, computer services and hire-purchase, is the use of deflators which have been specially constructed to reflect more closely than those officially employed developments in the activities in question. The official practice for both construction plant hire and finance leasing has been to base indicators on output developments in user industries. Instead of this approach the new measures are derived from gross output in the case of construction plant hire and the value of assets newly leased and of the stock of leased assets in the case of finance leasing, each deflated by price indices specifically compiled for the activities in question. The new measures for the covered financial and business services are set alongside the official indicators.

The basic date series from which these were derived are such that not all of them cover the full span of years, 1971 to 1986, so that it is convenient to combine them into three groups: five industries-building societies, hire-purchase, insurance, advertising and construction plant hire-for which growth rates are available for the whole period 1971-86; six industries where the information is shown for 1973-86; and all ten covered financial services, architects, finance leasing and computer services-for which alternative and official growth rates can be compared for the period 1978-86.

In the case of the first group, for which measures extend over the full period 1971-86, whilst there are some very significant differences between alternative and official growth rates-for building societies the former is appreciably higher than the latter whilst the opposite is true for hire-purchase-the arithmetic average growth rate for all five services, at 4.1 per cent per annum, is identical for both alternative and official measures. The same generalisation applies to the group of six industries over the period 1973-86: for hire-purchase, advertising, construction plant hire and banking the two measures yield quite different results but these contrasts offset each other so that the average alternative growth rate is identical with the average official growth rate.

Results for the group of ten industries, relating to the period 1978-86, paint a very similar picture; of individual industry diversity but overall similarity. In this case only for building societies, insurance, advertising and accountants do alternative and official methods yield rates of output change that are at all akin. Yet, overall, the average alternative growth rate, 7.4 per cent per annum, is not much greater than the 7.0 per cent registered officially. The official measure for finance leasing is constructed to minimise distortion in GDP measurement whilst the alternative measure has been compiled in such a way as to enhance the reliability of the industry's growth indicator *per se*. If this service industry is left out of account, the average alternative growth rate, at 6.6 per cent, is below the average official rate, 7.6 per cent.

This set of results contains a further point of interest. Whilst, as pointed out, there are substantial differences in the case of most industries between the alternative and official measures, the inter-industry growth patterns are remarkably similar whether gauged by alternative or official indicators: again leaving out finance leasing the correlation coefficient for the remaining nine pairs of, alternative and official, growth rates is +0.95. Although comparisons of unweighted average growth rates can be quite instructive more attention should be focused on differences between alternative and official measures revealed by weighted aggregate indices of the kind. These output indices, derived from the alternative and official measures for individual industries and relating to the same groups of industries and periods specified have been obtained from an aggregation procedure which is based on 1985 contributions to GDP.

The results contained are summarised in the form of average annual rates of growth that also contains growth rates obtained from weights derived from 1980 industry contributions to GDP and 1985 industry employment levels, to test the sensitivity of the results to alternative weighting systems. In the case of the five industries for which there is full coverage over the period 1971 to 1986 the alternative growth rate is 4.4 per cent and the official one 4.8 per cent on the basis of 1985 GDP weights.

A discrepancy of no more than a tenth between the two versions is also suggested by 1980 GDP weights. This group of five industries accounted for only 20 per cent of the contribution to GDP and an estimated 27 per cent of employment of all financial and business services in 1985. In contrast the group of six was responsible for 56 per cent of output and an estimated 42 per cent of employment and the group of ten for as much as 74 per cent of output and 56 per cent of employment. Greater significance should therefore be attached to the results obtained for these latter two groups. All three weighting systems show that for the group of six industries, over the years 1973 to 1986, the official measure understated growth by about a fifth when compared with the aggregate alternative measure; much the same picture emerges for the group of ten industries during the period 1978 to 1986 where, on the basis of both 1985 and 1980 GDP weights, the official measure, compared with the alternative, under estimates growth by about a fifth.

When considering this disparity two industries merit special attention: banking which is by some way the largest of the ten industries; and finance leasing on account of the fundamental difference in the methods underlying the alternative and official measures. In fact if banking-with alternative and official growth rates of respectively 8.2 and 6.5 per cent per annum for the period 1978 to 1986-is left out of account the picture hardly changes at all: the alternative aggregate growth rate for the remaining nine industries over the period 1978 to 1986 emerges as 8.0 per cent per annum compared with an official growth rate of 6.0 per cent.

This is in sharp contrast to the effect of excluding finance leasing. In this case the alternative growth measure for the nine remaining industries falls to 7.5 per cent whilst the official measure rises to 7.2 per cent so that most of the differential disappears.

Recreational Services

In 1985, recreational services, SIC class 97, contributed almost 6 billion pounds sterling to GDP and provided employment for 430,000 people. Apart from cinemas, for which the official output indicator is based on numbers of attendances, the measures used by the CSO rely for the most part on deflated series of turnover or consumers' expenditure on the service in question. In the case of local authority libraries, however, employment-based indicators are used. In the search for alternative measures it has proved possible, for these services, to base the new indicators largely on numbers of service units.

Thus the output index for 'group' 974, broadcasting and theatres, reflects changes in numbers of radio and television hours transmitted and of attendances at theatres etc, whilst that for libraries and museums has been founded on numbers of books issued and numbers of visitors. The new measures for sport, 'group' 979, an activity that accounts for almost half of the output of recreational services, has been derived from a variety of indicators which reflect, inter alia, changes in numbers of attendances at paying spectator sports, sports hours transmitted by television and radio, membership of participatory sports clubs and measures which trace changes in numbers of betting slips and football coupons.

Only in the case of local authority leisure facilities was recourse made to conventional deflated value series. The output series set out for cinemas and for authors and artists are those used officially: that for cinemas being already based on numbers of service units whilst no alternative measure could be readily identified for 'group' 976. For comparison with the overall official measure for recreational services the five component output measures have been combined into a single output index using weights based on 1985 contributions to GDP. The official measure suggests that the output of this service industry complex grew, between 1973 and 1988, at an average annual rate of 2.9 per cent; the alternative points to a significantly slower rate of increase of 2.0 per cent.

One factor which may go some way towards explaining this discrepancy is that whilst in principle the alternative measure includes local authority libraries and leisure facilities throughout the period, the official indicator embraces these activities only since their transfer to class 97 of the 1980 SIC. Yet it can be seen that even in recent years the official measure has registered a significantly higher rate of growth for this industry than that shown by the alternative measure.

THE CATERING TRADES

In 1985 the catering trades' contribution to GDP totalled 7-1/2 pounds sterling billion and the industry employed more than a million people. Output measures for these trades are summarised, in terms of average annual growth rates. In the early years of the period covered the official indicator was based on turnover data supplied by a voluntary panel of catering organisations deflated by price indices specific to each of the catering trades.

From the beginning of the 1980s the official measure has been derived from changes in the margins of the individual catering trades as recorded in the DTI's annual catering trades' enquiry, again deflated by specific price indices. Although in principle it should be possible to measure output in the catering trades on the basis of numbers of service units-resort bed occupancy, numbers of bar transactions etc-attempts to use this approach proved, for practical reasons, to be fruitless. Therefore to test the sensitivity of the official measure alternative output series were constructed using the price indices officially compiled but applying them throughout to turnover data yielded by the catering trades enquiries, interpolating results for early years where no such enquiries were conducted.

It is clear that these alternative measures alter the picture quite significantly for some trades. Whilst for restaurants, clubs and catering contractors changes in output are not greatly different whether measured on the official or alternative bases, sharply contrasting developments emerge for public houses and the resort trade: the substantial growth recorded for public houses by the official measure virtually disappears with the alternative, whilst the opposite occurs in the case of resorts. These quite significant modifications to the subsectoral picture, in effect, cancel out: on both official and alternative methods catering output increased over this period by about 1 per cent a year.

The reliability of catering output changes cannot, however, be allowed to rest there. For when these changes are compared with labour force developments there would seem to have been substantial long-term declines in labour productivity: taking the official output measure in conjunction with changes in the number of employees in catering, labour productivity appears to have fallen by as much as 1.7 per cent a year between 1971 and 1986. To help determine whether these results reflect real developments in this service industry or whether they arose from statistical series which are sufficiently unreliable as to produce a misleading picture of events, alternative, more sophisticated, full-time equivalent labour force series have been constructed.

Since both part-time working and self-employment are important features of the catering trades' labour force, allowance for developments in both these aspects has been made in the FTE series shown. Whilst the introduction of FTE labour force series improves the productivity picture there nevertheless remains an apparently substantial fall in catering productivity: an annual average decline of 1.7 per cent a year using numbers of employees is modified to a deterioration of 1.2 per cent on an FTE basis. Of the individual trades only catering contractors emerge with enhanced FTE productivity, displaying an improvement of 1.7 per cent a year.

The other four trades register deteriorations: restaurants by 2.1 per cent a year, public houses 0.1 per cent, clubs 3.6 per cent and resorts 1.2 per cent. It is theoretically feasible, on the basis of most formulations of the production function, that in certain circumstances output in any economic activity might increase over the long term at a rate below that registered for labour inputs.

This could arise in particular if there were a fall in capital intensity but such a development does not appear to have been a feature of catering during this period. A measure compiled for the industry suggests that between 1971 and 1986 the stock of equipment grew at an annual average rate of 3.6 per cent a year which, in conjunction with an annual rise of 2.3 per cent in the FTE labour force, points to a 1.4 per cent annual increase in capital intensity.

In these circumstances it is difficult to accept that either the official or alternative output measures presented adequately reflect output growth in the catering trades. A probable explanation of this deficiency is that the measures fail to take sufficient account of developments, in some general sense, in the quality of catering output, be it a reflection of changes in the range of services offered, the milieu in which they are provided, the nature of the food and drink supplied or the standards of customer service. It is relevant that following comparatively little change in its size during the 1950s and 1960s the catering industry's labour force has grown substantially over the last two decades, especially during the early 1970s.

These developments have generally been explained by contrasts in the nature of the labour market between, on the one hand, the earlier decades and on the other the 1970s and 1980s. The earlier prevalence of full employment meant that because catering work was notoriously unattractive and ill-paid the industry was able to adjust its labour force towards its basic manning requirements. This kind of effect was reinforced by the impact of the selective employment tax which led to a significant fall in catering employment when it was implemented during the later years of the 1960s and a rapid increase in the early years of the 1970s after its abandonment. This thesis is also supported by case studies of the impact on the industry of technological innovations.

A recent survey of organisations operating in the catering trades revealed that rather than causing redundancies 'the time saved by new technology and improved productivity was being used wherever possible to enhance customer service'. A stagnant productivity performance in catering is equally difficult to reconcile with the rapid growth of both take-away food facilities and self-catering accommodation. In the event it has been decided to use labour inputs, to be precise the FTE measure shown, as a surrogate output measure for this industry.

It is felt that whilst far from ideal it provides a less unsatisfactory output measure, over the period in question. On this basis an annual average growth rate of 2.3 per cent emerges for catering output, hardly an unreasonable achievement for what is largely a leisure industry during a period when GDP increased, on average, by 1.7 per cent a year. Furthermore when applied to the individual catering trades this labour force based method yields results, for changes in real output over these years, which are intuitively much more plausible than those derived from either the official or alternative methods. It suggests that between 1971 and 1986 output in all five trades increased substantially: in restaurants by 2.4 per cent a year, in public houses by 2.5 per cent, in clubs by 3.1 per cent, in catering contractors by 2.8 per cent and in resorts by 1.6 per cent.

Measure for All Covered Services

The alternative output measures compiled for financial services, recreational services and the catering trades are combined and compared with their official counterparts. Group 1, for which the series relate to the full period 1971-86, comprises five financial services and the catering trades. Group 2 covering the period 1973-86 includes in addition banking and recreational services. Whilst group 3, for which the output indicators are available for the period 1978-86, embraces all the service industries for which alternative measures have been compiled.

These aggregate output indices, both official and alternative, are derived from those presented in the relevant tables using as weights the 1985 contribution of each activity to GDP. The results are summarised in the form of average annual rates of change. To check the sensitivity of these final results alternative and official measures of growth are also compared using as weights the services' 1985 employment levels and 1980 contributions to GDP.

The picture which emerges is one in which the alternative measure consistently points towards a higher growth rate than that indicated by its corresponding official index. Moreover the size of the differential varies comparatively little regardless of the group, period or weighting system to which attention is directed. If most attention is attached-in view of the size of their coverage-to the results for groups 2 and 3, it appears that compared with the alternative methods the official indicators have understated growth by between 13 and 18 per cent.

Given that in most cases the alternative measurement methods differ radically from those officially employed it is perhaps remarkable that, overall, the discrepancy should be no greater than this. To what extent, as it stands, would the official measure of GDP growth be changed if the alternative measure is substituted for the official indicator?

The answer is: very little. Basing this adjustment on the alternative/official differential revealed for group 2 the annual average GDP growth rate for 1973-86 is unchanged at 1.3 per cent per annum, and using the group 3 results the annual growth rate for 1978-86 rises from 1.6 per cent to 1.7 per cent. If the disparity between official and alternative growth rates depicted held for the commercial services excluded from this exercise then the official GDP growth rate of 1.3 per cent registered for the period 1973-86 is boosted to 1.5 per cent per annum and the GDP growth rate of 1.6 per cent for the years 1978-86 is raised to 1.9 per cent a year.

There are good reasons for supposing that these upward revisions to the GDP growth rate will understate rather than overstate the actual shortfall. In the first place output measures which lean towards numbers of service units will to some extent be biased downwards compared with those derived from deflated sales or turnover values because the data sources in question tend to cover any new services in the latter but not the former.

Secondly whilst official output measures which rely on employment series usually incorporate some productivity improvement, this has not been applied to the FTE based measure compiled for catering so that it may well underestimate actual output growth in this activity. Thirdly salary indices which have been used as surrogate price deflators in the case of accountancy and computer services will tend to overestimate actual output price increases-and therefore bias downwards the resulting output measure-since no allowance is made for the impact on unit labour costs of any productivity improvements in these services.

While the implications for GDP measurement of the substitution of alternative aggregate service output indicators may not be unduly significant it is clear that they are more substantial for the commercial service sector as a whole. They are even more significant for individual service complexes. Although the new measure for financial and business services differs relatively little from the official measure, especially if account is taken of the contrasting conceptual treatment of finance leasing in the respective approaches, the alternative obtained for recreational services points to a significantly lower growth rate and that compiled for catering is about twice the official growth rate. Contrasts between alternative and official measures are even more pronounced for individual service industries.

Service Output Measurement

Substitution of the new output measures for those officially compiled would have made little difference to GDP growth rates in recent years. In effect discrepancies which emerged between alternative and official output measures for individual service industries have tended to offset each other. There is no guarantee that this condition would hold in the future and for this reason alone the search for alternative, improved, measures of service output change should be pursued. In contrast significantly large differences between alternative and official output measures have emerged for particular services and these have very important implications for the analysis of economic developments in individual service industries.

The validity of the economic analyses to which these activities are now widely subjected depends crucially on the accuracy of the output and productivity measures that are employed to map their development over time. For this reason, especially, new and improved service output measures are required.

The research which lies behind the results is that new service output measures can be further developed both extensively and intensively. Whilst the service industries examined were chosen as systematically as possible on the basis of specific criteria, only limitations imposed by time and resources prevented other service activities being subjected to a similar kind of scrutiny.

Moreover in many of those service industries which have been surveyed scope for further measurement improvements remain. In this connection attention needs to be drawn to the results obtained for building societies and the catering trades.

In the case of the former serious doubts attach to the alternative measure which, although it yields a growth rate higher than the official one, nevertheless implies, as it stands, a long-term fall in labour productivity in this service industry. Also it is clear that the search for improved catering output measures needs to be continued: the labour force indicator adopted for the purpose of this exercise must be regarded as no more than a stop-gap strategem though on the basis of existing statistical sources there is at present little immediate prospect of new measures being based on numbers of service output units.

None the less the data deficiencies are essentially practical, not conceptual, in nature and with appropriate statistical arrangements could no doubt be remedied eventually: already there is some experience of collecting data relating to resort room utilisation which some time in the future might form the basis of a service unit-based measure. Generally there seems to exist a large reservoir of data relating to both output indicators and weights, collected by a variety of service industry organisations, which lies outside the purview of official sources.

It is difficult to avoid the impression that the current exercise has barely scratched the surface of this fund of material and that, in particular, much is available at the firm level which has yet to be systematically collated in a way that it can be used to measure developments for whole industries. Certainly it is clear that within the firms in question most service outputs are documented in detail, increasingly in computerised records, so that alternative measures based on numbers of output units should become progressively more practicable. There appear to be two basic options for tapping into this kind of data base. One would comprise an official periodic survey of each of the main service industries in which, as in the case of some industrial censuses, questionnaires would seek information about numbers and values of those output units which are best measured for each service. The enquiries into the distributive, catering and service trades periodically conducted by the Business Statistics Office might be developed in this direction.

The alternative is to adopt the approach followed, in the main, in this exercise and base new output measures on the information which is collected by trade associations and other industry organisations. This option is less attractive than the systematic collection of the requisite data, on a comprehensive and consistent basis, by means of an official census.

IMPORTANCE AND USAGE OF DRESS CODES

A survey was conducted to investigate the nature and use of employee dress codes of organizations that market professional services. The study sample consisted of personnel administrators employed in selected service organizations that are members of the American Society of Personnel Administrators; the total sample included 1000 administrators. The analysis of responses revealed that dress is important in marketing services and that compliance to a dress code is a criterion for employee performance evaluation.

While most administrators agreed that dress is a significant factor in their companies' success, few organizations had formal written dress codes; dress codes are most often communicated orally. Traditions in the professions, the expectations of customers, Chief Executive Officers of the organizations, and past experiences were the factors that dominate the development of dress codes. On the question of dress code requirements for male vs. female employees, the study revealed that more service organizations specify dress for males than for females.

For traditional business attire, comparing the dress codes of the different service organizations revealed several significant relationships. In recent years much emphasis has been placed on the importance of dress and appearance for professional success. Often organizations make an effort to manage dress and appearance so as to communicate to the client/customer in the most effective manner. Such controls have traditionally been manifested in policies called "dress codes." The responsibility for the administration of dress codes has conventionally been treated as a personal function. "Proper" business dress has long been a part of the norms of professional services practitioners such as bankers, accountants, stock brokers and management consultants. However, it is interesting to note that in the marketing literature there is little attention devoted to dress as it relates to the marketing of professional services.

This is particularly interesting when one considers the growth of professional service industries as a part of the U.S. economy and the broadscale increases in attention focused on services marketing by practitioners and academicians. The marketing literature does, however, address the issue of personal appearance as it relates to the personal sales interview.

It is well documented from a behavioural standpoint that dress has a significant impact upon perception and image formation as a part of the interpersonal communication process. Peak discovered that when personality traits are correlated with clothing styles, persons who wear conservative clothing are perceived as being more intelligent, mature, generous, sincere, trustful, understanding and dependable than those wearing more "daring" styles. Premeaux and Mondy, dress establishes a level of respect and authority. This is often necessary to get the work done.

In a study on occupation and grooming it was found that less positive characteristics are attributed to those who were groomed "poorly" than to those well groomed. There is an essential difference between the professional salesperson and the professional service practitioner which underlies the justification of this study.

Sales personnel are designated as the "front-line" customer contact persons for an organization which markets goods. Management, as well as salespersons themselves, are not only aware of the role of personal appearance and dress in interpersonal communication, but have employed the resources necessary to incorporate dress codes into promotion and marketing strategies. On the other hand, it is argued that professional service practitioners see themselves as "doers" rather than, sellers". Therefore, it is felt by some that these employees do not focus the necessary attention on those behavioural factors important in selling or marketing as would designated marketing personnel.

As Denny states: One of the fundamental misconceptions many accountants have about marketing is that...someone else can bring in the new clients and then they can take over and do the work. Unfortunately they are wrong...It takes an accountant to sell accounting services. The literature dealing with services marketing ends support to the premise that the dress behaviour of employees could be a salient attribute of the buyer when involved in the purchase process of a professional service.

Two commonly cited characteristics of services, intangibility and inseparability, give credence to this postulate. Because services are intangible in nature, perceptual and communication problems exist during the exchange process which make the true quality of the service difficult to evaluate and distinguish. Pricing and valuation problems result, leading the buyer to feel uncertainty.

With complex technical services such as legal, financial or consulting research, the problem is magnified because of the lack of knowledge of the buyer. It can be argued that because the buyer cannot see the true quality of the service for evaluation that he might use surrogate criteria such as the behaviour of the practitioner, the physical appearance of the facility or other tangible cues. Dress behaviour, then, can become a tangible evaluative criteria for the buyer, regardless of the relationship dress has to the skills of the practitioner or quality of the service performed.

Another theoretical argument offered which distinguishes services from goods is that of inseparability. Often production and consumption of services cannot be separated temporally or spatially. Consequently, personal contact exists between the producer and consumer, allowing the buyer to have the perceptual exposure necessary to observe behavioural and physical characteristics of the seller. The premise set forth as the rationale for this study is that through their behaviour, each practitioner in a service organization which has customer/client contact plays a role in marketing that organization's service. Since dress is an important aspect of that behaviour which plays a role in the communication process during this interaction, dress behaviour can be a salient factor in the exchange process.

If this premise is accepted, and dress is perceived to be important in marketing of professional services, then the question of management or control of employee dress arises. One would assume that organizations would make an effort to manage appearance so as to communicate to the client/customer in the most effective manner.

The purposes of this study were to identify the nature and extent of usage of dress codes among selected service organizations and to determine the importance of dress in the marketing of professional services as reflected in the attitudes and opinions of personnel administrators and in the policies of their organizations. The study sample consisted of personnel administrators employed in selected service organizations that are members of the American Society of Personnel Administrators; the total sample included 1000 administrators. The study involved a questionnaire designed to secure information about the perceived importance of dress codes among selected service organizations.

Questions concerned the importance of employee appearance for service organizations, the factors used in developing dress codes, the requirements of dress codes, the effect of dress codes on employee performance evaluations, and the dress code requirements for male and female employees. Questionnaires were returned by 304 personnel administrators, a 30.4 per cent return. Data was analysed using frequency distributions, and cid-squares were computed to determine statistical significance. The number of respondents from various types of service industries which were used in this study: Type of Service Organization Number in Sample Management/Marketing Consultants 51 Health Care and Human Services 47 Resort/Restaurant/Entertainment 40 Financial 39 Employment Agencies 39 Other 35 Engineering and/or Computer Services 30 Legal 13- Total 304 The personnel administrators responding to the questionnaire clearly indicated that appearance of professional employees was a significant factor when a potential client or customer evaluated their company's services. Most of the respondents indicated that personal appearance was a "very important" factor in this evaluation process.

Of the 304 responding personnel administrators, 73 per cent indicated that a dress code, either formally or informally communicated, had been established for their service organizations. Among those respondents whose organizations employed any type of dress code, 67 per cent noted that individual employee compliance to the code was a criterion for employee performance evaluation.

Eighty-five per cent of the respondents indicated that compliance to a dress code was either absolutely necessary or very important when employers underwent performance evaluation.

The employment of an established dress code varied little by type of services, ranging from 66 per cent for management consultants to 83 per cent for employment placement services. But the differences in the formalization and use of compliance varied more dramatically. While only 19 per cent of management consulting firms had established written dress codes, 60 per cent of the resort/restaurant/entertainment groups used written codes.

The data revealed that differences in the use of written codes existed between types of services, and that these were statistically significant at the.05 level. Only 42 per cent of management consulting firms considered dress code compliance in evaluation of their employees, while 80 per cent of employment placement/personnel services considered dress compliance as a factor in performance reviews. The respondents were asked to rank the level of importance of eleven factors when developing a dress code. The scale ranged from "very important," "fairly important," "of little importance," to "no importance," with each given numerical weights of 1, 2, 3, and 4 in corresponding order. Mean scores and the percentages responding to each level of importance are reported. Customer expectations, tradition/convention in the profession, and the opinion of the organization's C.E.O. were the three most important factors listed by the respondents in the development of dress codes.

Among those respondents whose organizations employed any type of dress code, chi-square analysis was performed to compare the classifications of the companies to the formality of the dress codes. Though not statistically significant, the study revealed that more of the local/independent service organizations used formal written dress codes, while more of the multi-located firms utilized dress codes which were informally communicated. Over one-third of the respondents indicated that their dress codes had been established within the last 20 years.

Many of the companies had made changes in their dress codes within the last 10 years. Though not statistically significant, it was found that the firms with revised dress codes were more relaxed in requiring a traditional business look. The differences in the degree of requirement for wearing a "traditional business suit" by type of business organization. Of all types of services in the sample, financial services most required business suits, and engineering/ computer least. Those organizations classified as personnel services expected the wearing of suits with skirts more often than others, and again the engineering/computer services required the traditional suit with skirt to the least degree.

Most of the respondents indicated that dress is important in marketing services and that compliance to a dress code is a criterion for employee performance evaluation. While most administrators agreed that dress is a significant factor in their companies' success, few organizations had formal written dress codes; dress codes are more often communicated orally. The results of this study lend support to the premise that dress and appearance of employees could be a salient attribute of the buyer when involved in the purchase process of a professional service. Although the usage of dress codes differed among service organizations, many administrators agreed that dress and appearance are particularly important in making an initial impression and in progressing in a business career. More needs to be known about the actual impact of dress and appearance on the communication process with clients and customers in professional service organizations.

QUALITY IN SMALL- AND MEDIUM-SIZED RESORTS

Total Quality Management can be defined as a satisfaction of social shareholders via implementing effective planning, programmes, policies, and strategies, as well as using human and other assets efficiently and continually within an organization.

This approach will continue to be one of the hot topics among practitioners, academics, and professionals in the new millennium. This presents how a new TQM readiness model can be utilized for providing social shareholders' satisfaction and continuous improvement in small- and medium-sized resort organizations.

Five-star resort staffs appear to have better organizational strengths than four-star resort staffs in North Cyprus. Four-star resort employees indicate substantial differences in their perceptions concerning TQM readiness elements. An extensive literature review has been conducted.

Issues examined include the following:

- Where to start?
- Is it valuable to bring such a total system?
- Should some parts be imported instead of the whole? and
- Is there any cheap way to bring TQM to small- or medium-sized organizations?

Oakland, the first decision of where to begin can be daunting, referred to as the Total Quality Paralysis problem in quality-management literature. This has been confirmed by other experts and academics who state that small- and medium-sized enterprises generally are less comfortable in bringing TQM into their organizations than large companies are due to limited managerial knowledge, skill, ability, incentives, resources, and time. Only a few studies have been developed on TQM readiness assessment criteria in small- and medium-sized firms. Scholars and others have a common understanding that the more clearly the TQM readiness factors are assessed, the healthier a transition can be achieved to the TQM process. The TQM literature states, "Organizations, which are ready for change in climate, have more opportunity to achieve a successful implementation in a shorter period of time". A common point endorsed in the literature is that there must be a readiness survey before designing, developing, and implementing a TQM programme. This may help to determine TQM factors within an organization and to identify potential problems that may create resistance to TQM and will help to develop a database for future comparisons. Walker and Salameth have stated that only a small percentage of resorts have heard "the siren call of TQM implementations" even in the U.S. It is interesting to note that after 10 years, the literature regarding resorts is still sparse.

Although some viable resorts in limited geographical areas have reported that their TQM performance resulted in profit increased, employee satisfaction, and better usage of economic resources, only a few case studies have been published. As Bloomquist and Breiter indicate, "While those case studies are important in elaboration on the theme of quality management, there remain no reliable statistical data on industry-wide performance credited to quality management."

CHALLENGE FOR RESORT ORGANIZATIONS

Cyprus is the third-largest island in the Mediterranean. Cyprus has a great historical heritage, conserved environment beauties, and a good climate, and after the war in 1974, the island was divided into north and south parts. No study has been conducted on how TQM can be applied in small- and medium-sized resort organizations in North Cyprus, which is a major deficiency since tourism is the leading sector. North Cyprus is certainly not the only country where tourism is the most important business sector. The World Tourism Organization statistics, tourism in the world is expected to reach a volume of $US 4 trillion after 2000. This will mean that one out of nine people in the world will be employed in tourism industry in 2010.

The aim of this analysis is to provide a better understanding of how different groups of managers, chiefs, and employees perceive their readiness towards the TQM philosophy in North Cyprus four and five-star resorts. In June 1999, a preliminary investigation was carried out through one-on-one interviews with several assistant general managers, department managers, chiefs, and other lower-level employees from the four- and five-star resorts of North Cyprus. The aim was to design a more realistic TQM readiness model, as well as to prepare a better quantitative questionnaire for the targeted resorts.

The hypotheses of this study are as follows: There is no difference between small-and medium-sized hospitality organizations' hierarchical levels concerning their TQM readiness. There is a difference between small-and medium-sized hospitality organizations' hierarchical levels concerning their TQM readiness. A new model with its first selected eight factors of TQM culture was identified.

These factors are leadership, participation, teamwork, employee satisfaction, empowerment, influence, change, and training. It is important to mention that the assessment factors may not represent all the TQM readiness culture factors. In time, other related factors may be added to this group.

THE ASSUMPTIONS UNDERLYING THE MODEL

The assumptions underlying this model include the following:

- The readiness model factors are iterative; in other words, every organization may use several different preassessment factors, and the rank of these factors also may be different.
- TQM is not a completely new strategic system but rather is a process of developing the current system, opening its way to continuous improvement.
- The readiness model will decrease the total cost, time, and energy of an organization in transforming it into a new TQM culture.

The model involves two important stages. The first stage is to understand and to monitor the present organizational system, especially when dealing with the factors of TQM philosophy and its soft components such as leadership, teamwork, participation, influence, empowerment, and employee satisfaction.

The second stage is the process of examining the gap between upper, middle, and lower layers of personnel in order to prevent possible resistance from different layers at the time of transitioning to a new TQM culture, as well as preparing a database for future assessments. This database may serve as a benchmark where yearly data can be compared with the previous year, necessary precautions can be taken against weaknesses, and the organization can open its way to a continuous improvement process.

Of course, if the necessary proactive precautions can be taken successfully every year, the actual gap among the layers of staff will be narrowed in terms of employee resistance and inefficient use of time, money, and energy. As a result of successful TQM applications, the social shareholders will be more satisfied, and effects of internal challenges will be minimized for the organization.

The data in this study were obtained from four- and five-star resorts. In these resorts, the general manager, usually the owner or a relative who has a very close relationship to the investors, has overall responsibility for all activities. The department managers work under the control of the general managers and report directly to them.

Department chiefs largely serve the role of supervisors, reporting to the department manager. The rationale for selecting four- and five-star resorts is because they attract the majority of tourists in North Cyprus. A total of seven out of 10 resorts were included in the study. There are two resorts that are identified as five-star resorts; the remaining five are four-star resorts. All seven of these five- and four-star resorts were sampled, which provide an overall 100 per cent sampling ratio among five-star resorts and 87 per cent sampling ratio among four-star resorts. This stratified-sampling ratio is very high, and therefore the research is designed to be representative. Stratified sampling has been used in determining the number of employees of four- and five-star resorts. The stratified sampling technique "separates the population into relative homogenous groups".

The resorts employed approximately 550 permanent staff according to statistics gathered from the tourism ministry at the time of the research. The average return rate from the quantitative survey collected from the managers, chiefs, and employees was 73 per cent, 85 per cent, and 39 per cent respectively. Among the 500 questionnaires distributed, 267 were returned, 10 were not completely answered, and 13 were considered biased. Consequently, 23 responses were deleted from the analyses.

The net return rate of 43.8 per cent was quite adequate for the set of questions. A perception survey, a self-administered questionnaire addressed to all managers, chiefs, and employees of the targeted resorts, was prepared in order to collect the necessary readiness data from a more comprehensive perspective.

Respondents were asked to indicate their degree of agreement with each statement on a five-point Likert scale: 1=strongly agree, 2=agree, 3=somewhat agree/disagree, 4=disagree, and 5=strongly disagree. Furthermore, three questions were asked about the ranking of the resort, type of ownership, and the job position. Items for each subscale were subjected to a reliability assessment. The Cronbach coefficient alpha value for the total scale was 9602, and the subscales were 9092.8425.8812.7177.6993.7164.6976, and.7744 for leadership, team, influence, empowerment, participation, training, change, and satisfaction.

Usually, a reliability coefficient above 0.50 is considered to be a sufficiently high reliability. A factor analysis of the TQM readiness questions in the survey was performed. In order to identify the actual factors in the survey, all questions that did not load cleanly on one factor were dropped from further analysis, which left 61 questions. The frequency and one-way analysis of variance were calculated as a second statistictical technique. Levin and Rubin, ANOVA tests are used for determining the significance of the differences among more than two sample means.

The critical mean scores of the TQM readiness survey for the four- and five-star resort mangers, chiefs, and staff. A one-way ANOVA analysis is used to explore whether there is a significant difference in the perceptions among upper-, middle-, and lower-level employees of the resorts. In terms of highest and lowest scores, it has been observed that there is little consistency in perceptions among the three staff levels. Results for five-star resorts indicate that employees have significantly higher scores on seven items: teamwork, leadership, and influence.

For those seven items, employees had the highest mean scores. Considering all 61 questions, four-star resort employees are less positive than five-star resort employees. They have significantly higher scores on 32 items. For those 32 items, all staff has different scores on each item. Interestingly, the managers have higher mean scores than chiefs and employees on eight items, which are mainly dealt with through satisfaction, empowerment, participation, and leadership.

The chiefs gave negative scores to change, empowerment, teamwork, and participation factors through six questions. Four-star resorts had aggregate means for the 61 items indicated by managers, chiefs, and employees. Both managers and chiefs expressed a moderate level of TQM readiness, while employees exhibited a low level of TQM readiness. However, in five-star resorts, the aggregate means for the same items were managers, chiefs and staff, where all expressed a moderate level of TQM readiness.

Therefore, the null hypothesis was rejected, and the alternative hypothesis was accepted. North Cyprus is a suitable island for tourism because of its undeveloped industry, rich historical and cultural heritage, natural beauty, and relatively unspoiled environment. The various governments that have come to power all have stated that tourism is the primary sector in achieving economic development. The aim of this research was to find out how different groups of managers, chiefs, and employees of four- and five-star resorts in North Cyprus perceive their readiness towards the TQM philosophy With this study it is possible to point out to the owners arid managers the weak and strong aspects of the TQM soft side components they are practicing, and it also provides an opportunity to remove the resistance and conflicts that arise because of perception differences about this philosophy Some researchers point out that in many cases, TQM has been applied without any readiness research and has thus resulted in failure.

As Weeks, "The perceptions of managers, chiefs, and employees are crucial because individuals act as if their beliefs or perceptions are real." Social shareholders are defined by the author as interested or chain parties who are in the same business arena and are a part of the same business life in a free market economic system such as customers, owners, employees, suppliers, government, municipality, and so forth. Two of the five-star resorts are in the same complex and therefore are considered as one resort. Two resorts have been excluded from the research due to extraordinary reasons.

COMPETITIVE ADVANTAGE

This offers an in-depth treatment of conversion franchising, where new franchisees are added to a franchised system by recruiting existing independent entrepreneurs or competitors' franchisees. The first part of the paper examines conversion franchising as a source of competitive advantage. This discussion leads to the articulation off our propositions. The second part of the paper looks at the empirical results of our study of 72 North American franchisors.

Seventy-two per cent of these firms use conversion franchising in their domestic markets, and 26 per cent use conversions in international locales. The propositions relating to a franchisor's decision to use conversions based on increased levels of experience, economic resources, and to a lesser extent skills! knowledge, all were supported. These results lend support to the literature indicating that resources and skills serve as sources of competitive advantage. Implications for research and practice are discussed. Franchising is emerging as a preferred method of doing business throughout the global economy.

A recent study by the International Franchise Association estimated that, by early in the new millennium, nearly 50 per cent of every U.S. consumer dollar would have been spent in franchised locations. Business franchising has spread rapidly to most continents during the past decade. Given the widespread use of franchising, how can firms leverage better this method of doing business? Some firms have gained increased advantage by adding mobility to their franchised operation by bringing their products/services to the customer where and when they demand them.

But increasingly, firms are turning to conversion franchising as a way of enhancing growth and of gaining competitive advantage in multiple markets. Conversion franchising occurs when a franchisor adds new franchisees to the system by recruiting existing independent businesses or competitors' franchisees.

The purpose of this paper is to examine closely this emerging phenomenon by drawing on relevant literature and by reporting the results of an exploratory study of conversion franchising. Before discussing some of the competitive advantages that can accrue from employing conversion franchising, it first is instructive to review some of the advantages of traditional franchising. Franchising's longevity and success also may be due to the fact that, organizationally, it represents a collaborative alliance.

The alliance depends on the cooperation of two entrepreneurs in order to be successful. Further, these partners depend on cooperation among a network of entrepreneurs to advance common methods and goals, like the sharing of information on innovations that potentially could benefit all franchise partners.Franchising traditionally has offered many competitive advantages over independently formed and operated businesses. The franchisor has access to capital at lower risk; cost sharing with the franchisee; rapid market penetration at a relatively lower cost than establishing one's own distribution system; economies of scale; a motivated workforce of indigenous entrepreneurs; and reduced monitoring and control costs. The franchisee gets an opportunity to enter a business at less cost with a proven product or service and brand name. Additionally, the franchisee frequently receives management assistance in the areas of business location, facilities design, operating procedures, purchasing, and marketing.

These advantages have been born out by a superior survival rate for franchising over independent ventures. Next, we turn to a discussion of conversion franchising and its competitive advantages. Conversion franchising occurs when a franchisor adds new franchisees to the system by recruiting independent businesses, chains, and/or franchisees from other franchised systems. Conversion franchising offers additional advantages to those discussed under traditional franchising. The use of conversion franchising appears to be expanding in recent years, as several industries have experienced changing environmental conditions that often have combined to favour this form of franchising.

The environmental conditions fostering conversions include economic, market, competitive, and technological changes. A contracting economy can mean tight credit policies, making it difficult to raise funds for new projects. During one such period, 3.7 per cent of the domestic resorts converted to a new brand affiliation. A restricted real estate market has led many fast food franchisors to convert existing urban locations to their system rather than to devel op new sites. Saturated markets and increased competition coupled with the growing consumer demand for rejuvenated brand names have generated conversions in the real estate and hospitality industries.

Independents have converted to ReMax and ERA, while Holiday Inn has converted some Ramada Inns and vice versa. Keeping abreast of changing technology has forced firms to seek conversions with systems on the cutting edge of technology, such as Century 21 and Coldwell Banker in Real Estate or Marriott's reservation system in the lodging industry. Resource-based models of organization indicate that established know-how serves as a basis for competitive advantage. Experienced franchisors have developed such managerial capabilities.

Moreover, experienced firms often operate in more competitive arenas, in turn forcing them to try innovative strategies such as conversions. Experienced franchisors have learned to share their know-how with franchisees and have established a record of strong performance, in part because they have taken the time to build brand equity and economies of scale in purchasing, advertising, and distribution, all of which are attractive to independent businesses.

Thus, we suggest the following proposition: Proposition 1: The decision to use conversion franchising is associated positively with the experience of the franchisor.

Once a business has converted to a new franchise, is the conversion likely to lead to sustainable competitive advantage? Possible answers to this question are examined in the ensuing discussion. Using the framework of competitive advantage from the field of strategic management is consistent with the view expressed by Castrogiovanni and Justis that researchers need to consider findings from outside the franchising field to assess their generalizability to franchisors.

Competitive advantage is concerned with developing a value-creating strategy by uniquely combining bundles of valuable firm resources and skills to yield positional advantages that result in positive outcomes. Firm resources include both tangible and intangible assets. Firm skills include organizational, technical, and market knowledge, among others.

Aaker argues that a retail location superior to the competition's can act as a key asset, leading to competitive advantage. Barney suggests that a valuable location can act as an imperfectly imitable physical capital resource for the firm, while Day and Wensley see location as a tangible resource that can enable a firm to exercise its capabilities, leading to positional advantage. An existing location may be the only space available on a crowded playing field. This is particularly true in the restaurant, retail, and resort industries, where location is a key element. Franchisors can acquire location resources in tight real estate markets by converting independents or chains that possess strategic locations.

A strong brand name may be regarded as a superior resource or as a key asset, leading to competitive advantage for today's firms. Consumers in every industry are increasingly brand conscious. At the core of the franchising concept is the bundling of a brand or a trade name with a good or service to sell to entrepreneurs in return for fees or royalties. The need to maintain brand equity motivates franchisors to grow their systems in order to develop promotion economies and, therefore, to spread promotion costs over more units. Converting independents to a franchise system allows for rapid growth and increased name recognition.

For example, in the resort industry converting members of other chains has been shown to lead to increased occupancy rates. Thus, conversions permit firms to reposition themselves under a new brand to enhance their competitive position. Human resources are critical to the proper execution of any strategy Franchising taps into entrepreneurs who sign on as franchisees to manage individual business units. Sen provides an extended discussion of the franchisee as a source of managerial talent. While entrepreneurs may be motivated to do well, they often are inexperienced and require considerable training on the part of the franchisor.

Using inexperienced franchisees poses a risk of adverse selection, that is, the franchisee misrepresents his/her abilities to the franchisor. Conversion franchising enables the franchisor to bring in experienced franchisees who already have managed a similar business in the industry, either as an independent or as a franchisee for a competitor, thereby reducing the risk of adverse selection. Experienced managers are more likely to enhance a repositioned unit's performance than one with less industry experience. Furthermore, such an experienced franchisee requires less training support. An existing customer base is a major resource that independents and members of other chains possess that can be internalized by the franchisor upon conversion. Since converts can resume business rapidly with existing customers, royalty streams also can begin flowing quickly to the franchisor.

Of course, an additional benefit is that a competitor now has been co-opted into the system instead of working against it. We suggest the following: Proposition 2: The franchisor's decision to use conversion franchising is associated with the potential resource advantages provided by conversions. It has just been argued that conversion franchising brings together key resources of the franchisor and franchisee that have a high potential for improving the competitive positioning of each alliance member.

We now will examine important skills that can play a role in creating competitive advantage. As a cooperative alliance, conversion franchising facilitates the sharing and enhancement of skills to improve the competitive position of both the convert and the franchisor in expanding markets. Skills or capabilities are those attributes that enable the firm to coordinate and to exploit its resources. At the core of the firm's capabilities are its knowledge base from which the skills originate. Thus, we now examine the role knowledge of markets, technology, and organization plays as key sources of competitive advantage provided by a firm's skills.

When a franchisor enters a new market, he or she does so with a limited knowledge of local market conditions and consumer preferences. Since cultures, consumer behaviour, and marketing methods are often different in various markets, franchised systems may need to be adapted to fit local requirements better. Feltenstein argues that firms need to think globally but to act locally and that much of the variability in sales, service, costs, and margins is determined by local market knowledge. Experience in growing the business provides enhanced knowledge for franchisors in areas such as market and site selection.

Acquiring experienced converts helps leverage the advantage of such experience. Moreover, converting independents or other chain members who have been operating in the local market for some time allows the franchisor to internalize these skills into the franchise system. Newly allied members also can aid the franchisor in maneuvering around local rules and regulations that otherwise could slow down or could block a venture. Since conversions typically are of firms operating in the same type or in closely related businesses, converts bring their technical knowledge and expertise to the partnership.

Two general types of technical knowledge are especially relevant in the case of conversions: industry and franchising knowledge. Knowledge relevant to the industry in terms of competitors, substitutes, methods of distribution, and general industry practices are critical to determining competitive advantage. A convert brings new perspective on industry knowledge to the franchisor, broadening the latter's knowledge base and vice versa.

Experience in a particular type of franchising is critical to a system's competitive advantage. The franchise concept is developed on what is believed to be a successful set of practices, and then knowledge bundles are replicated for franchisees. Independents who convert may obtain the immediate advantages of competing with a proven franchise concept. Converts who are previous franchisees presumably have switched because they perceive the new franchisor to have a superior franchise concept.

Such franchise-experienced converts, however, also may provide additional knowledge from their prior franchising experience to enhance the concept of their new franchisor, thereby providing advantages for the entire system. Converts' technical skills are enhanced by the franchisor through extensive training of new members through operating manuals and procedures, and through technical guidance and support.

For example, PIP Printing, a leader in the quick-printing industry, offers its franchisees training workshops. The technical skills of the franchisee are enhanced further by the introduction of sophisticated computer systems. In real estate, 20 per cent of the firms in the U.S. are organized as a franchise. New franchisees in this industry gain access to nationwide databases of existing housing stock. Franchising enables a firm to harness the efforts of entrepreneurs while reducing the costs of monitoring a large multiunit organization. Thus, organizational skills revolve around monitoring to prevent franchisees who either may under invest in their units or may shirk on product quality because these actions affect the entire franchise system.

The scale or size of the system contributes to improved organizational coordination. Increased size of the firm enhances monitoring capabilities of the franchisor by reducing the lower per unit costs of monitoring. Conversions enable a franchisor to expand more quickly, thereby strengthening the organizational monitoring skills of the franchisor. Another way to control opportunism is through the payment of fees to the franchisor; this provides financial incentive not to behave opportunistically because the franchisor risks forfeiting the fee if the franchisor suspends the relationship.

Monitoring capability also can be enhanced by learning how best to control the franchisee's behaviour over time. Thus, the longer the franchisor has been offering franchises, the greater the likelihood of improved monitoring skills. Independents can gain other improved organizational efficiencies, such as increased purchasing power, joint or pooled advertising, and other benefits of similar economies of scale, by joining a franchise system. We offer the following proposition: Proposition 3: The franchisor's decision to use conversion franchising is associated with the potential skill advantages provided by conversions.

The literature on competitive advantages stresses those factors that facilitate the development of competitive advantage. However, traditional strategic management theory also notes that the acquisition of skills and resources may also be seen as threats or as challenges confronting the firm when undertaking a new strategy. Anecdotal evidence from franchise experience suggests that certain problems may be encountered when making conversions. Some of the resource-related challenges posed by conversions include the added time it takes to implement a programme or to socialize or to retrain converts. Newly acquired entrepreneurs may be experienced but may be unwilling to work as part of a team or to readily adopt new business methods, thus diluting the advantages of a conversion.

Market, technical, and organizational capabilities may be threatened because of the need to adopt new rules or methods to accommodate a new local market or to attract a convert to join. In short, the franchise concept and standard contract may be changed for opportunistic rather than strategic reasons in order to attract and retain new converts. The reality of the existence of such threats or barriers suggests the following: Proposition 4: The franchisor's decision to use conversion franchising will he associated negatively with the perceived existence of threats posed by the conversion.

The purpose of this empirical part is to provide a description of the current nature and extent of the use of conversion franchising among North American franchisors; and to provide an initial examination of the propositions relating to the factors behind the decision to use conversion franchising by franchisors. A random sample stratified by size and industry of 250 North American franchisors were selected for the study from the Franchise Annual. The top manager of each firm was sent a cover letter and a two-page questionnaire concerning their use of conversion franchising; one follow-up mailing was sent three weeks later.

Seventy-eight firms responded. Six decided not to participate because of mergers, company policy, etc.; 72 firms returned useable questionnaires for a 29 per cent response rate. This compares favourably with other surveys of franchise companies that have reported similar return rates. The profile of franchisors in our sample reveals a good distribution of firms across eight broad industry sectors.

The firms are large, averaging 746 total units and having an average of 23 years experience in franchising. The majority of responding managers hold sufficiently high level positions in their organizations to be considered knowledgeable about their firm's franchise strategies. A comparison of respondent firms to a random sample of 40 non- respondents in terms of industry, size, and age revealed no significant differences. This should reduce concerns of response bias in our sample. The survey instrument consisted of 10 questions. After defining conversion franchising, the first question asked the respondents to indicate their agreement concerning 18 characteristics of conversion franchising.

These characteristics represented the advantages and barriers of conversion franchising. Responses were made on a Likert-type scale ranging from 1 = not at all to 5 = highly descriptive of your experience. Other questions asked whether the firm used conversion franchising and explored the extent and reasons for doing so. The last three questions explored the use of conversions in international markets. We describe the variables used to explore the four propositions. The decision to convert was assessed by the following survey question: Has your firm used conversion franchising now or in the past?

A simple yes/no response was recorded. This is the categorical dependent variable for investigating the propositions. The remaining variables serve as the independent variables. Franchisor experience was expressed as the number of years the firm had been in business. These were combined further into two factors using principle components analysis with varimax rotation; these factors explain 50 per cent of the variance in conversion advantages. One factor represents "market/location skills" and is comprised of 4 items and has an eigenvalue of 1.58 and a reliability of =.60. The second factor represents "economic resources" and is comprised of five items and has an eigen-value of 2.87 and a reliability of varies =.73.

Two items did not load on any factor. A third item was dropped from the market factor due to reliability problems. These latter three items were not included in any tests of the propositions. Other sources of competitive advantages based on skills were drawn from the Franchise Annual. Technical advantages included seven dummy variables representing eight industry sectors. Franchising knowledge was assessed by the number of years the firm had been franchising. The organizational skills assessed were monitored through scale and financial bonding. Scale was measured by the number of franchised units possessed and financial bonding was measured using the initial franchising fee charged by the franchisor. Competitive barriers/threats were assessed strictly with subjective measures drawn from the eighteen conversion franchising characteristics described earlier. Seven of the items represented potential barriers or threats.

These were reduced to two factors using principle components analysis. The factors explain 49 per cent of the variance in conversion barriers. One factor was labeled "changes" because of the adjustments to existing procedures required by conv ersions. This factor was comprised of three items and has an eigenvalue of 1.52 and a reliability of infinity =.50. The second barrier was labeled "effort" because of the extra effort required by the franchisor to make conversions and was comprised of four items and possesses and eigenvalue of 1.89 and a reliability of infinity =.60 The nature and extent of conversion franchising is described using descriptive statistics. The exploration of the propositions was analysed using discriminant analysis.

The decision to convert represents a nominal dependent variable. The analysis derives a linear combination of independent variables that will discriminate best between the firms that use conversion franchising and the non-users.

The analysis determines whether the competitive advantages and barriers posed by conversion franchising account for a significant variance in the decision to convert. In addition, this method of analysis determines both the predictive accuracy of the independent variables and their relative importance in explaining the decision to convert.

Seventy-two per cent of the firms surveyed use conversion franchising in their domestic markets. Almost half began using conversions prior to 1987; the remaining firms have started using conversions since that time. Among the firms using conversions, an average of 26 per cent of their units are conversions. In responding to an openended question as to why businesses converted to their franchise, our respondents identified eight major reasons. The most frequently cited reasons were to acquire a brand name, which represents one of the major competitive resources conversions can provide businesses.

Awareness, identity, and recognition on a national or global level were cited as the chief benefits of branding. Franchisor characteristics and operating results were tied for second as the most frequently cited reasons for conversion. Key franchisor characteristics included proprietary products and quality of operation and system. Operating performance benefits of conversions included better pricing, leading to increased sales and profitability.

Support services such as technology and research and development, as well as training, each were tied for third in importance for conversions. These represent technological and organizational skills frequently mentioned as advantages of joining a good franchise system. Cost savings and other marketing benefits represented the fourth and fifth major reasons why franchisors believe that businesses convert to their system.

These reasons appear to be congruent with the expected competitive advantages of conversion franchising discussed previously. One of the difficulties in using conversions is that franchisors may have to make adjustments to their normal franchise plans in order to attract well-run businesses to convert. However, less than 25 per cent of the franchisors using conversions needed to make any changes to their normal conversion franchise plan.

Most changes made to attract converts included reduced fees; added training; reduced royalties; covered remodeling costs; additional capital; longer contracts; and other. Thus, a variety of changes are made by a minority of franchisors in order to attract businesses to convert to their system. The majority of franchisors who are currently using conversions to grow plan to continue using them in the future. Thirty-one per cent plan to increase their use of conversions; 25 per cent plan to use them at the same rate as in the past. Only two per cent of the franchisors plan to decrease their use of conversions in their domestic markets. These intentions indicate that franchisors are satisfied that conversion franchising delivers distinct advantages over other forms of doing business. The survey also briefly explored the franchisors' use of conversions in international markets.

Twenty-six per cent of the respondents use conversion franchising in international markets. Half of these franchisors began using conversions internationally in 1990 or after, and currently an average 5.8 per cent of their overseas units are conversions. The country markets in which they have the largest number of conversions include Canada, Germany, France, and the U.K.. Importantly, of the franchisors using conversions internationally, 61 per cent intend to increase their future use of conversions internationally.

By way of summary, the descriptive data reveal that a substantial proportion of North American franchisors are using conversion franchising. Businesses were attracted to convert because of numerous competitive advantages associated with conversion franchises. The future of conversions appears to be quite promising, especially in international markets, as the domestic market becomes more saturated.

All four propositions advanced regarding the factors associated with a franchisor's decision to use conversion franchising were examined using discriminant analysis. Since there were only two categories for the dependent variable, a single discriminant function was derived. The function, using competitive advantages and barriers to predict the decision to convert, is meaningful. The function accounts for 55 per cent of the variance in the decision to convert.

The validity of the function is ascertained by how well it predicts the classification of firms between those that use conversion franchises and those who do not. The derived function correctly classified 93 per cent of the firms. This is almost a 33 per cent improvement over chance alone. A statistically significant and valid function also may be interpreted. For interpretation, we use the discriminant loadings from the structure matrix. These loadings are simple correlations between each independent variable and the discriminant function. The loadings can be interpreted similar to factor loadin gs to assess the relative contribution of each independent variable.

The analysis of the discriminant loadings and their ability to discriminate between franchisors who convert and those who do not reveals five variables that significantly explain the decision to convert. Proposition 1, the decision to convert is associated with franchisor experience. Only experienced franchisors with an established reputation and system can use conversions meaningfully. Proposition 1 is supported as "experience," has a relatively high, positive loading, and is also a significant discriminator between franchisors who use conversions and those who do not.

Proposition 2, concerning the resource advantages associated with conversion franchising, is supported. "Economic resources" has a high positive loading, and its mean is also significantly different between the two groups of franchisors. Firms that use conversions perceive that they derive greater competitive resource advantages than firms who do not u se conversions. Proposition 3 concerning the association of "skill/knowledge" advantages of conversion partially is supported. Franchise skills market skills, and industry knowledge all are associated with the decision to convert.

Franchise and market skills have the two highest, positive loadings and are significant discriminators as indicated by tests of mean differences. The retail industry sector has a moderate but negative loading. The negative loading suggests that non-retail industry experience is more relevant in the decision to convert; other industry categories did not have high loadings, however.

The ability of this variable to discriminate between the two groups is marginal. Organizational monitoring skills achieved through scale and bondings had relatively weaker loadings and were not significantly different among the two groups of franchisors, contrary to our proposition. Finally, competitive barriers did not add significant discriminating information to the decision to convert, contrary to Proposition 4. Neither effort nor changes had strong loadings, nor were their means significantly different between the two groups of franchisors. However, the negative sign of the loadings for effort was in the predicted direction.

Overall, our implicit model of franchisor experience and the competitive resources and skill advantages provided by conversion franchising appear to be significant predictors of the decision to use conversions. Although competitive barriers appear to exist, they do not appear to contribute significantly to the decision to convert, at least among this sample of franchisors. Although conversion franchising appears to have been used for some time, its use has accelerated recently. Over half of the firms have started using conversion franchising since 1987.

While conversions appear to be more prevalent in domestic rather than international markets, a greater proportion of firms intend to increase their use of conversions in international versus domestic markets. The descriptive data also seem to support the franchising and strategy literature regarding why firms convert to a franchise system. Resources such as brand identity, franchisor support, and training were among the most frequently cited reasons.

Three of four propositions concerning the factors affecting the decision to use conversion franchising were supported in whole or in part. The most significant discriminant variables explained 69 per cent of the variance accounted for by the discriminant function. Our results confirm that firm experience, economic resources, market skills, franchising knowledge, and selected industry experience all contribute significantly in explaining why franchisors use conversion franchising as part of their growth strategy.

These results support the strategy and marketing literature, indicating that resources and skills serve as sources of competitive advantage. The results also support the franchising literature regarding the various benefits of this form of business organization. Competitive barriers were related negatively to the decision to use conversions but did not have strong loadings, nor did the means of the barriers differ significantly between those firms that use conversions and those that do not. It seems reasonable to assume that franchisors tend to focus more on the advantages rather than on the threats when considering whether or not to use conversion franchising.

The results of this study should be examined in the light of its potential limitations. The sample size may be considered somewhat small, especially when analysing the propositions due to missing data. The results are pertinent only to North American franchisors. However, North American franchisors are the most mature and therefore are the most likely to consider conversions.

Our data reveal that business experience is a significant factor in the decision. Our respondent companies had similar profiles to non-respondents, minimizing response bias. Our measures of competitive advantages and barriers were drawn mostly from the field rather than the literature; this may reduce their explanatory power. However, both subjective and objective measures of competitive advantages were used to reduce same-source bias.

Slightly more than half of the variance in the decision to convert was accounted for by the variables examined in this study. Thus, these results provide a partial but not a complete picture of the factors affecting a firm's decision to use conversion franchising. With the limitations in mind, we offer some implications for practice and research. North American franchisors considering the use of conversions should possess significant experience in their business to develop both their business concept and a strong identity for their brand.

Having done so, franchisors then have something to offer to businesses seeking to join their franchise system. When investigating potential businesses to convert, franchisors must evaluate carefully the resources needed to attract technically qualified businesses with a good track record in order to gain resource advantages. Conversions may enhance the franchisor's market skills if the new franchisees are located in more distant markets and possess a prime business location. Conversions appear to be more attractive in non-retail sectors such as business and personal services and lodging. However, additional research is warranted to confirm these results. North American businesses seeking to convert to a new or different franchise system are advised to seek a franchise with a proven concept and a strong brand identity in the markets in which they want to expand.

Successful business converts should have a proven track record of financial performance. These potential converts should demonstrate that their management team is well experienced and qualified in their industry; however, they may lack some key resource or skill that the franchisor can provide. This has demonstrated the relevance of employing theories of competitive advantage to guide systematic studies of conversion franchising. Future studies should develop more robust measures of competitive advantages and threats.

Larger samples from other parts of the world also should be included to determine if the factors affecting the decision to use conversion franchising are the same in other national or regional markets. A particularly fruitful avenue for future research suggested by our data is the use of conversion franchising for international expansion.

While a minority of the North American firms currently are using international conversions, the majority of these firms intend to increase the use of conversions for international growth. Studies examining the factors affecting the international conversion decision also would be a valuable addition to the franchising knowledge base.

CATERING AND FOOD SERVICE

Catering is the business of providing food service at a remote site. Mobile catering is the business of selling prepared food from some sort of vehicle. It is a feature of urban culture in many countries. The food service generally encompasses those places, institutions, and companies responsible for any meal eaten away from home. This industry includes restaurants, school and hospital cafeterias, catering operations, and many other formats. The companies that supply foodservice operators are called foodservice distributors. Foodservice hard goods like ovens and refrigerators are often sold by large buying groups.

Some companies manufacture products in both consumer and foodservice versions. The consumer version usually comes in individual-sized packages with elaborate label design for retail sale. The foodservice version is packaged in a much larger industrial size and often lacks the colourful label designs of the consumer version.

Foodservice sales to restaurants and institutions are estimated to be approximately $400 Billion, about equal with consumer sales of foods through grocery outlets. A food cart is a motorless trailer that can be hauled by automobile, bicycle, or hand to the point of sale, often a public sidewalk or park. Carts typically have an onboard heating or refrigeration system to keep the food ready for consumption.

Foods and beverages often served from carts include:

- Halal food such as lamb or chicken over rice, or in a gyro
- Ice cream and other frozen treats
- Coffee, bagels, donuts, Egg sandwichs and other breakfast items

Food Truck is a mobile kitchen, known colliqually in some regions as a "X" Truck, is a mobile venue that sells food. Some, including ice cream trucks, sell mostly frozen or prepackaged food; others are more like restaurants-on-wheels.

Food trucks make frequent appearances at carnivals, construction sites, and other temporary venues where large numbers of people gather. Some college campuses and surrounding areas boast many food trucks with loyal followings; for example, visitors to Harvard University or MIT in Cambridge, Massachusetts or the campus of the University of Pennsylvania in Philadelphia may see some very popular trucks parked outside the main entrances to buildings at lunchtime. At Rutgers University, the Grease Trucks serve "fat sandwiches" that contain an ensemble of ingredients such as steak, cheese, chicken fingers, french fries, mozzarella sticks, jalapeño poppers, and more. In the United Kingdom, these are known as burger vans and can be found on nearly all major trunk roads at the side of the road selling their food. A 1/4lb burger can be purchased for about £2.

Many people prefer to stop at one of these Burger vans when travelling due to the cheap price, rather than stop at a motorway service station where prices can be extremely high. Sometimes also called "maggot wagon," "roach coach," or "gut truck," these rolling restaurants can frequently be found at or near construction sites. An early version of the food truck was the US Army's mobile canteen and before that the old West's chuckwagon.

A mobile kitchen is a modified van with a built-in grill, deep fryer, or other cooking equipment. It offers more flexibility in the menu since the vendor can prepare food to order. A vendor can choose to park the van in one place, as with a cart, or to broaden the business's reach by driving the van to several customer locations. Examples of mobile kitchens include taco trucks on the west coast of the United States, especially Southern California, and fish and chips vans in the United Kingdom.

A concession trailer has preparation equipment like a mobile kitchen, but it cannot move on its own. As such it is suited for events lasting several days, such as funfairs. In addition to being operated as private businesses, mobile catering vehicles are also used after natural disasters to feed people in areas with damaged infrastructure. The Salvation Army has several mobile kitchens that it uses for this purpose. An event caterer serves food with waiting staff at dining tables or sets up a self-serve buffet.

The food may be prepared on site, made completely at the event, or the caterer may choose to bring prepared food and put the finishing touches on once they arrive. The event caterer staff isn't responsible for preparing the food but often help set up the dining area. This service is typically provided at banquets, conventions, and weddings. Any event where all the attenders are provided with food and drinks or sometimes only hors d'oeuvres is often called a catered event.

A catering company or specialist is expected to know not just food preparation, but how to make it attractive. Many events require working with the entire theme or colour scheme. Catering companies have moved towards full-service taking charge of not only food preparation but also decorations, such as table settings or lighting.

It's not that food is no longer a focal point, but rather that it is part of a broader mission. Many suggest that catering is about satisfying all the senses. A caterer and his or her staff should be friendly and coorperative because, after all, they are in the food service industry and should follow the motto "the customer is always right". Catering is typically sold on a per-person basis, where adding additional people is a flat price per person.

Keeping the cost of the food and supplies below this is required to make a profit on the catering. With the correct atmosphere, professional event caterers experience can bring clients satisfaction of all the senses in a way that makes an event special and memorable. Of course, beautifully prepared food can appeal to your sense of taste, smell and sight—perhaps even touch, but the decorations and ambiance should play a significant part in the clients enjoyment as well. Industrial catering includes providing food for airline passengers, schools, prisons and other institutional settings. It can include contract management of client foodservice facilities.

Airlines often have divisions or hire third parties to provide food for passengers. Catering is covered by two different groups. "Independent caterers and companies with a catering business on the side" is a phrase that could be combined with the previous sentence.

CATERING TIPS AND TRICKS

CHOOSINGRIGHT CATERING SERVICE

Food is an integral part of any party so one must choose a catering service wisely. But how does one choose the right caterer for an event? It is important to do a lot of research, check references, and often request a sampling to make your final decision. List your catering needs In order for a caterer to provide an accurate estimate for your party or event, you must communicate your needs clearly. Do you have a location for your party/event reserved and is there a kitchen on site? How many guests are coming to your event?

Find out if the potential caterer has a minimum guest requirement. Take into consideration that some of your guests may have special dietary needs and be certain to communicate this with your caterer. A great caterer will be ready for any surprise that may surface, but at what cost to you? Discuss your budget with your caterer and what options are available. Ask yourself, do you prefer a buffet style or a silver-service sit down dinner for your guests?

Be clear about your proposed menu, do you have a theme or style at the event that will be reflected in the cuisine? Your budget may or may not determine how flexible your caterer is to meet your needs. Keep in mind; it is the type of food that often determines the bulk price of the catering job. Find out, and possibly request, if the caterer will provide a detailed contract of service and outline what the payment terms will be. Does the caterer use fresh or frozen food for recipes? Is the produce grown locally? Is it organic? Will any of the dishes be pre-made and then frozen until the party/event? Does anything come from a can?

Does the potential caterer supply decorations, linens, tables and chairs? Very often there will be a brochure catering services supply with examples of past event and table decorations. It is important to be very clear in what your event needs and what the caterer will be supplying. Is a menu board provided for the guests that describes the ingredients of the dishes being served?

Will the catering company provide a wait-staff? What is their required dress code? What is the ratio of servers to guests? A rule of thumb is one server for every 10 guests. Be certain to ask your potential caterer if taxes and gratuities are included in the final bid. What happens to the leftovers? Often, upon request, a catering service will compile a food basket at no additional charge for the host or hostess of the event. Remember, it is critical that you communicate with your potential caterer exactly you want; the result, you get what you want and the caterer can provide an accurate bid for the job as well as the exceptional service your event deserves.

SERVING ALCOHOL AT YOUR EVENT

When one commits to planning an event or party, one must decide whether or not to serve alcohol to the guests. There are a few considerations to keep in mind and discuss with your caterer. Where will your event or party be taking place? It is important to confirm that your event or party site will allow alcohol on its premises. Once you have made certain that you can serve alcohol at your chosen site, ask your caterer if he or she holds a liquor license.

He or she must have a valid liquor license. If he or she does not hold a liquor license, then you must contact a liquor-licensed dealer. Prepare to provide a guest estimate for your caterer to work with. The caterer in turn will supply you with a quote for the number of bartenders that must attend bar and the quantity of ice, glasses, and mixers necessary.

The amount of bartenders depends on the number of guests. Your caterer or licensed liquor dealer will be responsible for setting up the bar. You must now determine what you wish to be served from the bar as well as if you require your guests to pay for alcohol themselves. A cash bar requires the guest to pay for their drinks. Guests tend to consume less alcohol when it isn't free. This is a basic bar with all the works and at no charge to the guests. The open bar includes hard liquor for mixing drinks, wine, beer, and soft drinks.

A limited bar will set boundaries on what will be served and in what moderation. An example of a limited bar is an event in which beer and wine is offered to the guests at no charge and hard liquor is offered at a pre-determined price. Whatever you decide in regards to serving alcohol at your event or party is up to you.

WEDDING CATERING

After watching the happy couple exchange vows and begin their married life together, your guests will be hungry. Many of the guests may have scaled back on eating in order to look good for pictures or just because they were so busy during the day. When you're putting together such a large assortment of people, there are bound to be those that have certain ways or preferences of eating. You may find that there are vegetarians or those that can not eat dairy.

You might have a diabetic in the crowd or some other health restriction. You should certainly try to have options for any sort of eating arrangement. In the case of those that don't eat meat, you might want to have a cheese lasagne available or other pasta dish. This is becoming widely popular to have two options anyways, so why not offer them?

Another way to cope with varied needs is to serve dinner in a buffet style. This allows each person to pick only what they want or what they can eat. A lot of wedding caterers rely on word of mouth to get their services recognized. If you can, talk to other people that have gotten married in your town to see who they recommend. Of course, you will still want to see them for yourself, but this list can be a great starting point. Another way to find good catering is to talk to the reception hall coordinators.

Many times they will either require the use of a particular caterer or they have a list of those that they recommend. Of course, you will want to schedule an appointment with all of the catering candidates in order to do a taste test of their menu options. At that point, you can pick what you think your guests will enjoy. A good meal is a great way to send your thanks to your guests for coming to your wedding. This is the part that shouldn't be skimped on for any reason.

Of course, that doesn't mean that you can't find moderately priced options. Try your favourite restaurant, for example. If they're able to cater, then you may be able to get a better deal because you're buying food in bulk. Having a friend who is a cook is even better-so long as they don't mind working through the wedding. So you've tasted the offerings of the caterer and you've selected your main menu options. What about drinks? Much like selecting the menu options, you will need to factor in what kinds of drinks everyone would like to drink. The easiest way to take care of this is to offer a full service bar.

In this way, guests can have mixed drinks of all varieties or they can stick to wine and beer. You want to plan this option out carefully as you may end up paying more than you would like. Check with the provider as to how many drinks each guest can have, or can expect from the supply that will be brought. In most cases, there is no limit. A word of advice: Don't ever have a cash bar. Making your guests pay for their drinks when they may also have paid for their outfits and transportation is just a lot to ask.

In terms of wine and beer, tastes and varieties are enormous-how does someone choose? The best advice is to select four to five different kinds of beer with each one having enough to fill everyone's glass. This may surprise you, but sometimes all of your guests will like the same thing and you may want to make sure that they can have it. As for wine, you may want to have at least one of each a red varietal and a white varietal.

This ensures a milder and more acidic selection. A way to make sure that everyone is happy is to find blends of each of these wines. By blends, this means to find a red that includes a merlot, syrah, and pinot noir, while the white might include a chardonnay, reisling, and zinfandel. These can be tricky to find, but they are crowd pleasers. Toasts are just not toasts without a little glass of champagne. It's common sense to make sure that the new couple and their wedding party have the very finest in champagne, while the rest of the guests have another variety. In many reception halls or catering services, the champagne for the wedding party is provided. Of course, there will also be designated drivers at the wedding, so you will also want to have water, sodas, coffee, and juices available as well. When you're planned it thoroughly, everyone will be well-watered throughout the evening.

HOW TO START A CATERING BUSINESS

The catering industry in the United States is estimated to be worth $5 billion a year. Caterers are hired to perform an assorted number of jobs-everything from cooking to serving, mixing drinks, and whipping up delicious desserts. Functions range from dinner parties that serve a handful of guests to enormous events that serve thousands of guests. Normally a caterer will define their niche, meaning a caterer will choose what type of functions to specialize in as well as their job description.

For example, you may offer the best fondue table for up to 100 guests, perhaps you would rather prepare meals for business catering parties that are held within banker's hours. There really are no limits in regards to catering styles.

Once you have arrived to the idea stage it is great to begin a business catering plan. Be meticulous when you detail how the catering business will be operated, managed and capitalized.

The following checklist can help you organize your ideas into the beginning of a business catering plan:

- What services will your catering business offer? Will you run a full service catering business, corporate catering service, custom event catering service, or a scheduled events catering business?
- Research necessary permits and requirements your local government imposes on a catering business.

- Determine your start up costs of your catering business. Remember to include everything-permit fees, catering equipment, marketing, uniforms, catering supplies etc.
- Construct a budget, forecast and projection.
- How will you finance the start up of your catering business?
- Research liability insurance needed to protect your catering business.
- Where will you house your catering business office and how will you manage your business? Prepare to think about cancellations, payment policies, consultations, menu-planning as well as samples, contracts and the transportation of food.
- What food suppliers do you intend to work with?
- Will your catering service rent equipment for special requests?
- What will you name your catering business?

  Owning a catering service not only includes cooking but also be prepared to wear many hats such as: accountant, manager, marketer, sales representative, and bill collector. Additional questions to consider when constructing your catering business plan:
  - Is my business idea practical and is it in demand?
  - What is my competition?
  - What is my advantage over existing services?
  - Can I deliver a better quality service?
  - Can I create a demand for my business?
  - What will be my legal structure?
  - How will I compensate myself?

Your answers to these questions will help you create a focused, well-researched catering business plan that can serve as a blueprint for your new catering service. Whatever you choose to specialize in, running a catering business offers creativity, flexibility, and growing opportunities. Maybe you've got the details of the actual wedding ceremony worked out, but what about the reception?

One of the major costs of the wedding reception will definitely be the food, so you'll want to make sure you'll have enough food for everyone without spending too much money. Here are some top ways to cut on your catering bill that will ensure that your guests enjoy your reception-and you save money. Most couples want to order an extra tray or two of hors d'oeuvres in case extra guests show up.

This is fine but you should still make sure that you're not order more appetizers than you actually need; use your discretion based on the guest list. For instance, if you know a number of your guests are vegetarian, you may not need to order as many appetizers with meat. Also, ordering two or three types of hors d'oeuvres will help to reduce your catering bill. If you buy more of the same dish, you can usually save money with most catering companies-different kinds of foods will increase the bill, so it's important to keep it classy but simple at the wedding-even when it comes to food. Caterers will also try to encourage you to spend more than you may need to on the actual meal as well.

You may not need a five course meal if you've already purchased three types of appetizers and a salad, or three extra desserts if you already have a pretty large wedding cake. The time of day that you hold your wedding will give you a good indication of how much food to serve; if you're having the ceremony in the afternoon or early evening, you may want to serve more food.

There are some foods that are always going to be expensive, even if you only order small amounts. So, since you have to order a considerable amount of food, ordering dishes that aren't so costly will help you to keep your catering bill reasonable. Certain seafood, like shrimp, lobster and salmon will definitely make your catering bill higher, so if you have to have them, try to use them as only one of the course choices for dinner, or purchase these fo1ods as appetizers to save on costs. Food stations are a unique way to serve a variety of foods at your wedding reception, and you can be sure that everyone will find something they like to eat. This way, you won't have to worry about people changing their minds about their meal choices once they arrive at the reception. A food station with different types of pasta is usually a hit with most guests, and can be very economical.

You can also include food stations with other types of the ethnic foods, such as Mexican or Indian fare, to celebrate the cultures of the people who will be attending your wedding, or to acknowledge your backgrounds. You may also be able to cut your catering bill by not requesting an elaborate setup for your food stations and tables. Using a single colour for tablecloths, usually white, will cut down on labour costs.

8

Marketing and Associated Activities

INTRODUCTION

For most resort companies, it was only during the 1980s that the word *marketing* was anything more than a euphemism for sales. Indeed, in the competitive landscape of the not too distant past, an aggressive and knowledgeable sales staff could accomplish most activities that related to putting guests in rooms. In the competitive environment of the present time, this has become impossible. Resort companies that design and market a sophisticated inventory of hospitality services need a similarly sophisticated scheme for letting potential clientele know about their services.

For most resort companies in the twentyfirst century, true marketing has evolved to reflect this sophistication. This development also acknowledges increased sophistication on the part of guests and potential clientele.

Business travellers, travel agents, and meeting planners who represent and book group and convention business are educated and informed consumers.To serve this clientele, resorts have had to develop marketing efforts and product segmentation, first to interest the market, and second to allow people representing that market to make intelligent choices among competitors.

Increasingly, individual consumers and small businesses are becoming more sophisticated in arranging their own travel plans over the Internet. This represents yet another challenge to resort marketers: How do we market most efficiently to all groups? Good question.

Marketing has become an umbrella term that covers a number of strategic and tactical activities designed to tell the clientele the story of the resort's services and to encourage that clientele to make choices based on how one resort's marketing message matches their needs better than the available alternatives.

In any given resort or resort company, marketing includes a range of sales activities, public relations, advertising in all media, design of symbols and images, and the departments of convention services, reservations, revenue management, and, perhaps, catering. It should be noted that research plays a major role in designing marketing strategies and tactics. The monograph presented in this edition by Bianca Grohmann and Eric Spangenberg has a research orientation at its core.

It is designed to assist managers in choosing and generating data that are useful to staying successfully competitive. It is important that managers understand the range within which this data may be interpreted and applied. Successful managers and high-quality organizations are always seeking information and data that allow them to make accurate decisions and design effective marketing and managerial efforts.

These data can take a number of forms but, for the most part, deal with the characteristics of the resort's target market segment that affect their choice of resorts. In this case, the research seeks to understand how consumers make choices among resorts based on the value of their various attributes.

Among other data that resorts find mechanisms to accumulate and interpret are these kinds:

- *Geographic:* What sorts of communities are represented; what parts of the country or world; how far people travel
- *Demographic:* Age, sex, occupation, income, ethnicity, family, education
- *Psychographic:* Client's self-image, social or peer group, lifestyle, personality traits
- *Behavioural:* Whether the resort choice is a routine or special occasion; what guest seeks in terms of quality, service, economy; user status; usage rate; loyalty.

While many of the specific details or programmes implied under the marketing umbrella may be farmed out to agencies that specialize in advertising or public relations, the genesis of the resort's strategic marketing plan must be within the resort organization itself.

The object contributed to this part by Fletch Waller provides a strong argument for broadening the definition of *marketing* to include all operational aspects of the resort.This object is an excellent overview of the marketing process. Waller shows the relationship between marketing and operations as a "continuing process" without which resorts probably cannot remain competitive.

Yield management, long a practice of the airline industry, has found total acceptance by resort marketing and reservations systems. Indeed, it has become an industry standard.The object in this part by Paul Chappelle can be read in conjunction with that by Quain and LeBruto for a comprehensive primer on yield management. Together, these objects explore various aspects of that practice from the viewpoint of Chappelle, current practitioner. Chappelle lives the theory of yield and revenue management on a daily basis and provides insights about how it works in practice. As the revenue manager for over 30 resorts, Chappelle has the experience to back up the theory.

The Sinclair thesis on resort pricing should be read in the context of the issues and suggestions raised by the contributions on yield management. But it goes beyond that. Drawing on Sinclair's deep experience in resort operations, particularly sales, this contemporary work on pricing is up to date and useful not only from a conceptual standpoint but a practical one.

Shaw and Morris bring their collaborative talents in academe and industry to the thesis on the organization of the sales function in resorts. Because, as noted elsewhere in this text many times, the potential markets for a resort's services and the types of resort are so numerous, sales efforts can be complicated. Shaw and Morris present this complex departmental function in a clear, straightforward fashion that is both theoretically relevant and operationally practical.

Traditionally, the function of public relations for any organization, particularly resorts, was oriented towards the generation of favourable—usually free—publicity and the suppression or management of bad news. Louis Richmond proposes the different and expanded but not necessarily contrary position that public relations activities can positively enhance the resort's sales and marketing efforts.

He discusses his experiences in the case of the Seattle Sheraton Resort and Towers.Using that example, he argues that through creative cooperative efforts with local charity, cultural, and volunteer organizations, resorts can serve the activities of those groups' fundraising efforts and simultaneously position themselves to show the arbiters of potential business how well the resort can perform.

His examples are instructive. Richmond, who is president of his own very successful public relations firm in Seattle, retains the Sheraton and other hospitality concerns as clients. All in all, the strategies, tactics, activities, personnel, and concepts described in objects and thesiss in this part provide an overview that only hints at everything important to effective management of the marketing function.

Marketing is perhaps the most written-about topic in hospitality literature. Because of the great diversity of opinion, it can be argued that there is no one "right" way to market, nor is any single piece of literature generally considered seminal to resort marketing. The reader is urged to consider the references cited by contributing authors, the suggested readings, and active perusal of recent hospitality journals to achieve greater understanding of this fascinating process— and, by extension, its management.

BUILDING MARKET LEADERSHIP: MARKETING AS PROCESS

The resort business has changed enormously over the last 30 years, embracing special niche forms of lodging, new ways of segmenting markets brand proliferation and consolidation, new tools for acquiring customers distribution innovations and globalization. These changes in markets and in ways resorts relate to and capitalize on them have put new demands on marketing.

Marketing, as addressed herein is not the sales and marketing department; I mean marketing in its broadest sense of how resorts respond to and seize on market opportunities.

Definition? Marketing is a process of creating and sustaining productive relationships with desirable customers. Its goal? To produce such relationships more effectively than competitors do. Let's examine the definition and its implications.

Marketing is:

- *A process*: A process, a series of functions and actions for approaching and dealing with opportunities. *Marketing,* as used herein, is not a job but a way of proceeding to create and operate a resort focused on customers and competitors, a way that incorporates all members of the resort staff and its support.
- *Of creating*: The essence of marketing is creation: imagination, insight, willingness to change and evolve, and, yes, discard.
- *And sustaining*: Loyalty over time and repeat customers are the key to productivity and optimal contribution margins.
- *Productive relationships*: A relationship must be two-sided, with benefits for both partners in the relationship. In the case of customers, the benefits are wants and needs consistently fulfilled and full value received; in the case of staff, professional satisfaction and operating profits sufficient to fund improvements provide attractive compensation, and provide returns on investors' or owners' capital.
- *With desirable customers*: Not all customers are equally desirable; we want those who are willing to pay, growing in numbers, making multiple purchases, and whose needs we are able to fully satisfy. And the goal?
- To produce such relationships. *Production* implies inputs, outputs, and the measurement of productivity. Marketing productivity has been lagging for the last decade; the rising costs of acquiring customers must be reined in.
- More effectively than competitors do. Marketing success is judged in relative terms, using competitors and similar resorts as

benchmarks. As a creative process, especially in a field like hospitality wherein innovations are unprotected and easily copied, the benchmarks and goals are always moving targets. Besting the competition is the constant challenge.

It will be clear that successful marketing of a resort requires the orchestration of a wide variety of talents and skills, of which sales and marketing personnel are only a part.

Chain resorts approach the process one way; independents must do so another. But in either case, market success depends on an effective integration of marketing and operations at the property level under the direction and leadership of a marketdriven general manager.

THE MARKETING PROCESS

BACKGROUND TO EXMAR

Professor Malcolm McDonald of Cranfield University School of Management, a world authority on marketing planning, has produced numerous publications on the marketing planning process over the last 10 years.

His best selling book, *Marketing Plans - How to prepare them: How to use them*, now in the Fourth Edition, describes *The Ten Steps of the Strategic Marketing Planning Process* as follows:

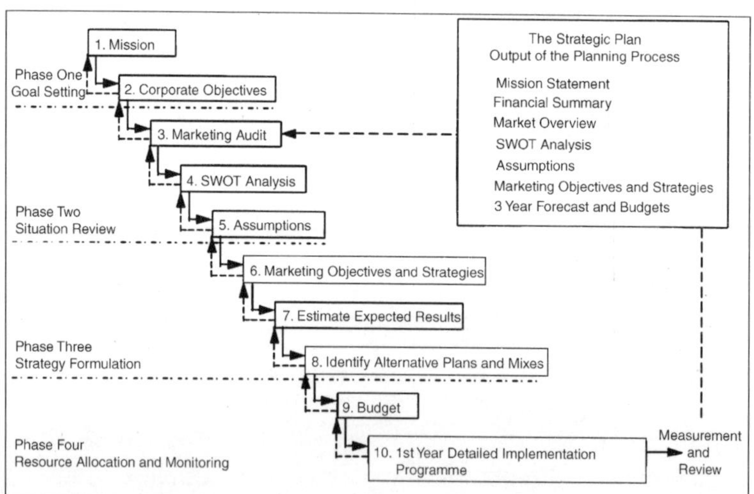

Fig. The Ten Steps of the Strategic Marketing Planning Process

In order to assist companies with the implementation of an effective Strategic Marketing Planning Process many of the techniques were implemented in software programmes. Several prototypes were developed at the Cranfield School of Management, which were widely tested in a variety of commercial environments over a number of years, in order to produce a complete and robust specification of the requirement.

EXMAR

PRODUCT DESCRIPTION

EXMAR is a process, supported by a set of associated services, for developing Strategic Marketing Plans.

It assists companies by:

- Guiding them through a logical marketing planning process
- Prompting and defining key data requirements
- Displaying information graphically to aid understanding of the business
- Providing advice at key stages
- Allowing 'what-if ' analyses
- Automatically outputting the report resulting from the analysis.

There are a number of techniques and methodologies incorporated in EXMAR including:

- Gap Analysis
- SWOT Analysis
- Ansoff Matrix
- Boston Box
- Directional Policy Matrix
- Market Segmentation
- Perceptual Maps
- Porter Matrix
- Objective and Strategy setting.

BENEFITS OF EXMAR

The competitive differentiation derived from EXMAR has been the subject of extensive research by Cranfield School of Management and can be summarised as follows:

- Provides a planning framework which ensures consistency across divisions and each division covers all the key aspects of the planning process
- Takes the 'number crunching' out of marketing analysis
- Gives new insights into the markets particularly through the market segmentation techniques
- Gives powerful graphical display which makes large volumes of data understandable
- Enables easy 'what-if ' iterations as strategy options are explored
- Facilitates team work and multidisciplinary involvement in the marketing planning process

- Improves marketing skills within the company
- Focuses planning on the customer
- Gives a clear vision of markets and the company's position in them
- Adds value to marketing database investment.

IMPLEMENTATION OF THE STRATEGIC MARKETING PLANNING PROCESS USING EXMAR

The successful introduction and implementation of the Strategic Marketing Planning Process within an organisation is dependent on management commitment and high quality process consultancy and training, as well as the EXMAR process support tools. This ensures that key members of staff are familiar with, and trained in, all the marketing processes and integrated techniques that have been developed in conjunction with Cranfield School of Management, and that a first class strategy is produced. Experience has shown that the most efficient and beneficial method of implementing the Strategic Marketing Planning Process supported by the EXMAR software is to follow the steps shown below:

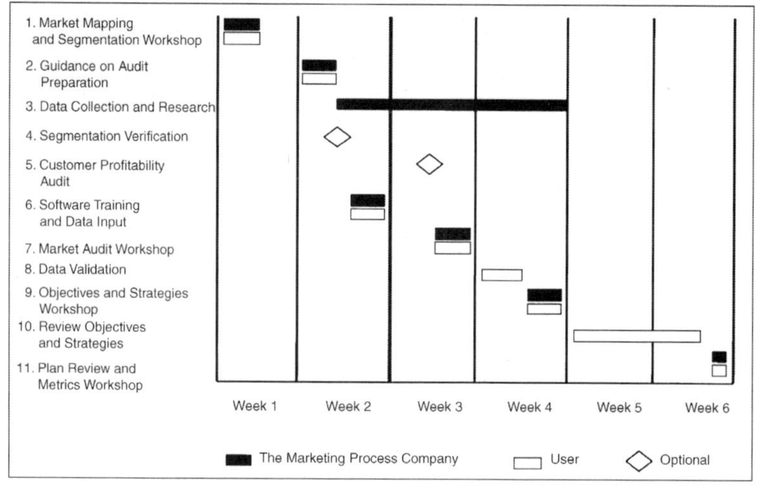

Fig. Project Plan for a Strategic Marketing Planning Process Implementation

MARKET MAPPING AND SEGMENTATION WORKSHOP

The objective of the workshop is to produce a structure for the defined market, which clearly identifies the different requirements that customers look to be satisfied. These different requirements can then be used to develop the alternative strategies that need to be implemented to better access the segments and tune the product offers to suit the customer requirements. It should be noted that most organisations do not have access to the information to produce a definitive segmentation structure that is 100 per cent accurate.

However most organisations do have sufficient internal knowledge to produce something that is 'roughly right' and a reasonable starting point. Where this is not the case, the process makes it very clear where the information holes are and the importance of that information. If research is required, the process ensures a rigorous and very targeted brief can be produced.

Market Definition

A market is defined in terms of a need that can be satisfied by the products or services customers' view as alternatives. Once this is clear, the boundaries for the segmentation project can be set.

Market Mapping

A market map defines the distribution and value chain between supplier and final user, which takes into account the various buying mechanisms found in a market, including the part played by 'influencers'.

Market maps help focus attention on key decision makers within a market, and identify key target market segments within a market segmentation project. Market channels and the key players within channels can be easily identified with the help of a graphic presentation of a market. A market map can help deliver key customer and consumer insights, and ensures full awareness of the the total market place.

Market Segmentation

Market segmentation is a concept in economics and marketing. A market segment is a sub-set of a market made up of people or organizations with one or more characteristics that cause them to demand similar product and/or services based on qualities of those products such as price or function. A true market segment meets all of the following criteria: it is distinct from other segments, it is homogeneous within the segment; it responds similarly to a market stimulus, and it can be reached by a market intervention. The term is also used when consumers with identical product and/or service needs are divided up into groups so they can be charged different amounts for the services.

The people in a given segment are supposed to be similar in terms of criteria by which they are segmented and different from other segments in terms of these criteria. These can be broadly viewed as 'positive' and 'negative' applications of the same idea, splitting up the market into smaller groups.

Examples:

- Gender
- Price
- Interests

- Location
- Religion
- Income
- Size of Household

While there may be theoretically 'ideal' market segments, in reality every organization engaged in a market will develop different ways of imagining market segments, and create Product differentiation strategies to exploit these segments. The market segmentation and corresponding product differentiation strategy can give a firm a temporary commercial advantage.

Bases for Segmenting Consumer Markets

- Geographic segmentation
- Demographic segmentation
- Psychographic segmentation
- Behavioural segmentation

Geographic Segmentation

The market is segmented just as to geographic criteria- nations, states, regions, counties, cities, neigborhoods, or zip codes. Geo-cluster approach combines demographic data with geographic data to create a more accurate profile of specific

Psychographic Segmentation

Psychographics is the science of using psychology and demographics to better understand consumers.Psychographic segmentation: consumer are divided just as to their lifestyle, personality, values. People within the same demographic group can exhibit very different psychographic profiles.

"Positive" Market Segmentation

Market segmenting is dividing the market into groups of individual markets with similar wants or needs that a company divides into distinct groups which have distinct needs, wants, Behaviour or which might want different products and services. Broadly, markets can be divided just as to a number of general criteria, such as by industry or public versus private. Although industrial market segmentation is quite different from consumer market segmentation, both have similar objectives. All of these methods of segmentation are merely proxies for true segments, which don't always fit into convenient demographic boundaries.

Consumer-based market segmentation can be performed on a *product specific* basis, to provide a close match between specific products and individuals. However, a number of generic market segment systems also exist, *e.g.* the system provides a broad segmentation of the population of the United States based on the statistical analysis of household and geodemographic data.

The process of segmentation is distinct from positioning. The overall intent is to identify groups of similar customers and potential customers; to prioritize the groups to address; to understand their Behaviour; and to respond with appropriate marketing strategies that satisfy the different preferences of each chosen segment. Revenues are thus improved.

Improved segmentation can lead to significantly improved marketing effectiveness. Distinct segments can have different industry structures and thus have higher or lower attractiveness

Once a market segment has been identified, and targeted, the segment is then subject to positioning. Positioning involves ascertaining how a product or a company is perceived in the minds of consumers.

This part of the segmentation process consists of drawing up a perceptual map, which highlights rival goods within one's industry just as to perceived quality and price. After the perceptual map has been devised, a firm would consider the marketing communications mix best suited to the product in question.

Behavioural Segmentation

In Behavioural segmentation, consumers are divided into groups just as to their knowledge of, attitude towards, use of or response to a product.

- *Occasions*: Segmentation just as to occasions.we segment the market just as to the occasions.
- *Benefits*: Segmentations just as to benefits sought by the consumer.
- Users status: non-users, ex-users, first time users, etc.

Using Segmentation in Customer Retention

The basic approach to retention-based segmentation is that a company tags each of its active customers with 3 values:

1. *Tag No.1*: Is this customer at high risk of canceling the company's service? One of the most common indicators of high-risk customers is a drop off in usage of the company's service. For example, in the credit card industry this could be signaled through a customer's decline in spending on his or her card.
2. *Tag No.2*: Is this customer worth retaining? This determination boils down to whether the post-retention profit generated from the customer is predicted to be greater than the cost incurred to retain the customer. Managing Customers as Investments.
3. *Tag No.3*: What retention tactics should be used to retain this customer? For customers who are deemed "save-worthy", it's essential for the company to know which save tactics are most likely

to be successful. Tactics commonly used range from providing "special" customer discounts to sending customers communications that reinforce the value proposition of the given service.

Process for Tagging Customers

The basic approach to tagging customers is to utilize historical retention data to make predictions about active customers regarding:

- Whether they are at high risk of canceling their service
- Whether they are profitable to retain
- What retention tactics are likely to be most effective

The idea is to match up active customers with customers from historic retention data who share similar attributes. Using the theory that "birds of a feather flock together", the approach is based on the assumption that active customers will have similar retention outcomes as those of their comparable predecessor.

Niche Marketing

A niche is a more narrowly defined customer group who seek a distinct set of benefits. Ýdentified by dividing a segment into subsegments,distinct and unique set of needs,requires speciallization, and is not likely to attract too many competitors.

Price Discrimination

Where a monopoly exists, the price of a product is likely to be higher than in a competitive market and the quantity sold less, generating monopoly profits for the seller. These profits can be increased further if the market can be segmented with different prices charged to different segments charging higher prices to those segments willing and able to pay more and charging less to those whose demand is price elastic.

The price discriminator might need to create rate fences that will prevent members of a higher price segment from purchasing at the prices available to members of a lower price segment. This Behaviour is rational on the part of the monopolist, but is often seen by competition authorities as an abuse of a monopoly position, whether or not the monopoly itself is sanctioned. Examples of this exist in the transport industry where business class customers who can afford to pay may be charged prices many times higher than economy class customers for essentially the same service.

Ansoff Matrix

To portray alternative corporate growth strategies, Igor Ansoff presented a matrix that focused on the firm's present and potential products and markets. By considering ways to grow via existing products and new products, and in existing markets and new markets, there are four possible product-market combinations. Ansoff's matrix is shown below:

Table. Ansoff Matrix

	Existing Products	New Products
Existing Markets	Market Penetration	Product Development
New Markets	Market Development	Diversification

Ansoff's matrix provides four different growth strategies:

1. Market Penetration - the firm seeks to achieve growth with existing products in their current market segments, aiming to increase its market share.
2. Market Development - the firm seeks growth by targeting its existing products to new market segments.
3. Product Development - the firms develops new products targeted to its existing market segments.
4. Diversification - the firm grows by diversifying into new businesses by developing new products for new markets.

Selecting a Product-Market Growth Strategy

The market penetration strategy is the least risky since it leverages many of the firm's existing resources and capabilities. In a growing market, simply maintaining market share will result in growth, and there may exist opportunities to increase market share if competitors reach capacity limits. However, market penetration has limits, and once the market approaches saturation another strategy must be pursued if the firm is to continue to grow.

Market development options include the pursuit of additional market segments or geographical regions. The development of new markets for the product may be a good strategy if the firm's core competencies are related more to the specific product than to its experience with a specific market segment. Because the firm is expanding into a new market, a market development strategy typically has more risk than a market penetration strategy.

A product development strategy may be appropriate if the firm's strengths are related to its specific customers rather than to the specific product itself. In this situation, it can leverage its strengths by developing a new product targeted to its existing customers. Similar to the case of new market development, new product development carries more risk than simply attempting to increase market share.

Diversification is the most risky of the four growth strategies since it requires both product and market development and may be outside the core competencies of the firm. In fact, this quadrant of the matrix has been referred to by some as the "suicide cell". However, diversification may be a reasonable choice if the high risk is compensated by the chance of a high rate of return. Other advantages of diversification include the potential to gain a foothold in an attractive industry and the reduction of overall business portfolio risk.

GUIDANCE ON AUDIT PREPARATION

The objective of these two days is to ensure that the data required has been identified in detail and the format of the data is consistent.

DATA COLLECTION AND RESEARCH

The following information needs to be collected and input into EXMAR for each product-market as defined in the Ansoff Matrix. This information is then used to drive the market audit.

For each product-market the following information is required:

- Market size and growth Volume
- Revenue
- Market share

Current figures are requested. Historical data is also useful, as far back as available. If only some of these data items are known, the system will estimate data values where possible. In order for EXMAR to construct the Boston Box and the Directional Policy Matrix, it is necessary to define and gather the following information:

- Market Attractiveness Factors - defined once for the business unit
- MAF scores
- Critical Success Factors
- CSF scores for yourself and important competitors.

SEGMENTATION VERIFICATION

Often our clients sell products and services into horizontal segments. In these cases, the product-offer maps onto how the customers run their business, and segments are often hard to identify in a way that will give maximum leverage in the marketing plan. To help solve this problem, we have developed a set of tools and processes for analysing existing and potential customer data, and generating and sizing segments.

CUSTOMER PROFITABILITY AUDIT

This is an optional audit and will develop a more realistic view of Customer/ Segment Profitability as opposed to Product Profitability. It is often the case that a few segments generate more than 100 per cent of the profit and it is important to identify which segments are actually profitable.

SOFTWARE TRAINING AND DATA INPUT

Two days of hands on training are provided on the EXMAR software including the use of the extensive help system. Data from your company can be entered into EXMAR at this stage.

MARKET AUDIT WORKSHOP

The objective of this workshop is to produce the Market Audit and Trend Analysis, *i.e.* What will happen if we do nothing over the plan period? For each product-market the following information is analysed:

- Financial performance
- Market share
- Relative strengths and weaknesses
- Competitor strategy
- Relative costs
- Market attractiveness trends
- Opportunities and threats
- Assumptions and sensitivity analysis.

Additionally the portfolio of products and services is analysed using various tools including the Directional Policy Matrix and the Boston Box.

DATA VALIDATION

The sensitivity analysis on assumptions, whether they be in terms of relative strength, market growth, or profitability are used to highlight those areas where it is most important to verify the data, as wrong assumptions could lead to inappropriate strategies being developed.

This may require highly focused Market Research studies on the particular issues identified.

OBJECTIVES AND STRATEGIES WORKSHOP

The objective of this workshop is to set the overall strategies and those that operate at the product-market level. Objectives are defined as the financial performance and market share required from each product market. Strategies are defined as the set of costed actions required to improve competitive performance in order to reach the objectives. It also includes assigning responsibility for the actions.

The process is iterative and can result for example in the identification of generic problem areas, where one set of actions and investments can affect competitive performance in several productmarkets. These usually provide the best ROI. Additionally the output of the workshop often results in several scenarios, each with its own investment profile, *i.e.* these are the anticipated results of this level of investment as opposed to a larger or smaller sum. These can highlight the implications of the spread of the investment and resources.

REVIEW OBJECTIVES AND STRATEGIES

This phase of the project involves the Client in performing a 'sanity check' on the strategies. This can be both in terms of the viability of implementation, given the internal processes and constraints on the organisation and investment available, as well as a management review.

PLAN REVIEW AND METRICS WORKSHOP

On completion of the project, a day is set aside to review the Strategic Marketing Plan and to identify key metrics for monitoring the implementation and success of the strategies. For example, if 'service levels' are an important Critical Success Factor, then key performance indicators need to be defined that can be measured, such as 'response times to customer requests' or 'adherence to committed delivery schedules'. If required we can offer our Clients further services to help them design and implement appropriate KPIs in their organisation.

DECIDING WHAT TO BE AND WHAT TO OFFER TO WHOM

In an existing resort, the developer and architect already may have decided many of the things it is—high-rise or resort, in the business center or on the edge of town, large rooms and baths or smallish, one restaurant or several, wood or marble, with ballroom or not, and so on. Even so, the management team must still consciously examine what they intend the resort to be and offer to whom.

The type of customer originally in mind may not be available now in enough numbers to support the resort.

Perhaps a competitor has come in and taken away a piece of the market. Perhaps the business center has shifted to another part of the city. Perhaps new customers from Korea or California have replaced the original ones from Europe and the East Coast. Even though the owner has provided a basic envelope within which to operate, there still are options—many things the resort team can control, many choices to be made on what to offer and to emphasize to various market segments. Is the resort the place to be seen or the place that guards privacy? Is it better to stress family style or crisp, professional business style?

Should the resort add services, like a Japanese breakfast, to meet the needs of one particular group? Should the team put in meetings express and add more small meeting spaces to tap the short-lead-time corporate meetings market? Should it drop some services the market no longer wants to support?

The answers to what to be and offer are found by studying the marketing situation, which comprises three parts:

1. Strengths and weaknesses,
2. The kinds and numbers of customers available in the marketplace, and
3. The other resorts with whom this resort competes for these customers.

Careful analysis yields a picture of which segments the resort is best able to attract and serve. These become the *target markets*—the “to whoms”—and their needs and wants become the “what to be's.” The key to successfully deciding what to be and offer to whom is a matter of strategic selection of, focus on, and commitment to a well-defined set of markets for whom the resort is best suited to compete. Trying to be all things to all potential customers is a guarantee of ineffectiveness.

A good example of focus and targeting is Starwood's W. At risk of turning off a sizeable portion of the business and leisure travel market and leaving families well behind, Starwood focuses tightly on a lifestyle segment of professional and business people, with remarkable success.

The talents required to assess the marketing situation, create a data model of the market's segments, calculate a feasible share of each, and select the targets on which to focus are comfort with data, the ability to observe and infer, creativity, patience with detail, comfort with the hypothetical, and an analytic curiosity. Usually, such analyses are uncomfortably foreign to people with backgrounds in sales, and often to operators as well. It is essential that we teach, motivate, and reward curious, careful, insightful analysis of history and market information—skills that are not natural to those typically attracted to hospitality management. the *target markets*—the “to whoms”—and their needs and wants become the “what to be's.”The key to successfully deciding what to be and offer to whom is a matter of strategic selection of, focus on, and commitment to a well-defined set of markets for whom the resort is best suited to compete. Trying to be all things to all potential customers is a guarantee of ineffectiveness.

A good example of focus and targeting is Starwood's W. At risk of turning off a sizeable portion of the business and leisure travel market and leaving families well behind, Starwood focuses tightly on a lifestyle segment of professional and business people, with remarkable success.

The talents required to assess the marketing situation, create a data model of the market's segments, calculate a feasible share of each, and select the targets on which to focus are comfort with data, the ability to observe and infer, creativity, patience with detail, comfort with the hypothetical, and an analytic curiosity. Usually, such analyses are uncomfortably foreign to people with backgrounds in sales, and often to operators as well. It is essential that we teach, motivate, and reward curious, careful, insightful analysis of history and market information—skills that are not natural to those typically attracted to hospitality management.

SETTING PRICES

Having decided what to be and offer and to whom, the next most important decision is price. Pricing is a critical decision because it determines, first, whether or not the intended customers will purchase, and second, whether they will be satisfied with the value offered and, thus, be willing to return. Third, it determines whether the resort will be financially healthy enough to maintain itself and reward its employees so customers can once again be satisfied when they do return.

Three factors must come into consideration in pricing—the Three Cs of pricing, if you will: costs, competition, and customers' comfort zones. In F&B, costs drive pricing of menu items and beverages. Drucker says American industry has too much cost-driven pricing, and that it needs more price-driven costing. Doesn't F&B have the opportunity to build and test menus to discover where price points should be set, and is not the chef challenged to manage ingredients and portion size to deliver the cost and margin structure desired? Yet the cost-driven practice continues.

In rooms, competition is most often the dominant factor. Costs play a role, but changes in variable cost of an occupied room are generally small and rooms' contribution margins are large, typically 65 per cent or better. Moreover, resort accounting does not measure discounts from a standard price, as do almost all other industries. So there is no visible cost in reducing price to meet competitors. Remember: Any damn fool can cut his price, and some damn fool always will.

Must everyone follow? No. The key is to get in the head of the customer. The truly controlling factor is customer comfort zones, and all too often resort management leave money on the table because they don't know what those comfort zones are. At what price does the offer attract and deliver value? That is the key question in setting prices.

Price setting requires talent and skill in data gathering and analysis, accounting and building pro formas, interpreting and drawing inferences, and decision making. Do not let salespeople set prices; do not let controllers set prices. Only one person—the GM—can pull together the inputs of sales, control, operations, reservations, and the rest, and make this crucial judgement call. Also, build at least three price scenarios and have the controller and marketing director agree on occupancy impacts. Then run a GOP pro forma on each.

Out of that exercise will come a sense of the best pricing approach to take. Setting prices is the one task the GM cannot delegate, for he or she must live with and be accountable for all that results from this critical decision.

CREATING AWARENESS AND STIMULATING DEMAND

Herein are the typical roles of the marketing department: using sales, communications, and promotions to attract the target markets. But creating awareness is not only marketing's job. Everything the public sees and hears about the resort—its name or brand, its signs, its restaurants, the public activities of its managers, its charitable support and festivals—all create a meaning, a picture of what this resort means and offers.

Starwood's W again offers an example: Every element of their presentation expresses the "to whom" they target. In decor, uniforms tone, and attitude, they focus and send a coherent message. It is critical that every department understands the target markets and agrees on the idea, the meaning the resort intends to have for each of the target customer groups. This is called *positioning;* it's something done not to the product but to the mind of the prospect.

The team should prepare written positioning statements, including a compatible but individual positioning statement for each market segment they intend to target. These statements are the blueprint against which each ad, promotion, and sales call is tested to assure consistent messages are being sent.

And those statements should be shared with all employees.When all parts of the resort are sending a coherent and consistent message of what the name or brand means and what underlying promise is being made, the resort establishes a clear position in the mind of the prospects—ideally, one that is attractively distinctive from competitors.

Marketers can use a variety of tools to create awareness and stimulate demand—for example, sales blitzes, telemarketing, newspaper ads, Internet sites and ads, partnership alliances, radio ads, and price promotions. The marketing mix is the range and balance of tools selected and resources devoted to each to achieve the resort's marketing goals.

In most resorts, direct selling is still the primary marketing tool used to create awareness and stimulate demand.There are two parts of effective direct selling: sales skills and sales management. Consider one the weapon, the other the shooter.

Sales skills are not natural; enthusiasm may be natural, liking to meet people may be natural, but selling is a process that anyone can learn and that must be practiced. Make sure your salespeople are taught how to research their prospect, to listen for needs and purposes, to acknowledge that they have heard the prospect, to transform relevant features into benefits and to sell the customer's success, to anticipate objections and prepare responses, to negotiate, to ask for the order, and to thank the customer and facilitate delivery.

Sales management is quite another thing; often the top salesperson does not make the best sales manager. The sales manager must be able to select salespeople; reinforce their training; coach, counsel and motivate them; assign them to prospects and market segments; set goals, manage compensation, review performance; and troubleshoot. He or she must also be the gatekeeper on contracts and rates, making sure that inventory Compensation of salespeople need not be complicated. *First principle:* Tie compensation to goals set in terms of what you want them to do—that is, produce contracts and roomnights.

Don't just set room-night goals; add measures of relationship or share of a specific customer's business. Have salespeople suggest their own goals for the coming year; participation builds commitment. *Second:* Provide them near-term reward and reinforcement, not postponed rewards. Pay out bonuses quarterly. *Third:* Build teamwork so that one salesperson supports and encourages another. Add a team bonus multiplier to personal performance measures. *Last:* Separate performance bonuses from overall job appraisal. No one attends to suggestions for performance improvement if he or she has just received a big check for exceeding goal.

Many full-service resorts are overresourced in group sales and underweighted in transient market tools. Sales efforts should be balanced with other parts of the marketing mix—advertising, publicity, and promotions.

The range of communication options increases geometrically with proliferation of new media—cable television, news magazines and national papers, the Internet, and direct mail and telemarketing. But the eyeballs are not growing apace, meaning the audience for any one medium is steadily shrinking, putting increasing demand on measures of productivity, care in allocating resources, and creativity to get through the clutter. As audiences of prospects become increasingly expensive to reach through advertising, the tools of publicity, the Internet, and direct marketing are increasingly the media of choice.

The Internet is a demanding medium for communication; use professional help to design, maintain, and market the resort's web site as though it were, itself, a product for which awareness must be created and demand stimulated. To draw audience to the site and manage its visibility in search engines are skills beyond the property team.

Set specific goals for the site:They might be to attract qualified prospects, to sell services, to provide customer service. Don't just have a site. And measure the experts against those goals.A passive, unmanaged, and undermarketed site is a waste of money.

Promotions can powerfully stimulate demand, but too often, price promotions are resorted to as a last-minute attempt to prop up a weak demand period. Promotions should be planned, justified on a breakeven basis, and used sparingly. Not all promotions need be price promotions; customers invest energy and time in transactions, too: value-added promotions that offer non-monetary savings can be used to avoid habituating consumers to buying only on sale or shopping only on price. Well-forged alliances for copromotion can increase both productivity and absolute sales volume.

The skills and talents necessary in a comprehensive effort to create awareness and stimulate demand include:

- *In sales:* Initiative; being goal-directed; listening with empathy and imagination; time management; self-confidence.
- *In sales management:* Coaching and counseling; quantitative skills; priority setting, time management, and sense of urgency; leadership and problem solving; ability to manage incentive programmes.
- *In communications:* Ability to write clearly; ability to select, engage, and manage professional creative talents; ability to evaluate and allocate resources among options; comfort with and appreciation of the Internet and the Web.
- *In promotion:* Ability to analyse breakevens; creativity; anticipation; conceiving and selling partnerships and alliances.

MAKING THE RESORT AVAILABLE

Once a person in one of your target markets is interested in buying, how does he or she reach you? Your resort's reservations office, the central reservation system, airline global distribution systems, corporate sales offices, and your property sales office are all parts of a distribution network. Travel agents, corporate travel managers and secretaries, meeting planners, and travellers themselves reach your resort through this network.

Travel industry distribution channels are in chaos by virtue of the shift of travel agencies from commission to fee-for-service models, the rise of the Internet as a consumer's direct booking channel, and online thirdparty intermediaries like Expedia and Travelocity.

Increasingly, the Internet will become your key distribution channel, but in the meantime, you must manage two parallel systems, the traditional central reservation and travel agency channels and the new electronic channels. Are the rooms you want to offer available in both systems, with helpful and upto-date information? Are your prices sensible in each outlet? Making the resort available is no longer a passive stance but an active part of your marketing.

In other industries, distribution channel revolutions have brought efficiencies that benefit both consumers and suppliers. In the travel distribution revolution now underway, the consumer has benefited, but costs to resorts—the suppliers—have skyrocketed. Since 1993, full-service resort costs of distribution more than doubled, to $1,377 per occupied room per year in 2002.

Along with these new channels and thirdparty room merchants has come pressure on prices. In the downturn of 2001–2003, this was devastating. Price comparisons are quick and easy for the consumer. Packagers and auction sites unconsciously cultivate the destructive idea that a resort room is a commodity, as is an airline seat. But resorts are not commodities; each differs in location, features, and benefits. A resort team must resist the idea that a room is a room is a room, must emphasize their resort's distinctive positioning, and must resist the urge to simply match the lowest price offered.

For the foreseeable future, both the traditional and Internet-based distribution systems will coexist and have to be managed. This raises a new question:What channels do you want to encourage, and what ones discourage? Conventional wisdom, in recent years, has been to make the resort's inventory and rates available via as many channels as possible so as to capture from anywhere in the world the last drop of demand for arrival on a given day. Given their sharply differing costs, however, and the difficulty of managing coordinated presence in these new and overlapping channels, the time may be coming for a new strategy. One possibility is to starve undesirable channels with limited information and access while being fully open and transparent to others. Another approach might be to price differentially among channels to reflect their different costs. A large Hawaiian resort group is already doing that by explaining to consumers what comparative options and costs are. Other chains advertise a guarantee that the lowest price will be found on their own web site, which is a low-cost channel for them.

Reservations, revenue, and channel management constitute the fastest-changing part of resort management today. Channel management requires a comfort with and interest in technology and systems, and a knack for problem solving, anticipating, and risk taking.

CLOSING, CONFIRMING, AND MANAGING REVENUE

How one commits space—a room, meeting space, ballroom, or even a restaurant table— and at what price—determines the revenues and financial health of the resort and determines the customer's expectation of value.

Revenues must be managed to optimize financial returns and customer satisfaction— that is, the customer's willingness to return. No one department controls the tools of revenue management. They are shared among salespeople, catering and banqueting managers, front desk agents, reservation agents, and so on. To manage properly requires frequent and open conversation between managers, good forecasting, skillful selling by customer contact people, and an appreciation of each week's goals and targets for the resort. Poor forecasting, inflexible inventory policies, and conflicting approaches by different departments with whom the customer deals can undo all the best advertising, selling, and promotion.

Through the same forecasting disciplines, resort teams manage their revenues to maximize the productivity of the resort and assure its financial health. Revenue management tools and increasingly affordable yield systems can have a major and salutory effect on the financial health of the resort.

Another part of revenue management is incentives for reservations upselling, conversion of callers, and average rate increases, and for front desk agents upselling. In the same way, F&B staff should be viewed as salespeople and given training on suggestive selling. Inventory policies for tier price quotes by forecast levels of occupancy, for stay-through restrictions, for same-rate substitutions and upgrading to clear demand inventory categories— all these are tools through which reservation and revenue managers optimize the RevPAR performance of the resort.

It is in the area of revenue management that chains, especially multibrand management companies, have achieved significant advantage over independent resorts and franchisees that do not participate in cluster or regional revenue management. Decisions on pricing are still the domain of the property GM, but with a centralized expert staff collecting data and forecasting, the advice and guidance available has brought yield and RevPAR premiums to the chain member properties.

Revenue management requires attention to detail and analytic and forecasting skills; tolerance for ambiguity and comfort with change; and managing, training, leading, and motivating reservations agents. This is one of the most critical and dynamic areas of resort management, one with which every aspiring general manager or director of sales and marketing should take pains to become familiar.

PREPARING TO DELIVER AND DELIGHT

A marketer of a product can count on the factory quality-control system to deliver a consistent product for sale. When the sale is closed, the customer takes the product away and uses it. In a service business, however, the product is human Behaviour, and the customer uses the product in the resort. Because we are humans, both customers and employees, our interactions are never the same one time to the next. The job of the marketer is to help employees understand what the customer will want, need, and expect, and to sell employees on doing their job with enthusiasm.

In a full-service resort, the conference services department embodies this preparing idea as its primary function. Conference service managers are the essential group business brokers between sales and operations. Conference services people can create loyal and repeat meeting planners; the job requires empathy, attention to detail, willingness to work unusual hours, action orientation, internal relationship building, and persuasiveness.

Preparing the resort to fully satisfy and regularly make customers happy is as much a marketing task as attracting customers in the first place.What makes marketing hospitality services harder than marketing a tangible product is that for every market segment there must be two marketing programmes, one directed externally to customers, the other internally to employees.

RETAINING CUSTOMERS

The key to both financial health and market leadership is retaining a higher proportion of customers than do any of your competitors. Retain more customers than others do, and over time your costs drop—because of efficiency, lower advertising and selling costs, better forecasting—and your occupancy and rates rise. Numerous studies validate the high correlation between profit leadership and customer retention.

Frequent-stay rewards are often mistaken for retention programmes. They are not. Rewards can motivate returns only as long as the customer values the points or airline miles or whatever. But they do not create loyalty.They are valuable only insofar as they give employees the opportunity to come to recognize and satisfy the guest, and insofar as they give the marketing department information on who the customer is and where he or she is coming from.

Retaining customers takes more than just doing the job well. Guests and customers must come to know they are valued. Management must build relationships—the tie that binds regardless of a new resort opening in the market or a hot promotional offer from across the street. Relationships are built on recognition and familiarity, on trust, and on appreciation.Thus, guest and customer retention must be a planned and creative activity that involves both sides of the relationship— the customers and the employees. It takes more than just smiling and trying hard. Among the talents and skills needed are analytic skills, curiosity, direct marketing planning, and management of data retrieval and direct marketing service providers.

MEASURING SATISFACTION AND EVALUATING PERFORMANCE

If the purpose of the business is, in part, to keep customers, does a financial statement of rate, occupancy, revenue, expense, and profit give enough information? No. Also needed is a scorecard of customer satisfaction, of how likely customers are to return or tell others about your good resort. That scorecard is the guest satisfaction survey. Accounting statements tell of the resort's financial health; a guest satisfaction scorecard tells of its reputation's health. The scorecard also helps management spot changes in expectations.

Customers are not the same from one visit to the next. Experience with a new resort, perhaps even in another city, may raise a customer's standards. To measure satisfaction, one needs quantitative skills for tracking, analysing, and reporting data, and the ability to manage the logistics of repetitive distribution, collection, and processing. The information helps management figure out what the resort needs to be and to offer next in order to remain competitive and keep customers. Note, now, the return to the first step of the marketing process.

THE CIRCULAR MARKETING PROCESS

In other words, the marketing process isn't the straight-line, step-by-step process, a continuous circle around which management must go again and again as competition improves and as the customer segments in the market change. Only by reviewing and renewing the marketing process will a resort get ahead and continue to be the leading resort in its market. This model of the marketing process applies to both the whole resort and to any revenue or profit center within it. Use it like a checklist when thinking through improving the revenue and competitiveness of any operation.

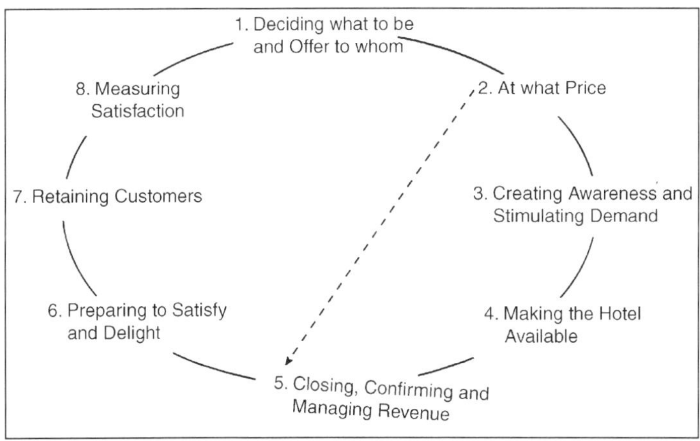

Fig. The Resort Marketing Process

THE MEASURES OF MARKETING

The health of the marketing process should be measured over a longer time than a month or quarter or fiscal year, and it should be measured by more than just profit and loss data.

A healthy marketing process results in:

- Rising room revenues per available room and rising F&B revenues per available seat and catering space.

- Rising market share to a share index over 100—that is, a larger share of a competitive set's occupied rooms than the resort's share of the set's available rooms, which is its "fair share."
- Falling costs of acquiring customers, not on a percentage-of-revenue basis but as dollars per unit of sale—for example, dollars per occupied room, dollars per cover, and so on.What is the acquisition cost? The total of the advertising and business promotion budget, plus commissions, reservation costs, franchise fees, and marketing fees. These costs in times of inflation may not actually decline but at least should grow more slowly than do gross operating revenues.
- Rising customer satisfaction ratings. • Increasing retention rates measured by the percentage of business from repeat customers.
- Growing top-of-mind awareness among target customer segments and, if the resort can afford to measure it, preference by segment rising to number one among your competitive sets.

Management and owners should ask for an annual report card on the health of the marketing process—of the resort, of a chain, of a franchise group.

MANAGEMENT OF THE PROPERTY'S MARKETING PROCESS

As should by now be clear, the marketing process is larger than any one individual's job. Further, no resort can afford the myriad talents and skills that must be orchestrated to create and sustain a healthy marketing process; a single resort is simply not a large enough business to afford having all those talents on staff.

Franchise companies and managed chains have the mass to employ a large proportion of those talents at headquarters, but even they must call on outside services in design, database management, advertising, direct marketing, and so on. But the chains' ability to invest in new tools and hire diverse talents has led branded chains, both management companies and franchisers, to collect increasing numbers of resorts under their umbrellas. The trend towards centralizing marketing functions to serve several resorts in a region, often even resorts of different brands, is accelerating, especially with the advent of Internet-driven information sharing. The advantages are the ability to integrate multiple sources of information, to hire experts that a single resort might not be able to afford, to share the cost of sophisticated systems for forecasting, revenue management and customer relationships, and to reduce the expense of marketing to individual properties.

Independents must counter such attractions with cooperative activities and aggressive local marketing. The Internet has leveled the playing field somewhat, allowing independents to be found and reviewed by consumers and travel agents in a way not possible when GDS systems were the only means of access.

PROPERTY RESPONSIBILITY FOR ITS OWN MARKETING

To optimize performance, a property can neither abdicate its marketing to a chain or franchise group nor passively rely on location and presence to bring customers to the door.

Each property, whether flagged or independent, must be responsible for creating and managing a marketing process tailored to its particular marketing situation—that is, its available customers; its inherent strengths, weaknesses, and employees; and its competitors. Each marketing situation is unique, even among cookie-cutter chain properties. Each has its own location, competitor, and customer dynamics.

So, given the wide range of talents and skills that must be orchestrated to create an effective marketing process, who is to lead it? Directors of sales and marketing cannot, for the process is much larger than the marketing department.

Only the general manager can lead his or her marketing process; only he or she can integrate chain supports, operating departments, human resources, the controller, and—yes, marketing and sales.

THE GM AS LEADER OF THE MARKETING PROCESS

General managers must come to see themselves as the leader of their marketing process and be comfortable in the role. This does not mean becoming expert in all tools and disciplines; it does mean seeing the whole and appreciating when to bring in what talents, when to apply what tools, and how to judge the effectiveness of the process. It means using the marketing process as an organizing concept for creating the management team and a unified viewpoint of mission and challenge.

When a resort is led by a general manager who sees herself or himself as leader of the marketing process, when that process is thoughtfully conceived and well executed, when all employees see themselves as joint operators/marketers, that resort becomes customer-centered, competitive, and a leader in its markets.

Few GMs are trained to do this. Many come to appreciate that location and flag are not enough; many intuitively pick up a smattering of sales, distribution, advertising, and customer retention. But it is the rare GM who weaves these parts into a coherent whole and thinks through the challenge of creating and leading the marketing process. As marketing continues to develop more complex tools and as marketing productivity becomes a more pressing matter, owners, universities, and chains must address this issue of how to develop GM candidates who are comfortable with and capable of leading a comprehensive marketing process.

THE MARKETING PROCESS MODEL AS A PROBLEM-SOLVING TOOL

One last word: The circular model of the marketing process is presented here mainly in terms of rooms marketing. But the model can be applied to every revenue department—to food and beverage outlets, catering, the health club, the business center, and even the laundry. The model can be used for planning, for business reviews, for presentations to lenders and owners, for troubleshooting, and as a checklist when preparing proposals for new services or facilities.

Use the model, make it part of your bag of management tools, and get your team to see their role in terms of this holistic and never-ending marketing process. If you achieve that, you will have gone far to create a customer- and competitor-focused organization, one in which employees see themselves as operators/marketers rather than just "in operations" or "in marketing" or "in HR."

The few resorts that achieve and nurture a well-tuned marketing process and whose employees see themselves as integral parts of it become leaders—in market share, in customer and employee loyalty, and in financial returns to owners.

CONSUMER DECISION RULES AND IMPLICATIONS FOR RESORT CHOICE

Consumers' choices are influenced by the goals they attempt to achieve. Once a person has recognized a need, such as the need for accommodation when traveling for business or pleasure, he or she engages in an information search to identify alternatives from which to choose. Understanding how consumers evaluate competing alternatives in their purchase decision processes enables marketers in the hospitality industry to design better advertising and promotional campaigns leading to a more favourable evaluation of their offerings in travellers' eyes.This is an important step in increasing the likelihood that consumers will choose their offering as opposed to that of competitors.

Given that most travellers' destinations offer several resorts, how do people choose among them? The answer to this question lies, in part, in research on consumers' attitudes and their relation to purchase intentions and subsequent purchase Behaviour. This stage describes several methods consumers may use to make choices based on the evaluation of identified alternatives.

Attitude is the tendency to respond in a consistently favourable or unfavourable manner towards a target. Important to marketers is that, if measured accurately, attitudes are predictive of Behavioural intentions and relatively stable over time.

Simply put, consumers generally form intentions to choose a resort brand towards which they hold positive attitudes. Behavioural intentions, however, do not always translate into corresponding Behaviour. For example, although some consumers have preferences and therefore form intentions to stay at Fairfield Inn when traveling across the country, they might end up choosing other forms of accommodation from time to time.Why would they act inconsistently with their intentions?

Traveling with friends who have different attitudes and preferences, temporary price reductions of competitors, or the fact that a Fairfield Inn is not readily available in a specific area might be reasons for inconsistencies between Behavioural intentions to stay at a Fairfield Inn and actual choice Behaviour.

Despite situational factors sometimes influencing travellers' choices, attitudes are ultimately useful in predicting actual Behaviour; changing or strengthening the basis of consumer attitudes may therefore increase the likelihood of consumers engaging in desired Behaviours. In order to change attitudes and subsequent related Behaviour, marketers must understand a few basic decision rules associated with consumer attitudes. We introduce decision rules likely to be implemented by different segments of consumers under varying market conditions.

DECISION RULES

Decision rules are strategies consumers use to choose among alternatives. Several factors can influence what decision rule consumers ultimately apply in a specific situation. Typically, the more important and less frequent a purchase decision is, the more time and effort consumers are willing to expend making that decision. Choosing a resort at which to spend a twenty-fifth wedding anniversary, for example, is a decision most consumers face only once and therefore are likely to take a relatively long time to make, and they are likely to be careful and thorough in evaluating alternatives.

On the other hand, a salesperson traveling frequently in a familiar territory likely chooses a resort using a routine process where far less time and consideration are given to alternatives. Further, brand-loyal customers might choose to stay with the same resort chain whenever possible, thereby avoiding a situation where they are forced to choose among alternatives. In general, the stronger a consumer is motivated to search and the greater the risk associated with a choice, the greater the complexity of the decision rule he or she implements.

Another important characteristic of modeling decisions is the fact that people often do not attempt to optimize choice. If a person's goal is optimal choice, considerably more time and effort is typically required to identify and evaluate alternatives. Therefore, consumers often choose a satisfactory alternative in order to save time and effort. The use of decision rules in these instances enables people to take shortcuts in making decisions in the face of the apparently unlimited or overwhelming amounts of information available regarding all possible alternatives.

Consumers usually work with a consideration set so they do not have to work as hard cognitively when required to make a decision in a given product category. They then make a final decision from this reduced set of alternatives.

Such decision rules are referred to as *heuristics* or rules of thumb. Employing heuristics, people save time and limit complex information processing while still making reasonable or satisfactory choices based on the few brand attributes or characteristics most important to them at the time of choice. In the context of resort choice, brand attributes are things like location, room rates, and availability of a swimming pool, restaurant, and so forth.

Although the number of consumer decision rules is almost infinite and likely varies by consumer, basic categories and a few specific examples serve as useful tools in modeling and predicting traveller decisions.

Two general categories of decision rules are:

1. Compensatory and
2. Non-compensatory.

Compensatory Decision Rules

Compensatory decision rules model consumers as deriving an overall brand evaluation such that alternatives performing poorly on one attribute can *compensate* for their respective shortcomings by positive evaluations of other attributes. For example, a high-priced resort might not be perceived positively on the dimension of room rates by some travellers; however, these same travellers might be willing to spend more money knowing they will receive better service or that the resort is conveniently located—that is, in this example, service and location compensate for the perceived disadvantage of high room rates. The multi-attribute attitude model described in the next part is perhaps the most popular compensatory decision rule.

MARKETING IMPLICATIONS

Once consumer evaluations of salient attributes are determined and their beliefs regarding a resort brand's offerings are known, managers can use this information to improve their resort's competitive positioning in the market. The goal of any marketing strategy is to increase positive attitude towards the offering or to encourage the use of certain decision rules, thereby increasing the likelihood of being chosen by consumers.

When consumers use a compensatory decision rule, the overall attitude towards a resort is determined by the sum of the products of evaluations multiplied by beliefs regarding salient attributes associated with the offering. Consequently, travellers' overall attitudes towards a resort can be rendered more positive by strategies targeted at increasing the evaluation of an attribute in consumers' decision making, or by changing consumers' beliefs about a resort's offerings.

Travellers' attribute evaluations can be influenced by stressing the attribute in advertising. This strategy of influencing attribute evaluations is effective in attitude change and also relatively easy to pursue. It is, however, not a strategy always recommended for changing consumers' attitudes when they are using a compensatory model.

The potential problem associated with this approach is that attribute evaluations are constant across brands in a consideration set. Travellers evaluating importance of the availability of an indoor pool is the same for all resort brands, E, F, G, and H. If Resort H were successful in a marketing message in increasing the evaluation of an indoor pool with a segment of consumers, say to a rating of _3, it would increase consumers' overall attitude towards its brand. At the same time, however, consumers' overall evaluation of Resort G would increase by the same amount, as both brands do not differ with respect to consumers' beliefs about their having a great indoor pool. In the end, the attempt to increase consumers' overall attitude towards Resort H would also benefit some of its competitors.

Thus, sometimes a more effective strategy for improving consumers' overall attitude towards a resort's offerings is to improve consumers' brand-specific belief ratings. For example, Resort F could strive to improve consumer belief that it offers a pleasant indoor pool by providing a picture of the pool on its web site, or by stressing the availability of the indoor pool in advertisements. While consumer brand-specific beliefs are then likely to increase, Resort F's competitors will not benefit from its strategy, and Resort F thereby improves its competitive position.

Assuming that Resort E cannot do anything to increase consumers' belief that it is not located in proximity of a skiing area, a strategy it may employ to increase consumers' overall attitude towards the property is to add a salient attribute to the set of attributes consumers consider when making resort choices. For example, Resort E could provide free accommodation for children staying with their parents. It is likely that parents would consider this option important when choosing a resort. As long as other competitors do not offer this service, Resort E enjoys some advantage in the choices made by its target market. It is essential that when adding a new attribute, marketers consider the following: First, the attribute added must be important enough to the resort's target market to be included in consumers' subsequent decision making. Second, the belief that a particular resort possesses this attribute must be stronger than the belief that any of its competitors do.

This marketing strategy, often referred to as a *strategy of differentiation,* is likely to be successful when these conditions are met. Differentiation, however, is unlikely to be sustainable— that is, over time, competitors identify what added attributes successfully attract customers and copy them, thereby creating consumer belief regarding their own properties. Thus, the resort that introduced the new salient attribute often can expect to lose its differential advantage over time unless it maintains a unique characteristic like a special location or a fabulous chef in the kitchen.

Increasing belief strength for a resort's attributes is not always a successful strategy, assuming a compensatory model is being used. For example, consumers may find it relatively unimportant whether the resort offers low room rates or not.

The importance rating for low room rates is _2—that is, consumers in this particular target segment evaluate low room rates negatively, perhaps because they associate low rates with low quality or with small, underfurnished rooms. In this case, stressing that a particular resort offers low rates, thereby increasing the strength of consumers' beliefs, may adversely affect consumers' overall evaluation of a property. If you compare Resorts F and H, you will see that the strong belief that Resort H offers low rates negatively affects its overall evaluation. Resort F, on the other hand, benefits from consumers not being aware of low rates.

It is important to note that importance weights associated with attributes vary across market segments. For example, while business travellers on corporate expense accounts or consumers on a once-in-a-lifetime vacation, such as a honeymoon, may attach less importance to low rates, more price-sensitive market segments usually weigh low rates more heavily in their resort choice. It is therefore important for marketers to carefully define the targeted market segment prior to conducting their research and applying evaluation weights and beliefs to similarly disposed consumers.

In general, it is crucial to find out what attributes targeted consumers feel are most salient to their decisions and, in response, increase performance regarding these attributes and commensurately inform market segments of this stronger position. The resultant positive attitude towards the offering should then increase the likelihood of the resort being chosen by travellers using a compensatory decision-making model. Alternatively, as a strategic move, particularly for special niche properties, marketers may want to encourage consumers to abandon the linear compensatory model. Niche market segments may exist or may be created through marketing communications; these target markets might be better served by resorts focusing on one or more of the non-compensatory decision rules presented.

For example, a segment of highly price-sensitive customers predominantly using a lexicographic decision rule with low rates as the most important attribute may constitute the primary target market for a property. In this case, travellers can be targeted by offering low prices and/or frequentstay loyalty programmes. At the same time, services deemed unnecessary or unimportant by this customer segment can be eliminated or minimized. The fact that some customer segments expect a minimal level of performance on several attributes when they use an elimination-by-aspect or conjunctive decision rule, however, implies that focusing performance and/or marketing on a single attribute may be inadequate for some segments of travellers. A resort would then benefit from creating a level of "at least acceptable" attributes in addition to providing stronger packages of the same attributes offered by competitors targeting the same market segment.

Overall, knowing how consumers make decisions should help resort managers to design better properties, packages, and services, and help them market those offerings to their respective target segment, thereby improving competitive position.

RESORT PRICING

TRADITIONAL APPROACH

The single most important criterion of success in any business, including resorts, is profit.The purpose of this object is to discuss the importance of resort pricing and its influence on yield or revenue management, especially in terms of profit generation, and because of inherent dangers to the industry worldwide, integrity of the established pricing structure.

Historically, price has been determined by the triangular relationship of cost and demand in the context of competition.

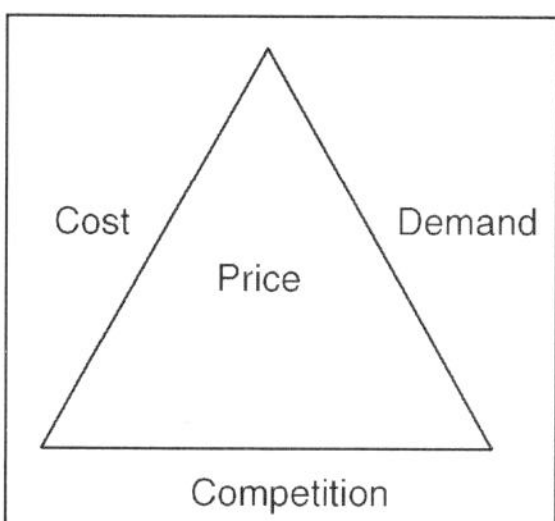

Fig. Three Forces of Pricing

The actual pricing structure is developed with one of these three components as the deciding factor while the other two play supplementary roles.

The traditional pricing strategy was largely cost-driven. Many resort operators tended to favour the rule-of-thumb method. This approach, also called the $1 per $1,000 rule, states that resorts should charge approximately $1 per night for every $1,000 of room cost, based on an average 70 per cent occupancy.

Although popular in its day, the calculation of cost was commonly misunderstood. Another widely used quantitative method was the Hubbart Formula, developed in the late 1940s as a guideline issued by the American Resort Association. It focused on computing an average room rate that would cover operational costs and yield a reasonable return on investment. These quantitative methods are fairly static and therefore suited for a stable economic environment. Qualitative pricing approaches, such as percentage increase of previous-year rates adjusted for inflation, payroll increases, and new cost of supplies, reflect more realistically the projected cost.

Other qualitative techniques are less exact but, by being competition-oriented, they offer more flexibility. The Pied Piper or Follow-the-Leader method uses competition as the basis for rate setting, while the Gouge 'Em approach tries to lure business away from other properties by undercutting their prices. If there is no competition to speak of, Hit or Miss fluctuation of rates tied to profitable occupancy levels could be employed.

The drawback of competition-driven pricing is its sole focus on rate comparison, ignoring differences in operating expenses and customer- perceived value. An effective approach, therefore, calls for a mix of methods adjusted for different situations. The fundamental question remains:What should be the driving force in formulating a sound pricing strategy? In today's dynamic business environment, which discards the traditional view that market demand for room rates is largely inelastic, demand orientation seems to provide the best fit.

CURRENT PRICING CRITERIA

"Our pricing is market-driven, not costbased," says Scott Farrell, corporate director of distribution with Fairmont Resorts and Resorts, a Toronto-based chain of luxury properties. When the chain is setting its prices, it starts with comprehensive market research. Based on the data, the correct price for each marketplace is determined. If there is a major shift in a market, then the prices will adjust for that. However, if there is a major shift in a demand curve, then a shift of price may have no effect.

It may actually leave more money on the table. For example, if the airlines go on strike, a significant shift in the demand curve would result. Under such conditions, decreasing the rate by $50, for example, would only result in a $50 loss. If there is an opportunity to go after a new targeted market with a specific offer, enabling the chain to capture a greater market share, then lowering the rate serves its purpose. Generally, however, lowering rates across the board is not the preferred pricing strategy.

PRICING: WHO IS IN CHARGE

While independently owned properties make their own pricing decisions, in case of a chain it is usually corporate headquarters (HQ) that sets pricing guidelines. Often, individual properties are still responsible for the actual pricing.

Because they are held accountable, they must balance corporate guidelines with their autonomy to set their prices. Caroline Shin, member of the revenue management team at Starwood Resorts and Resorts Worldwide, which operates a number of upscale brands, such as Sheraton and W Resorts, stresses the cooperative nature of this relationship. Successful pricing strategies arise from an ongoing interaction of both sides. Corporate HQ provides sophisticated tools and in-depth market analysis that would be beyond reach of individual properties. Property managers, on the other hand, offer their experience and knowledge of regional specifics that may have gone unnoticed by the corporate team."The people who have been in the property understand the dynamics of that market, and they have developed pricing intuition," explains Shin. Some experts view intuition as a valuable part of the pricing mechanism, and even managers who are technically savvy check the numbers against their gut feeling.

PRICING: SCIENCE, ART, AND INTUITION

Pricing distribution and revenue management techniques are a mix of science and art. Recent research shows that two-thirds of managers making strategic decisions under pressure and time constraints use a combination of analysis and intuition.

The advent of modern technology, such as yield management software packages, has further strengthened this link. "Even the most sophisticated analytical model for forecasting, may it be for resort pricing or for thermal dynamics of a nuclear plant, still needs variables based upon assumptions," says Shin, who used to work as a nuclear engineer.The more business- savvy resort management becomes and the more they understand the resort dynamics and the market, the more can be gained from training them how to define their experiencebased intuition and put it into numbers. In this respect, an interaction between the corporate revenue management team and individual resorts is paramount. "Every time I go out to a property, I learn something new. It only helps me when I build my analytical models to almost translate what they know into numbers," confirms Shin. The better resorts can do that, the better models they can develop. Nonetheless, inaccurate historical data remains a major limitation.

No model is ever going to be perfect, though.What seems to work best is to teach resort managers how to use the model and to understand the direction of the pricing decisions they need to make. That is the scientific part.The art piece comes into play when they infuse the model with their knowledge and intuition.

Staff training is an important part of this process. "We can't just have Ph.D.s sitting in one room coming with all these models and we just roll it out. At the same time, we can't just have people with intuitions run around and set prices," says Shin.

Revenue management teams must make sure that resorts understand how to employ the models in their daily pricing decisions. When science is applied, the revenue team can go to their experts, ask probing questions, and get solid results. Even though intuition is a part of this process, it is based only on a hypothesis that could have been triggered by a discussion with a customer, knowledge of what is happening in the marketplace, or historic trends. That is why pure intuition is not sufficient. "Managers must have reliable data to support their hunches," cautions Scott Farrell.

CUSTOMER NEEDS

Customer satisfaction is a crucial part of marketing, pricing, and yield management. Any pricing strategy established by the resort management must attract customers willing to pay the specified rate.While price is a determinator of the customer profile the resort is looking for, it is also an indicator of the quality of services and the market segment the resort is competing in.

Therefore, yield management uses information about targeted customers' purchasing Behaviour and product sales to develop pricing strategy together with inventory control that delivers products that are better matched to customer needs, create greater demand, and, on that account, produce greater revenues. Lieberman states that yield management is the process of maximizing profits from the sale of perishable assets, such as resort rooms, by controlling price and inventory and improving service through systemization.

An exact definition of the target market is essential. There is a definite and firm perception in the psyche of the customer, who views the price as the value forthcoming. Therefore, the eventual satisfaction of the customer is the paramount task of the pricing mechanism. This is the make-or-break factor of the entire resort, especially if the value expected does not match the price.

ROLE OF TECHNOLOGY

While the approach to resort pricing is still ruled by supply and demand, speed and sophistication of room-rate yield or revenue maximization is now much increased due to two technological factors: yield management software and Internet bookings.

Yield management software packages enable resorts to use a higher number of roomrate levels, or buckets, and to control inventory for rate availability in real time. Each level may consist of several room rates open under given conditions to yield a maximum profit. Traditionally, resorts used between three and five rate levels; otherwise, the adjustment became too complex for the human brain to work with.

The introduction of software removed this barrier, and some resort chains now use up to ten rate levels.This allows implementation of much narrower ranges for each bucket, thus optimizing price elasticity. This further means the software model recognizes the point at which the same number of bookings can be achieved at a higher rate.

Online monitoring of room inventory in real time facilitates the timing of the adjustment. So far, the biggest limitation is the reliability of historical data. Even in its imperfect form, the system has made a difference. However, resort managers are fully aware that it takes years to develop brand recognition and quality but just a push of a button to damage or even destroy it, if the pricing is not set up knowledgeably.

As the technology becomes more sophisticated, it will eliminate such questionable practices as overbooking, which aims at compensating for last-minute cancellations by taking in more than 100 per cent reservations. Besides the question of whether overbooking is ethical and, in some countries, even illegal, better technology would definitely improve the quality of service provided by properties that engage in this practice.

Another area where technological advancement had a great impact on resort pricing is the Internet. Its use as a booking tool has created a new level of pricing transparency and tiered competition. It also penetrated the negotiation of corporate rates.

Many resorts see the effect of the Internet as both good and bad.The good side is that web site bookings are growing every day. As more customers become familiar with their favourite resort web sites, resort companies have started investing heavily in web site development and upkeep, which gives them several advantages.

First, the cost of online bookings is lower than for bookings made through other distribution channels. Companies do not have to pay commission because the booking is direct, circumventing all intermediaries. Online booking also provides an opportunity to monitor inventory in real time without reliance on a distributor willing to share and regularly supply data. Last but not least, it generates loyal customers by making them eligible for bonus points, which they cannot earn if they use an Internet intermediary.

That is exactly where the flip side of the Internet lies. The intermediaries are getting more powerful and growing significantly in volume. Because most of them show all resort rates on their web site, they make the information accessible to any computer user. One way to meet the challenge of more powerful intermediaries, especially if resorts need to move inventory, is to utilize auctions where the name of the resort is not disclosed to the customer until the transaction is finalized. Such action, however, calls for extreme caution so that it does not damage a resort's reputation or threaten its strategic partnerships.

As intermediaries become bigger, rate transparency will increase to the point where it will drive the market, especially when computer literacy and Internet access become the norm.

Moreover, the Internet allows non-branded resorts to compete more heavily with the branded resorts because they can now be displayed just as readily. Without significant advertising expense, they can compete on price. For some markets this does not matter, especially when the brand is powerful enough to charge the premium and get the business.

In highly competitive markets, however, the competition creates an additional strain for the individual property. Many branded resorts must now compete with other brands through the traditional distribution channels and with non-branded resorts on the Internet, which, in principle, lowers resort rates. A frequently adopted strategy is to invest heavily in web site development and customer loyalty programmes, assuring excellent web site functionality and that customers are rewarded for booking directly through the resort web site rather than through the web site of a thirdparty intermediary. Both Fairmont and Starwood, for example, utilize their high-quality loyalty programmes in this way.

Internet booking also changed the way corporate accounts are negotiated. Because many companies now require that their employees make business travel arrangements via the corporate web site, the placement of a resort or a brand on this booking tool is of strategic importance. Being listed first in the accommodation part, for example, may bring in a higher volume of business and thus substantiate a lower negotiated rate.

LONG-TERM STRATEGY TOR THE INTERNET

Because resorts cannot expect that Internet distributors will go out of business, they smartly conclude that a partnership with the devil is better than a fight with him. Besides using their own web sites, resort companies are also making sure that the cost of their transactions goes down continuously so they can compete even at lower rates—while maintaining a good relationship with their carefully selected online intermediaries.

There is a large number of distributors to choose from. On one end of the spectrum is, for example, Expedia, which allows participating resorts to control their rates, meaning a resort can change its rates any time it wants.At the other end are companies, such as Resort Reservation Network that bind resorts contractually to a locked rate that cannot be changed. Some resort chains do not want to partner with these distributors because they like pricing flexibility and want to make sure their rates yield as much as possible.

Adaptation to new technology has been the biggest component of change for intermediaries as well. Companies that do not have the most current technology working in real time or allowing resorts to yield rates in real time are usually not considered a suitable distribution partner for some chains. On the other hand, companies that invest in real-time technology to yield rates are ideal partners because, as the industry sees it, they work with, not against the industry by permitting resorts to raise or lower rates in real time. "They work with us," says Caroline Shin.

"They give data to us very frequently so that we understand the travel pattern bookings on their web site.Then we compare it with what is happening on our web site and also what we are getting outside the Internet to make sure that our market mix is set appropriately." Pricing flexibility, compatibility with the desired resort image, and protection of its strategic partnerships, together with cost, play important roles in selecting an intermediary.

THE ROLE OF CREATIVITY IN PRICING

Creativity, either of an individual or a team, can and often does lead to innovative pricing ideas. However, its application must be specific, not just directional.

It is not enough to state,"We have to do something about our occupancy level." A pricing campaign must target a number of sold rooms or generated revenue that is required in order to break even or to do better. This specific approach injects efficiency into allocating marketing money to areas where it is most effective and in periods when it is desired.

If there is no task direction or overall pricing leadership, the most creative idea may book only ten roomnights instead of one hundred. It may generate more customer loyalty, but that is something the resort may not need at the moment, although it could be an acceptable outcome in a low-season month. Pricing leadership helps team members understand the resort's current situation and direct money and creativity to do exactly what is needed. Creativity comes up with the idea, which serves as a vehicle, but spending marketing money the smart way is a matter of experience in innovation, which turns the idea into a successful product. Creativity also plays a large part in employee satisfaction, and it lowers turnover.

In a sluggish economy, some resorts start paying attention not only to profit as the bottom line but also to revenue. This means they monitor closely the accrued cost as well as the generated revenue, thus achieving the maximum yield. Interestingly, contemporary price leadership may take different forms.

It could mean, for example, elimination of smoking rooms throughout the property. Many U.S. motels are revamping rooms, ripping off cigarette- damaged furniture and carpets, and designating them as non-smoking. This saves on maintenance and adds to overall packaging flexibility when the business is hurt by lackluster demand. This tactic means drapes, carpets, bedding, and other furnishings must be replaced less frequently; it also mitigates fire risk and enhances cleanliness and overall safety.

THE ROLE OF HUMAN RESOURCES IN PRICING

Some large chains recognize that pricing is a complex issue and that they need to get better at it.There is a new focus on analysing the culture of pricing and how it can be improved. This approach is reflected even in the kinds of people chains are hiring. Although the majority of staff involved in strategic pricing are in the resort industry and have a background in revenue management, others are in the airline industry and have indepth travel revenue management experience.

Some chains have sought access to this experience by hiring from outside the resort industry. This is to encourage diversification of thinking and new ways of thought—completely out of the box, as the traditional team members are joined by researchers doing a different kind of optimization analysis. The goal could be as radical as trying to manage risk or optimize towards the railroad industry and its scheduling.

On the surface, these tactics have nothing to do with revenue management *per se*.A lot of experience in optimizing difficult travel, however, can only be gained by bringing in people with different backgrounds in consulting or with in-depth Internet experience. In order to move pricing and revenue management to a different level of thought, a new mix of people is necessary. For this approach to work, adequate training must be in place.

In this respect, basic HR functions, such as hiring and training, have an impact on pricing. What is necessary is not only to train personnel in quantitative core skills but also in strategic thinking. For example, when a resort does not want to take a specific piece of business, it must ask such questions as:What is the revenue? What is the rate? What am I displacing by this decision? Where do I think this will go? How does it help my RevPAR?

Resort managers must become more analytical so they can use all the new tools now available. When reports are created, team members must be taught how to use them.A lot of training must be provided for corporate executives, general managers, and regional revenue directors as well. They all must be trained to think more strategically and to understand analysis and the reports so they can help their individual properties.

DIVERSIFICATION: THE IMPROVEMENT OF THE PRICING PROCESS

As noted, exclusive resort industry experience may lead to ossification due to one-sided judgement and the inability to see beyond the familiar. From this perspective, experience is both an asset and a liability. It is human nature to take for granted the way things are done after being in the same environment for a while. Therefore, resort chains are continuously creating and refining pricing strategies to accommodate not only different market segments but also different situations a resort may face based on occupancy levels. Corporate HQ tries to identify these different situations and associated variables. "It is almost like a bag of goods, a bag of pricing strategies that should be tested," says Caroline Shin. Resorts are given the full menu and encouraged to try a certain strategy if they are in a specific situation. Depending on the region, an individual property may use one set of strategies more than another. In a weak economy, however, the chains have to work harder and be more flexible because the market is overflowing with demand.

Adapting step by step, a resort may apply a different strategy every week.The problem for the corporate office is to identify situations a resort might be in and seek remedy. For example, if group bookings are low this week but competitors are full, how can the property make up the difference with transient or leisure business? The general manager may ask the corporate team, "What pricing strategies can I use in order to fill my house?" Then he or she may ask, "What else worked before for other resorts, and what may work for me based on my market specifics and market characteristics?" That way he or she can test each strategy using the provided tool and personal experience.

PRICING: SUPPORT AND PROTECT

The corporate pricing structure is also in place to support and protect members of the chain in a number of areas including pricing and partnerships. The corporate office sets guidelines for resorts in terms of pricing structure and the market segments they deal with. Fairmont Resorts and Resorts, for example, focuses on four segments: transient leisure travel, group travel, business travel, and wholesale. The corporate structure provides guidelines about how the segments fit with each other, how they cross over, and where they reside in the overall pricing structure.

This information is necessary because every segment acts differently. Most market segments are dynamic and require frequent rate adjustments. One exception is the wholesale market, where pricing is still largely done the traditional way: A wholesaler provides a net rate, marks it up, and sells it to the general population.There may be a hidden cost, however, if the distribution chain includes an operator acting as a middleman between the wholesaler and the supplier.

When setting up the overall pricing structure, one starts with the retail rate, which is a bucket of premium or best available rates charged on the open market. They usually do not carry any restrictions, such as cancellation fees, and they are fully billable. Depending on the level of occupancy, one of these rates is available on any given day when the resort is not fully booked. It is up to the yield management system to identify which BAR to offer. All other rate types, such as discount rates and prenegotiated rates, are determined in relation to the retail rate. For instance, a corporate rate for a high-volume client will be probably set lower than the BAR rate that is estimated to sell most during the period when the contract is in place. This way the rates are nested within each other in a manner that makes economic sense.

The corporate pricing guidelines follow two main criteria: to maximize revenue and to protect key partnerships.While the resort sales force negotiates contracts with key partners, such as longstanding corporate accounts or wholesale volume accounts, they make sure to protect these partnerships and provide them value. At the same time, they take every opportunity to maximize revenue. One cannot survive without the other, reiterates Scott Farrell. However, it is up to the resorts themselves, with guidance and additional research, to determine in their marketplace what their pricing structure should look like.

A diversified corporate team, with a mix of people with a resort industry background and others skilled in optimization modeling, fulfills an additional function. It acts as a risk prevention mechanism, a necessary prerequisite for managing the risk inherent in pricing. Any chain with a wide variety of resorts must make sure the properties are covered in all kinds of situations. One risk containment scenario might be that the chain, in response to a changing demand curve, acquires a type of business that the brand has not catered to traditionally.

Caroline Shin explains, "Sheraton did not take on airline crew business because we did not want crew members lingering in the lobby; it affected our brand image. But we thought maybe we could start taking that when our RevPAR index or occupancy slips to a certain point. So we are trying to change the standards of different market segments we are willing to take."

On the international scale, another risk management plan would be analysing operational cost and determining whether to close down part of the resort if market research shows occupancy will not be high enough. When

PESTEL (political, economic, sociocultural, technological, environmental, legal) analysis indicates demand will drop precipitously for an extended period instead of hoping for the best and running a full house with a full staff, the resort may decide to shut down floors or restaurants and save cost until the market picks up again. Selection of the appropriate strategy will depend on the market specifics and protection of the image. A property may opt to close down several floors over the weekend if it caters mostly to business clientele staying during the week. It would not, however, suspend room service, although unprofitable, if that is considered an integral part of the offered product. In a worst-case scenario, the chain may decide to sell properties in global risk areas when it determines the external circumstances make it difficult to raise occupancy on an ongoing basis.

BETTER UTILIZE YOUR DISTRIBUTION CHANNELS

The Internet creates a new level of transparency as it allows the opportunity to maximize profitability.There is now a multitude of channels to choose from. Understanding the cost of each channel in relation to the value of provided service has an impact on the quality of pricing decisions. Therefore, it is necessary to determine how much revenue bookings through an Internet intermediary generate and whether or not they justify the accrued cost.There is also a tremendous risk involved.

As discussed earlier, one of key guidelines of corporate marketing is that partners are protected. Just because there is a new Internet site it does not mean a chain can use it and advertise a lower rate, which would undermine a partnership of many years. In terms of cost, the chain must review its pricing strategy not only by market segment but also by distribution channel. "Several years ago, we would not consider the cost of distribution in our ROI.Today we do," concedes Scott Farrell.

Another challenge is to keep up with new Internet sites. The chains must reevaluate constantly and prioritize their yield so as to choose which channels to keep or drop. Fairmont Resorts and Resorts, for example, applies the 80–20 rule. They focus on the 20 per cent of the online wholesalers that capture more than 80 per cent of the business. As Scott Farrell puts it,"Why would I play with the other 10–12 per cent? I only have so many hours in a day to manage. I may as well work with the lion's share."

QUALITY ABOVE ALL?

Criteria for selecting an online distribution partner vary by price levels as well. Budget and economy properties are driven mostly by financial considerations, while upscale and luxury resorts are more concerned with compatibility.

As for chains, they ask two basic questions:

1. How can the partnership increase our brand recognition or a brand reach, and
2. How much is it going to bring us in terms of revenue or profitability?

Their choice has to match the brand first, and then it has to drive the revenue. If the brand is equaled with quality, online providers that project a connotation of cheapness will not be considered at all.The quality image refers not only to the resort asset itself but also to how and where this asset is sold.

Fairmont Resorts and Resorts, as a quality brand on the luxury side, cannot compete on price. The quality of their product and the offering of the experience must be considered by the customer at the price being offered.

When their resorts play with price, the corporate office watches closely. Scott Farrell explains, "If our property wanted to shift their rate by $50, I would ask why? Give me the case behind it and tell me what you are going to do to make up the additional $50 you are going to lose. If they come back to me and say they are moving their rate from $300 to $250 while driving a certain volume, I would make them go through the process of determining what incremental volume they will need to make up for the $50 in loss." In other words, pricing decisions must be driven by ROI, not only a feeling. Feelings and experience may be involved, but properties must present a strong case based on the estimated ROI and what they plan to get out of the proposed strategy. It allows them to go into the pricing change with their eyes open. They also must consider how the competition will respond.A carelessly lowered rate may lead to a price war.

SPEED AND STRATEGY

The speed and immediacy of exposure via the Internet have reshaped how marketing campaigns are conducted. Having eliminated the delay of exposure to marketing collateral material, such as brochures or newspaper advertisements, resorts can conduct targeted discount mini-campaigns on their own web sites when the yield management system indicates a drop in occupancy for specific dates. In a similar manner, brand recognition can be enhanced by a carefully orchestrated online auction. The South African hospitality group Protea was among the first in the industry using this method by offering their prospective guests the opportunity to bid on a limited number of weekend getaways in their properties that needed to boost occupancy.

By setting a minimum bidding price, the integrity of the resort image was protected. Similar auction systems, used to encourage room-night sales during slow periods, are nowadays available in the United States and Canada via several Internet intermediaries. For chains in particular, a long-term strategy in distribution pricing is paramount. It stipulates the criteria and accepts or rejects short-term adjustments depending on what is happening in the industry, what is new in the technology, and who the new players are.

In terms of corporate hierarchy, pricing is formulated and executed on three levels:

1. Strategy,
2. Tactics and execution, and
3. Measurement.

Strategy comes first, followed by tactics meant to support that strategy and their execution. Finally, the achieved outcome is measured against the set benchmarks. If the strategy is sound, it will last longer than the other two steps. Frequently, new tactics must be implemented; these drive the execution and the measurement. This requires a development of proprietary criteria for measurement and their continuous adjustment to changing conditions.

PRICE ELASTICITY

Contrary to the traditional view that resort rates are, in the long-term, generally inelastic, price elasticity is receiving a lot of attention nowadays thanks to yield management. Its goal is to take advantage of and to cover the entire spectrum of the customers' ability to purchase. Price elasticity allows resorts to capture customers who do not mind paying the high rate as well as those who are more priceconscious. This can be done in a number of ways. By using different room categories, a luxury resort can have on the same day suites available at $500 and entry-level rooms at $200. Every room rate category has a different value proposition associated with the incremental revenue. If the variance between a standard room and a deluxe room is $75, the latter should provide an adequately greater value to the customer. The result is a clear product differentiation, which can be also achieved by stay restrictions or by the use of fencing. Examples of physical differences, or fences, are room type, view, amenities, and location.

Non-physical fences may mean different customers, transactions, or consumption characteristics. These bear many similarities with airline pricing strategies, which differentiate the product by, for example, cancellation restrictions or last-minute availability of a prenegotiated corporate rate. The result is nested pricing, allowing properties to have a very high rate available on the same day as a rate that is more attractive to the lower-end customer.

NEW AREAS OF PRICING AND YIELD MANAGEMENT

Resort pricing strategies traditionally have been limited to setting and adjusting room rates and other ongoing activities. In order to survive in the current dynamic, competitive, and even dangerous global environment, resorts and resorts are taking on other types of business, some of which are one-time projects. Organizing shows, festivals, and conferences or undergoing renovations requires a new type of core competency. Therefore, in addition to mastering current pricing strategies, resort practitioners must acquire project management skills, such as those that are taught and practiced by Project Management Institute.

Mastering these skills will make resort team members capable of maximizing yield from project-type functions the same way as they optimize revenue from room rates.

RESORT SALES ORGANIZATION AND OPERATIONS

SALES AND MARKETING

Sales and marketing are related concepts, and each is an art and a science. Sales flow from marketing. Marketing, well stated by Lewis "is communicating to and giving target market customers what they want, when they want it, where they want it, and at a price they are willing and able to pay."The primary focus of sales is on the communication aspect of marketing. It involves direct personal selling to potential customers that you and your organization have the right product, in the right place, at the right time, and at the right price—be it a resort, a restaurant, a casino, or contract food services.

Marketing is getting and keeping a customer, a macro approach to managing a successful business. In a broad sense, marketing is the development and delivery of a successful product, that is, the development and delivery of a satisfied customer. Resort sales comprises finding that customer and matching his or her specific needs with the right product offering, a micro or one-on-one approach to customer satisfaction. For example, a meeting planner from Texas Instruments is planning an annual sales meeting to be held in Dallas. From a macro perspective, this planner has selected the city and is searching for full-service lodging accommodations for 200 TI sales representatives for a five-day conference. From a micro perspective, he or she visits several resort alternatives and meets with the resort sales representatives to find the best "fit." Various aspects of the meeting being planned are discussed including dates, rates, guest room accommodations, function room requirements, food and beverage services, and so forth. It is the job of the resort sales manager to learn the specific needs and wants of the planner and "create" the right product, place, time, and price for a successful conference.

A successful conference is what the planner is really buying, not bricks and mortar. Thus, successful selling is understanding the real needs of the buyer, communicating how your product and service can best respond to those needs, and then delivering it. In another context, McDonald's Golden Arches markets fun, simplicity, good service, and a good price.

McDonald's sells friendly service, good value for price paid, convenient locations, and those delicious golden chicken nuggets on which many of us grew up. Ronald McDonald is an ancillary product, a public relations endeavor, which augments and supports the idea or concept of kids and why they are special.

Public relations, advertising, and special promotions often support the selling effort. Advertisements for the Ritz-Carlton Resort Company are directed to their business traveller clientele. Such advertisements incorporate both the selling and marketing aspects of this upscale resort chain. The company is simultaneously selling resort rooms to busy business executives and marketing a resort that "remembers your needs," and is hallmarked by the vision implicit in their slogan "ladies and gentlemen serving ladies and gentlemen."

A travel agent, a corporate travel manager, or a secretary, however, may have handled the actual purchase of the resort room. Thus, the Ritz-Carlton advertisements support the sale, but they do not actually make the sale happen.

SALES AND OPERATIONS

Sales is the critical link between marketing and operations.While hospitality professionals may espouse marketing, all too often it becomes ignored in the daily hustle and bustle of operations. It is the role of sales to help bridge this gap and find ways for the key customer-contact members of the resort to keep the promise of marketing.

Selling starts by the professional sales managers prospecting, making contacts, establishing relationships with clients, uncovering their specific needs and wants. But it doesn't end there. Sales is also the host or hostess greeting restaurant patrons. Sales is the front desk clerk welcoming a guest at the local Holiday Inn or at the Waldorf-Astoria in New York City. Sales is the housekeeping staff delivering the extra set of towels requested by a guest. Sales is the sommelier in a gourmet restaurant recommending wines to complement an entrée choice. Sales is the front office cashier saying, "Thank you for staying with us. We hope you enjoyed your stay." It is amazing how a simple thank-you can express appreciation for a customer's patronage and bring them back.

All client-contact personnel of a hospitality organization perform personal selling either consciously or unconsciously. This includes staff who does not regularly have guest contact, such as the credit manager. One of the authors nearly lost a $100,000 annual account when a poorly trained credit manager called the client to collect a payment that had not yet been billed. A well-trained and motivated employee who understands how a resort works is key to successful selling. This is accomplished through the hiring and training process, and although the many facets of human resources are beyond the scope of this stage, its importance to guest satisfaction cannot be overstated.

In this particular context, however, the resort's human resources department can perform services on behalf of the sales department by recruiting sales associates who understand the nature of the resort industry and its place in the broader category of the services segment of business. Services are different from products and require specialized knowledge and training to be competitive.

Because hospitality is very much a part of the services industry, it is useful to understand how services differ from products. Those characteristics that are unique to the services industry product include perishability, simultaneity, heterogeneity, and intangibility.

Perishability refers to the short shelf life of the hospitality product. If it is not sold today, the potential revenue from the sales of that product is gone. A resort room has a 24- hour shelf life. A restaurant seat has a twohour shelf life. Manufactured goods have a much longer period of durability. If a television set is not sold today, it can be sold tomorrow or next week. The potential revenue from the sale of that product is not lost. But a Tuesday-night resort room cannot be resold on Wednesday.Tuesday has come and gone. If the resort guest room goes unsold Tuesday, the potential revenue lost from that vacant room cannot be recouped.

Simultaneity means that production and consumption occur at the same time. How can you produce a guest experience without the guest? Our customers, in a sense, are part of the assembly line.They need to be present for final production of the product offering.A vacant guest room produces nothing. Yes, the carpeting is installed; the bed is made, the bathroom plumbing works. But it all just exists until a guest arrives to use it. Simultaneous production and consumption is a unique challenge for successful operations in hospitality management. The guest needs to be present, because many of the facets of the service involve performances by resort staff. A related service characteristic in hospitality is *heterogeneity*. Heterogeneity refers to the variability of service delivery. Guest service agents have their moods. Customers have their moods. All have personalities of varying shapes and sizes. Hospitality is a very peopleoriented business. Service personnel change from shift to shift, typically on an 8-hour schedule. Though operational manuals exist in most hospitality establishments, rarely are policies and procedures followed in an exact manner. Guests' "personalities," too, can change throughout their stay, and it may have nothing to do with how they were treated by service personnel. Dealing with heterogeneity in service operations is dealing with reality.

Mistakes will happen. But more importantly, mistakes can be addressed. Often a simple apology can win back a customer regardless of who was at fault when a mistake happens. *Intangibility* is a fourth major characteristic of service businesses. Some consider it the most important component to recognize. Intangibility refers to the highly intangible nature of the service product offering. Intangibility is a feeling; it is having a sense about something that one cannot fully articulate.

The intangible nature of the service product cannot be prejudged. Consumers cannot really see, touch, smell, hear, or taste a service product prior to consumption. They can only anticipate. One can test-drive a car before an automobile purchase is made to see what it feels like to drive. But a hospitality customer cannot test-drive a resort weekend package or a restaurant meal prior to consumption. The intangibility aspect of hospitality emphasizes that service delivery is critical to customer satisfaction.

Most customers have an idea of what to expect. But, in the end, they are really not sure of what they are buying until the hospitality experience actually takes place. Finally, after the service has been consumed, the guest has only the memory of the performance.

The foregoing unique characteristics represent the foundational challenge to the resort's sales staff: they must find a way to promise performance and experience in such a way that the resort's operations departments can deliver on the promise. If the essence of marketing is finding and keeping a customer, then the sales promise is fundamental to that effort. Operations' most important role is the keeping of that promise to the customer— having that customer walk away with a positive and memorable experience and want to return again.

MANAGEMENT OF THE SALES PROCESS

Sales management is effectively directing the personal selling efforts of a hospitality establishment. It involves managing the sales process from both an individual and team perspective. In other words, sales management addresses the logistics of sales solicitation and the development of sales account executives to enhance their sales productivity.

Sales account executives need to manage their day-to-day activity, sales teams need to coordinate their efforts, and customers need to feel that they are working with a professional and well-managed organization.

There are several components to hospitality sales management. These include sales organization, sales account management, recruitment, training and development, goal setting, and performance appraisals. Sales organization refers to departmental and individual organizational issues and inventory management. The following part focuses on the sales organization aspect of hospitality sales management.

Sales Organization

Sales organization can be viewed from three perspectives. These include departmental organization, individual planning of sales activity, and inventory management. A sales department needs to be organized, and sales managers within that organizational setup need to coordinate their efforts. Sales managers need to plan or organize their individual activities on a daily, weekly, and monthly basis.

Allocating the sale of inventory to various customer segments needs to be managed, as well. These are important issues in hospitality sales management.

Departmental Organization

Organizing a sales department means determining who is going to do what. Sales solicitation needs to take place, administrative tasks need to be completed, and managerial decisions need to be made on a regular basis. In medium- to large-size hospitality establishments, a director of sales and/or a director of marketing coordinates these efforts. In smaller operations, it is not unusual to have one individual responsible for all of the above. For most bed and breakfast operations in the United States and Canada and the small boutique resorts in Europe, for example, the owner and/or manager of the establishment typically handle sales activities.

Sales organizational setup for a midsize urban resort targeting business clientele. The sales managers in this example are organized by target market and by geographic territory. Sales manager 1 is responsible for corporate accounts located in the immediate downtown and surrounding area. Sales manager 2 is responsible for national corporate accounts. This refers to companies based in other areas that conduct business or have the potential to conduct business at the resort. Both of these sales managers solicit group and transient business from their account base

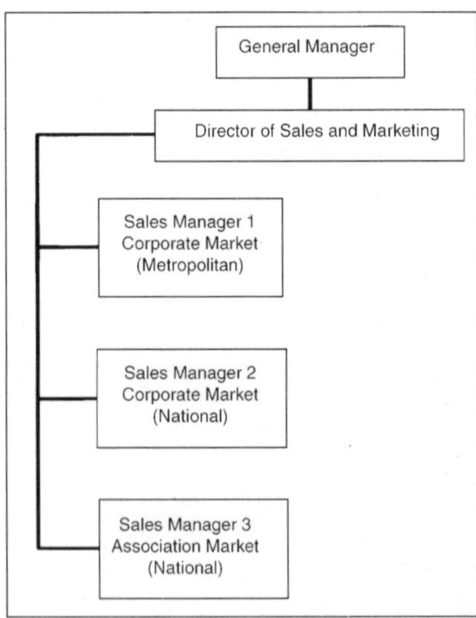

Fig. Organization of an Urban Resort Sales Department

Sales manager 3 targets meetings and convention business from national association accounts.This business may include executive board meetings, committee meetings, regional conferences, and annual conventions.

In this example, once group events have been booked they are turned over to the conference services department for service delivery. Both the sales managers and director of conference services report to the director of sales and marketing. The sales team meets weekly to discuss issues pertinent to achieving the department's sales objectives.

Weekly sales meetings are very much a part of a sales department's organizational structure, be it a sales force of two or twelve sales account executives. They are critical for effective communication within the department.

At these meetings, each team member highlights his or her weekly activity with regard to new prospects uncovered, tentative bookings, verbal definites, cancellations, etc. (Verbal definites are bookings where clients have verbally committed their meeting or function to the facility but a signed contract is not yet in hand.) In other words, sales managers share with each other progress reports on various accounts they are currently working on. Thus, each team member gets an upto- date informal report on the status of all current sales activity.

For example, one sales manager may be working on a tentative booking but considers it weak because of strong competition for this particular account. Call this Group A. Another sales manager may have a new prospect with similar space requirements interested in the same dates. Call this Group B. Assume, however, that the property has the capability of booking only Group A or Group B over the same dates because of space limitations.

When these types of issues surface at sales meetings discussion will occur raising the following types of questions:

- What is the likelihood that either group will eventually book its business at the property?
- What is the estimated profitability and/or contribution margin for each group?
- Is either group a regular client?
- What is the likelihood of repeat business from either group? In other words, what is the long-term profitability for each?
- Can either group consider alternative dates? What would incite them to move dates?
- Do convention history reports match their current space allocation requests?

These are just a sampling of questions that need to be raised and answered. It is a never-ending process in hospitality sales management to search for the best fit for both the buyer and seller.

The organization of sales management is the process of directing the personal selling efforts of a hospitality establishment. It involves effectively managing the sales process from both an individual and team perspective.

Sales or account managers need to manage their day-to-day activity; sales teams need to coordinate their efforts. Sales account management involves developing, maintaining, and enhancing customer relationships. Sales managers develop expertise for specific market segments, industry segments, and/or customer accounts, and common traits among successful sales account executives include self-confidence, high energy, empathy, enthusiasm, and a sense of self-worth.

This stage introduces the foundation for hospitality sales and marketing. First and foremost, sales flow from marketing. If management doesn't have a marketing mindset, then sales efforts will be all for naught.

Marketing is giving the targeted customers what they want, when they want it, where they want it, at a price they are willing and able to pay. Sales is direct communication with potential customers letting them know we have what they want. In many respects, sales is the link between marketing and operations.

Operations is essentially the delivery component of marketing and the final determination of a happy customer. Marketing begins, transcends, and ends with the consumer. Sales makes sure it happens.

9

Resort Taxes

ABOUT THE TAX

The use of resort/motel taxes to fund cultural programmes and facilities in the United States now is widespread and considered a popular way of dedicating tax dollars to the arts. The arts programming supported with these funds boosts local tourism and has a significant impact on local economies. Nationally, the arts are a $36.8 billion industry, which supports 1.3 million full-time jobs and generates $790 million in local government revenue. Expenditures by arts audiences on restaurants, resorts, parking facilities, and retail uses spur even more economic activity.

There are tremendous differences in the ways in which resort/motel taxes have been established, the levels of taxation that have been allocated to the arts, and the purposes for which funds have been disbursed. This article examines the emergence of the resort/motel tax with a general overview and a series of case studies from across the country. Each of these cases is unique, yet common themes and experiences can provide insights and direction to agencies and local governments now considering the resort/motel tax as a funding source for cultural development.

The resort/motel tax (also sometimes called a bed tax) has emerged over the last 15 years as a means of financing activities that attract tourists and visitors. With the phenomenal growth of tourism in the 1980s and the declining fiscal situation in many regions, communities have soughtnew means by which to promote and develop their tourist industries, without placing an additional burden on residents.

American and foreign visitors now are spending close to $450 billion ear in the United States. At the same time, federal contributions to cities and counties have dropped by more than two-thirds since 1980. Not surprisingly, then, state and local governments around the country have created and/or raised taxes on meals, rental cars, alcoholic beverages, and resort and motel rooms.

The resort/motel tax is considered the major generator of tourism taxes. A 1'992 survey by the National Conference of State Legislatures (NCSL) shows that 42 states have a local-option accommodation tax, meaning that local governments in these states can elect to add a resort tax. The local tax usually is collected and disbursed by that _jurisdiction. Ill a 1991 survey by NCSL, the resort tax in 25 cities ranged from a low of 6 per cent in Sioux Falls, South Dakota, to a high of 19.25 per cent in New York City and averaged 11.1 per cent (these rates include state taxes).

Resort/motel taxes, together with other tourism taxes, historically have been used for a broad range of services and activities, from operating support for visitors' bureaus to funding for summer concerts and fireworks displays.

For the arts, resort tax funding can be dedicated to a specific facility, to re-granting of programmes, or to events with some relation to local tourism. Funds also can be forwarded to the local arts agency or paid directly. to arts presenters and producers by a local commission, which manages fund distribution. The level of funding also can be fixed by statute or be left to the discretion of the taxing body. With these profound differences, it is best to consider specific examples.

"The arts are an important economic component in San Diego," says jack McGrory, city manager for the past five years. "They create an attraction in and of themselves. By supporting these organizations and helping them to grow, they in turn give something back to the city."

For many years, San Diego has had a transient occupancy tax. Starting in the 1980s, a portion of that tax revenue has been allocated to the San Diego Commission for the Arts and Culture for re-granting to local arts and cultural programmes. In 1988, in conjunction with the increase of the tax to 9 per cent, the city council awarded the arts commission a more substantial portion of the tax revenue. From 1988 to 1993, annual allocations ranged from $4.5 million to $6 million.

In 1994, the arts commission received a one-cent dedication of the tax, which concurrently was increased to 10.5 per cent. This amendment has taken effect recently and likely, will result in a 10 per cent increase in local arts funding. The 1995 allocation was budgeted at $5.6 million.

The commission splits funding into four pots: I per cent is a public art fund, which is in addition to capital improvement projects funded elsewhere; 2 per cent goes to neighbourhood arts programmes; 7 per cent goes to administration of the programmes; and the remaining 90 per cent is re-granted to local arts organizations as organizational support ($5 million in 1995). Of the 90 applicants for these funds in 1995, 84 will receive support.

According to the commission, the key to getting the increase and the dedicated income stream from the occupancy tax was a strong relationship with the convention and tourist bureau, which made a number of joint presentations with the commission to the council and has maintained a close relationship. The commission also maintains a standing committee on cultural tourism.

"Historically, our room tax has been spent principally on areas where the city could promote itself, particularly with respect to tourism," says McGrory. "We think the arts and cultural life in the city are key components to attracting people to it."

To receive room tax funds, local arts organizations and individuals must go through a rigorous evaluation process that involves an initial application, screening by a 15-member commission appointed by the mayor and council, and final council approval. Not only says McGrory, has this process brought the arts community together "but the council has a process they. can rely on. I think [the room tax] has helped our city. We're proud of the arts and cultural organizations that we have and the level of support that they get reflects that."

A 2 per cent bed tax was established in 1978 by state enabling legislation, a local referendum, and a county ordinance. By ordinance, 20 per cent of the annual proceeds from the tax are dedicated to the Dade County Cultural Affairs Council. Another 60 per cent goes to the countywide convention and visitors' bureau, with the balance going to the city of Miami for renovations to the Orange Bowl.

Funds are delivered to the Cultural Affairs Council to support a full range of cultural activities. Bed tax revenues to the council in 1995 will total S1.5 million, roughly 35 per cent of its annual budget. More than 700 individuals and organizations apply annually to the council's competitive grants programmes; on average, 350 applicants are awarded grants.

The council has managed the administration of this significant funding initiative successfully on behalf of the county, earning praise and support from county and community leaders. The arts council also has developed a strong relationship with the local tourism industry. The council and the industry have worked together to secure this funding stream, to pursue other dedicated revenues, and to build numerous programmes and services that link culture and tourism in Dade County. Representatives from the Cultural Affairs Council and the convention and visitors' bureau sit on each others' committees and boards.

Currently, these two groups have joined with economic development interests in Dade County to pursue the establishment of a food and beverage tax. This will provide an additional dedicated source of funding for the county's cultural activities, for its tourism advertising and promotion, and for economic development initiatives.

Finally, the county has committed proceeds from the convention development tax (an additional 3 per cent bed tax) to plan, develop, and construct the new performing arts centre in downtown Miami. This revenue is anticipated to yield $140 million in bond proceeds.

Columbus began arts funding in 1973 through the Greater Columbus Arts Council (GCAC). In 1978, the source of these funds was changed from general funds to resort/motel tax funds. In 1982, the city revised its tax code to increase the municipal room tax and to dedicate a 20 per cent portion to the GCAC and its grants programme. These changes resulted from an intensive advocacy effort undertaken by the GCAC and its member organizations.

In 1985, the allocation to the arts was increased to 25 per cent, and the total tax climbed from 4 to 6 per cent. Funding for the arts has continued to rise since the beginning of the programme. The 1982 allocation to the GCAC vas $425,000. For 1995, that allocation has risen to S2.2 million, which represents some 50 per cent of the total GCAC budget.

Funds are distributed to approximately 50 organizations each year. Grants are available for projects, management assistance, and operating support. Funds also help the GCAC deliver such services as technical assistance, training, information services, and residency programmes.

The GCAC maintains a close relationship with the tourism industry, in Columbus. Their premier annual event is the Columbus Arts Festival, which brings 500,000 people to the downtown. The industry and the GCAC also fund a number of downtown special events for residents and visitors. Arts council board members and staff also sit on boards of the convention and visitors' bureau and the chamber of commerce, acting as conduits between the arts and tourism industries.

Though there is no legislation that guarantees the arts allocation of the resort/motel tax, the income stream is relatively secure, thanks to the benefits that this allocation provides to the arts, the tourism industry, and the community as a whole.

Creating, increasing, or dedicating a room tax to the arts has proven to be a popular means of funding the arts as a basic city or county service. These arts programmes increase tourism and have a significant economic impact on the community. Because the Source of these funds can be identified specifically and because the funds are dedicated to a particular purpose, the tax is politically attractive, as it is not collected from local residents/taxpayers/voters but from renters of a city's local resort rooms. This dedicated revenue stream is also less competitive than a city s general fund, which supports core services like policing, fire protection, and garbage collection.

For a local government official or an arts advocate to obtain a portion of a local resort tax requires a strong argument that the arts contribute to local tourism, either through arts programmes or facilities. To make this argument, a close relationship between the arts and the tourism industry is mandatory.

This is a real challenge, as the resort operators who collect the tax must be convinced of its long-term benefit to their businesses.

The downside to a dedicated income stream is that funds can vary from year to year with the varying health of the local tourism industry. Yet, if properly, managed by a local arts agency, as one of several funding sources, room tax revenue can provide meaningful support for local arts groups, as well as capital and/or operating funds for arts facilities.

This article is based on a report by AMS Planning and Research for the National Assembly of Local Arts Agencies' (NALAA) Institute for Community Development and the Arts, of which ICMA is a partner. The purpose of NALAA's Institute is to educate local arts agencies, elected and appointed local government officials, and arts funders about the important role of the arts as community change agents for economic, social, and educational problem. NALAA's Institute also will identify innovative community arts programmes and non-traditional funding sources to enable local arts agencies and local civic officials to adapt these programmes to their own communities.

Resort lending

Banks are dipping their toes back into the resort-lending business. But inexperienced owners and operators need not apply. Banks are interested in financing people who have proven track records. Financing for construction of new resorts and motels, however, is frequently difficult to obtain. And where credit is being extended, bankers are striking tougher deals, putting more of the onus of bad performance in the borrower's lap.

Yet to the resort industry, this is good news. "Lenders are no longer hanging up when they hear the word 'resort'," says Kyle Draggoo, director of resort brokerage at Merimark Corp., Houston. "They'll at least listen to you."

Prices on the rise

Many banks are still smarting from the resort overbuilding of the 1980s that turned lenders into landlords.

It wasn't long ago that experts were suggesting the best thing that could be done with resorts involved dynamite and a detonator. Though some banks still have a fair share of seized properties to unload, prices are beginning to firm for resorts, and demand is up.

In September, Hospitality Valuation Services, Inc., Mineola, N.Y., released its latest "Resort Valuation Index." The lodging consulting firm's study found that U.S. resort values increased an average of 15 per cent across the country in 1993. This compares to an 8 per cent increase in 1992 and a 14 per cent decrease in 1991. The HVS index is based on analysis using occupancy and average daily room rate data to compute value.

The strongest comebacks were seen in Atlanta, which gained 39 per cent in value; Phoenix, 31 per cent; Denver, 28 per cent; and Washington, D.C., 23 per cent. On the other hand, Orlando, Honolulu, and Los Angeles saw values based on occupancies and room rates drop. Stephen Rushmore, president of HVS, sees the overall strengthening value of the business to be an indication that interested buyers should move now to obtain the properties still on lender's books.

"The beauty of lending to resort operators today is that the downside risk has been taken away," says Rushmore. Besides the improvements in value, the consultant notes, "there is virtually no resort building taking place." (The one exception in 1993 was the construction of three mega-resorts in Las Vegas. People in the resort trade believe they were an anomoly. The Resort and Motel Brokers of America estimates that if Las Vegas is subtracted from rooms opened in 1993, the total for that year comes to 23,500, which it says is a six-year low for new construction.)

What contributed to this improving picture? Business is better. In 1993, U.S. resorts annual occupancy rates hit 64 per cent, according to Hospitality Directions, a quarterly journal of the national hospitality group at Coopers and Lybrand. This was the highest occupancy rate reached by the industry since 1984, Coopers and Lybrand notes. The firm predicts steady improvement at least through 1996, when it expects occupancy rates to approach 70 per cent. Average daily room rates and growth in demand for rooms have also been steadily improving, though the firm observed that they were still behind the rates of growth seen before the recession.

Small Banks More Active

"Financing for resort real estate acquisitions and new construction was more attainable in 1993 than at any time since the late 1980s," stated a mid-1994 report by the Resort and Motel Brokers of America. "Currently activity is not widespread, but there is sufficient volume to speculate that the credit logjam is breaking up, and the future holds more promise."

The report, Transactions by HMBA, is based on a survey of the activity of HMBA members. Brokers belonging to the organization account for about 25 per cent of all resorts sold nationwide and about 35 per cent of the middlemarket segment of the business. Thus the study is considered a good proxy for the industry's experiences.

The HMBA survey indicates that the bulk of activity is actually centreed in the nation's community banks, rather than among the large banks.

"For loans of $4 million and under, local community banks were primary resources in 1993," states the HMBA report. "These lenders, who have a stake in building their local economies, treat the financing as a business loan, requiring personal guarantees from owner/operators. Rates and terms are generally more favourable than those offered by credit companies. Lower debt coverage ratios often can be negotiated, especially if the loan carries a Small Business Administration guarantee."

LTV ratios are down

Generally speaking, however, bankers from institutions of all sizes are playing harder ball.

"They're definitely trying to be more conservative in this recovery," says Merimark's Draggoo. He (and others) points out that underwriting has become much stricter than it had been during the 1980s. "We're finding that lenders are typically lending no more than 75 per cent," says Patrick H. Ford, Sr., a principal with National Resort Realty Advisors, Portsmouth, N.H. Others say they've heard of lenders going as low as a 60 per cent loan-to-value ratio. By contrast, lenders were frequently willing to go to 90 per cent and beyond during the 1980s.

"As lenders get back into business, they are being much more prudent," says Mark Woodworth, national hospitality industry chairman for Coopers and Lybrand. "They are basing decisions on current resort earnings, rather than on prospective earnings."

As mentioned at the outset, this is a difficult time for newcomers to the lodging business to obtain financing. Lenders are much less likely to entertain a newcomer's application than someone who knows the business. In fact, says Woodworth, just knowing the resort business isn't always considered sufficient.

Nowadays lenders look for expertise in the particular type of resort being financed: luxury, upscale, mid-price, economy, and budget. In addition, lenders are paying more attention than ever to the track record of the particular brand name a resort has decided to affiliate itself with, according to Woodworth.

Most of the financing referred to thus far consists of making loans to purchase existing resorts from current operators or from lenders. Other credits include renovations to an aging resort and refinancing of outstanding debt. Loans for construction of new resorts are scarce to non-existent, except in some pockets of unusual growth. Las Vegas is one, Branson, Mo., is another.

This is as much a matter of market demand as lender willingness. Coopers and Lybrand's Mark Woodworth notes that while resort values are rising again, it is only beginning to make as much sense to build a new resort than to buy one that's already up. Woodworth doesn't expect to see any meaningful amount of construction in the mid-price range for another year or so, and generally expects little construction of luxury resorts for another three.

As more than one expert noted, large-bank lenders still have a ways to go before they finish unloading the big resorts they got stuck with after the debacle of the late 1980s. Thus, most of the big domestic banks remain on the sidelines. "A couple of them are talking about getting back into the market, but they haven't yet," says Tom Arasi, executive vicepresident of finance and development at Tishman Resort Corp., a subsidiary of Tishman Realty and Construction. "There has been a great deal of equity trying to get into the hospitality business," says Arasi, "and it is way ahead of the debt side."

A particularly hot source of equity funding in recent times has been real estate investment trusts dedicated to resort properties. Much of what debt financing is available has come from resort mortgage conduits set up by major resort companies to provide financing to their franchisees.

Among big commercial bank lenders, says Arasi, what activity there has been has chiefly come from European banks operating in the U.S. Even they are very selective, however. Roderick Rohrbach, vice-president at Credit Lyonnais, New York, points out that even fast-growing markets can be risky. A property in a market where resorts still sell out on many nights of the year has appeal, he says.

But a hot market will attract new development, which could lead to a glut that would upset the economics that make a loan appealing at first glance. As a result, in some circumstances Credit Lyonnais would find the proposed acquisition of a high performer in a satisfactory market to be preferable to lending for acquisition in a roaring market. (In no event does it finance construction.)

While loans for big resort projects remain elusive, the hospitality industry has begun going directly to the credit markets with the assistance of Wall Street investment banks.

These players are forming resort mortgage conduits, similar in principle to the secondary mortgage market for residential loans. The Resort and Motel Brokers of America report cited earlier makes these observations about the relatively new conduits:

"The terms are restrictive and the loans are for only the highest-performing resorts, but the availability of funds is most welcome. Total loan volume, however, is only a trickle of the traditional flow of funds that it is replacing. Nonetheless, these loans are an important and needed interim step prior to the expected return of conventional sources of financing over the next few years."

One example of the technique is Richfield Resort Management, Inc.'s partnership with Lehman Brothers. In June the two companies introduced a programme that Richfield clients could use for acquisition, refinancing, and renovations. One advantage Richfield claims for its programme is that borrowers can operate their resorts as independent brands or under the national brand of their choice, whereas financing programmes offered by franchisors require that the borrower fly the franchisor's flag. Rates start at 290 basis points over the 20-year Treasury bill rate.

No deals had been closed in the Richfield programme as of mid-September, but several were in the pipeline, according to Roberta Griffin, senior director of corporate finance at Richfield. Industry observers reported that many conduits have yet to do a great deal of actual lending. Do conduits represent a threat to traditional lenders? Roderick Rohrbach of Credit Lyonnais doesn't see them as shutting banks out.

"Lenders such as ourselves will naturally cater to the borrower who seeks more of a customized approach than the conduits, which are less conducive to customized financing," says Rohrbach.

Richfield's Roberta Griffin acknowledges Rohrbach's point. "Right now, because the conduit programmes involve rated securities, there isn't a whole lot of room" for flexibility. However, she adds that investors' changing appetites might someday enable securitization programmes to become more adaptable.

Adaptable or not, right now conduit financing is expensive. Stephen Rushmore of Hospitality Valuation Services points out that a typical loan rate today is 9.5 per cent; by contrast, the conduits are charging in the neighbourhood of 11 per cent. "Conduits are very expensive," says Rushmore, "and you'd only use them if you had a gun to your head."

Bibliography

A.M. Sarma: *Industrial Relations*, Himalaya Publishing House, Delhi, 2010.

Aditya Jha: *Industrial Relations Democracy and Human Rights*, Dominant Publication, Delhi, 2012.

Ajit Kumar Ghosh: *Industrial Relations : Text and Cases*, Manas Publications, Delhi, 2011.

Aparna Raj: *Industrial Relations in India : Issues, Institutions and Outlook*, New Century Publication, Delhi, 2003.

Ashim Gupta: *Hotel Tourism and Catering Management*, Centrum Press, Delhi, 2011.

Asit K. Ghosh and Prem Kumar: *Personnel Management and Industrial Relations*, Anmol Publication, Delhi, 2003.

B.D. Singh: *Industrial Relations and Labour Laws*, Excel Books, Delhi, 2003.

Bipin Kumar: *Industrial Relations : Theory and Practice*, Regal Publications, Delhi, 2013.

C.S. Venkata Ratnam: *Industrial Relations*, Oxford University Press, Delhi, 2006.

Jerome Joseph: *Industrial Relations : Towards a Theory of Negotiated Connectedness*, Sage Publication, Delhi, 2004.

Jyoti. S. Sharma: *Catering Management Practices*, Akansha Publication, Delhi, 2006.

K K Jacob and S Mohanan: *Industrial Relations in Public Sector*, New Century Publications, Delhi, 2003.

K. Chitra: *Industrial Relations Under Globalised Economy*, Abhijeet Publication, Delhi, 2009.

Kavita Krishnamurthi: *Industrial Relations : Emerging Issues in Globalised World*, Global Vision Publication, Delhi, 2012.

L.K. Sharma: *Hotel and Catering Management*, Surendra Publications, Delhi, 2012.

M Arora: *Industrial Relations*, Excel Books, Delhi, 2001.

Md. Shahabuddin Usmani: *Industrial Relations in India*, Sonali Publication, Delhi, 2010.

Monappa, Nambudiri and Selvaraj: *Industrial Relations and Labour Laws*, Tata McGraw Hill, Delhi, 2012.

O.P. Kandari and Ashish Chandra: *Hotel, Tourism and Catering Management*, Shree Publication, Delhi, 2004.

P L Rao and P R K Raju: *Industrial Relations in India*, Excel Books, Delhi, 2003.

R K Arora: *Foodservice and Catering Management*, APH Publication, Delhi, 2007.

R. Jayaprakash Reddy: *Organisational Behaviour and Industrial Relations*, APH Publication, Delhi, 2004.

R.P. Saxena: *Food Services and Catering Management*, Centrum Press, Delhi, 2010.

S K Bhatia: *Strategic Industrial Relations and Labour Laws*, Deep and Deep Publication, Delhi, 2008.

Sawalia Bihari Verma: *Industrial Relations in Public Sector Undertakings*, Book Enclave, Delhi, 2002.

Shalini Goel: *Industrial Relations in Rural Industry*, Vista International, Delhi, 2006.

Tapomoy Deb: *Managing Human Resources and Industrial Relations*, Excel Books, Delhi, 1993.

Thomas Erickson: *Industrial Relations in Asian Perspective : Trend and Transformation*, Global Vision Publication, Delhi, 2012.

Varinder Singh Rana: *Catering Management*, Centrum Press, Delhi, 2011.

Index

G

H

I

K

L

M

N

O

P

R

S

T

U